JOURNAL FOR THE STUDY OF THE NEW TESTAMENT
SUPPLEMENT SERIES
81

Executive Editor
Stanley E. Porter

JSOT Press
Sheffield

The Law in Galatians

In-Gyu Hong

Journal for the Study of the New Testament
Supplement Series 81

Copyright © 1993 Sheffield Academic Press

Published by JSOT Press
JSOT Press is an imprint of
Sheffield Academic Press Ltd
343 Fulwood Road
Sheffield S10 3BP
England

Typeset by Sheffield Academic Press
and
Printed on acid-free paper in Great Britain
by Biddles Ltd
Guildford

British Library Cataloguing in Publication Data

Hong, In-Gyu
    Law in Galatians.—(JSNT Supplement
    Series, ISSN 0143-5108; No. 81)
    I. Title II. Series
    227

    ISBN 1-85075-391-1

CONTENTS

PREFACE

This study is a modification of my doctoral dissertation accepted by the Faculty of Theology at the University of Stellenbosch in South Africa in October 1991.

I am specially indebted to my promoter Professor H.J.B. Combrink for his careful guidance and constructive criticisms, to my co-promoter Professor B.C. Lategan for his critical reading and invaluable comments on the first draft of the manuscript, and to my external examiner Professor J. Lambrecht at the Catholic University of Leuven in Belgium for his penetrating criticisms, some of which I have been able to respond to in this book.

My thanks are also due to Dr D. Taylor and Dr D. Crutchley for their assistance in proofreading and in polishing my English, to Professor W.T. Claassen for his generous permission to make use of a Macintosh computer in the Department of Semitics, and to Mr J. Bronkhorst for his help in technical aspects of word processing.

Furthermore, I wish to thank the following people and institutions for their financial support: my parents Mr and Mrs C.S. Hong, Miss L. Bonthuys, Mrs E. Pieterse, Miss E. van der Merwe, Mr and Mrs A. VanGelder, my home church Kwangju Central Presbyterian Church in Korea, the University of Stellenbosch, the Dutch Reformed Church in South Africa, and the Centre for Science Development in South Africa.

Finally, my deepest appreciation is offered to my wife Kyung-Bok for her loving care and moral support, and to my children Nathan, Deborah, and Jonathan for their co-operation and cheerfulness which have often refreshed me.

Soli Deo Gloria

ABBREVIATIONS

AnBib	Analecta Biblica
ATANT	Abhandlungen zur Theologie des Alten und Neuen Testaments
BEvT	Beiträge zur evangelischen Theologie
Bib	*Biblica*
Bijdr	*Bijdragen*
BJRL	*Bulletin of the John Rylands University Library of Manchester*
BNTC	Black's New Testament Commentaries
BR	*Biblical Research*
BST	The Bible Speaks Today
BT	*The Bible Translator*
BTSt	Biblical and Theological Studies
BU	Biblische Untersuchungen
BZNW	Beihefte zur *ZNW*
CBQ	*Catholic Biblical Quarterly*
CTJ	*Calvin Theological Journal*
CwH	Calwer Hefte zur Förderung biblischen Glaubens und christlichen Lebens
EKKNT	Evangelisch-katholischer Kommentar zum Neuen Testament
ExpTim	*The Expository Times*
FRLANT	Forschungen zur Religion und Literatur des Alten und Neuen Testaments
HeyJ	*Heythrop Journal*
HR	*History of Religions*
HThS	Harvard Theological Studies
HTKNT	Herders theologischer Kommentar zum Neuen Testament
HTR	*Harvard Theological Review*
ICC	International Critical Commentary
Int	*Interpretation*
ITQ	*Irish Theological Quarterly*
JB	Jerusalem Bible
JBL	*Journal of Biblical Literature*
JBLMS	*JBL* Monograph Series
JETS	*Journal of the Evangelical Theological Society*
JSJ	*Journal for the Study of Judaism*
JSNT	*Journal for the Study of the New Testament*
JSNTSup	*JSNT* Supplement Series

JTS	*Journal of Theological Studies*
KBANT	Kommentare und Beiträge zum Alten und Neuen Testament
KD	*Kerygma und Dogma*
KEK	Kritisch-exegetischer Kommentar über das Neue Testament
KNT	Kommentar zum Neuen Testament
MQR	*Michigan Quarterly Review*
NASB	New American Standard Bible
NCB	New Century Bible
NEB	New English Bible
NICNT	The New International Commentary on the New Testament
NICOT	The New International Commentary on the Old Testament
NIDNTT	*The New International Dictionary of New Testament Theology*
NIGTC	The New International Greek Testament Commentary
NIV	New International Version
NovT	*Novum Testamentum*
NovTSup	*Novum Testamentum*, Supplements
NTAbh	Neutestamentliche Abhandlungen
NTS	*New Testament Studies*
PSB	*The Princeton Seminary Bulletin*
REB	Revised English Bible
RelSRev	*Religious Studies Review*
RGG	*Religion in Geschichte und Gegenwart*
RNT	Regensburger Neues Testament
SB	Skandinavische Beiträge
SBLDS	Society of Biblical Literature Dissertation Series
SBLSP	SBL Seminar Papers
SBT	Studies in Biblical Theology
SEÅ	*Svensk exegetisk årsbok*
SJT	*Scottish Journal of Theology*
SNTSMS	Society of New Testament Studies Monograph Series
SNTW	Studies of the New Testament and its World
SR	*Studies in Religion*
StANT	Studien zum Alten und Neuen Testament
STS	Stellenbosch Theological Studies
StTh	*Studia Theologica*
TBü	Theologische Bücherei
TDNT	*Theological Dictionary of the New Testament*
TEV	Today's English Version
THKNT	Theologischer Handkommentar zum Neuen Testament
TLZ	*Theologische Literaturzeitung*
TNTC	Tyndale New Testament Commentaries
TrinJ	*Trinity Journal*
TynBul	*Tyndale Bulletin*
TZ	*Theologische Zeitschrift*

WBC	Word Biblical Commentary
WMANT	Wissenschaftliche Monographien zum Alten und Neuen Testament
WTJ	*Westminster Theological Journal*
WUNT	Wissenschaftliche Untersuchungen zum Neuen Testament
ZAW	*Zeitschrift für die alttestamentliche Wissenschaft*
ZNW	*Zeitschrift für die neutestamentliche Wissenschaft*
ZTK	*Zeitschrift für Theologie und Kirche*

INTRODUCTION

The law occupies a central place in Paul. It is a subject which is closely linked with many other themes in his theology and ethics. A right understanding of Paul's view of the law is therefore essential for the study of Paul's thought.

The subject of the law in Paul is, however, an extremely complicated problem. Perhaps, as is often quoted, it is 'the most intricate doctrinal issue in his theology'.[1] The difficulty is largely due to the apparent contradiction in Paul's position regarding the law. On the one hand, he clearly disparages the law, sometimes very harshly: justification is not by the law (Gal. 2.16; 3.11; Rom. 3.28); the law is inferior to the promise (Gal. 3.15ff.); it is given to produce transgressions (Gal. 3.19) and to increase sinning (Rom. 5.20; 7.5, 8-13; cf. 1 Cor. 15.56); it cannot impart life (Gal. 3.21); Christians have died to the law (Gal. 2.19; Rom. 7.4) and been freed from it (Gal. 3.25; 5.1; Rom. 7.6); Christ is the end of the law (Rom. 10.4); and so on. On the other hand, Paul equally clearly speaks of the law in positive terms: the law is holy (Rom. 7.12) and spiritual (Rom. 7.14); it is the embodiment of knowledge and truth (Rom. 2.20); the commandment is for life (Rom. 7.10; cf. Gal. 3.12); Christians establish the law through faith (Rom. 3.31); the whole law is fulfilled in love (Gal. 5.14; Rom. 13.8, 10; cf. Gal. 6.2; Rom. 8.4); and so on.

It is not surprising, therefore, that an enormous volume of literature has appeared on the topic of Paul and the law, especially in the last few decades. Unfortunately, however, in spite of much labour scholars have thus far reached no consensus but have only succeeded in producing a wide variety of divergent opinions. Instead of providing a survey of all the different views, I would like here to outline the most important solutions proposed to date.[2]

---

1. Schoeps 1961: 168.
2. For a full survey of recent debates on Paul's treatment of the law, see Moo 1987: 287-307.

1. It is well known that a great number of biblical scholars have
long tried to find some consistency in Paul's understanding of the law
by making a distinction between the law as used in a legalistic way and
the law as an expression of God's will,[1] between ceremonial regulations of the law and its moral norms,[2] or between the Mosaic Torah
and the Messianic Torah.[3]

2. Some scholars admit inconsistencies in Paul's statements about the
law, but try to harmonize them within a developmental scheme.
According to Drane, Paul appears to be a libertine in Galatians which
he wrote under pressure from Judaizers, totally denouncing the law.
In contrast, he looks like a legalist in 1 Corinthians where he is confronted with Gnosticizing libertines, reintroducing 'the *form* of legal
language' in claiming in 7.19 that keeping the commandments of God
is essential.[4] In 2 Corinthians, however, Paul presents a combination
of a Galatians type of libertinism and a 1 Corinthians type of legalism.
This synthesis is accomplished more fully in Romans 'where we have
a more or less balanced and neutral expression of Paul's theology,
neither libertine nor legalist'.[5] In this letter Paul denies the saving
power of the law, but affirms its divine origin (Rom. 7.22, 25; 8.7)
and positive role in the believer's life (Rom. 8.3-4; 13.8-10).[6]

Hübner advances a similar theory, the basic thesis of which is that
Paul's thought on the law underwent a significant development
between the time of Galatians and Romans. He argues that in writing
Galatians Paul adopts an entirely negative attitude towards the law: the
law was given by demonic angels in order to provoke transgressions
(Gal. 3.19), and the Christian has nothing to do with the law but only
with the love commandment, a radical reduction of the demands of the
law (5.14). This hostile position invites severe criticism from the
Jerusalem Church, which forces Paul to rethink his view of the law.
The result is found in Romans. Here the law is presented as divine, its
function being to bring the consciousness of sin (Rom. 3.20; 7.7), not

---

1. E.g. Burton 1921: 443-60; Cranfield 1964: 43-68; Moule 1967: 389-406;
Ladd 1968: 50-67.
2. E.g. Haufe 1966: 171-78; Kaiser 1983: 307-14; Schreiner 1989: 47-74.
3. E.g. Davies 1948: 71-72, 136-46; Longenecker [1964] 1976: 128-32,
183-96.
4. Drane 1975: 65, italics his.
5. Drane 1975: 4.
6. Cf. Drane 1974: 167-78.

to stimulate sin. Moreover, in Romans there is no longer a contrast between the Mosaic law and the commandment of love. Instead, the love commandment is understood as a summary of the still valid requirements of the Mosaic Torah (Rom. 13.8-10). In commenting on Rom. 10.4 Hübner states that, whereas in Galatians 'Christ is the end of the Mosaic Law', in Romans 'Christ is the end of the carnal misuse of the Law'.[1]

Wilckens likewise sees a certain development in Paul's understanding of the law. In the polemical situation of Galatians Paul develops the contrast between Christ and Torah, faith and the works of the law, and between promise and the law to such an extent that the argument amounts to a radical abolition of the law. Simultaneously he sets the church over against Israel. However, in Romans Paul revises this totally antinomistic and anti-Jewish tendency. In this letter he presents the law as God's law, which is by no means abrogated by the proclamation of faith but rather is fulfilled (Rom. 3.31; 13.8-10). And he brings together the Jews and the Gentiles under the judgment of God.[2]

3. In contrast, Sanders does not find any straightforward development from Galatians to Romans. Instead, he perceives internal tensions and inconsistencies in Paul's statements on the law in Romans. For example, in 1.18–2.29 Paul argues for universal sinfulness; however, in 2.14-15 and 25-27 he claims that some can keep the law perfectly. Further, Paul states that in Romans 2 the law is required for sin to be taken into account while in 5.12-14 and 18 sin was taken into account even during the period between Adam and Moses. Furthermore, Paul produces three incompatible explanations of the function of the law in relation to sin in 5.20-21 and 7.7-13, 14-25.[3] For Sanders, all this indicates that Paul's theological reasoning moves 'from solution to plight rather than from plight to solution'.[4] That is to say, his thought on the law is not derived from analysing the human plight and then concluding that Christ is the only way of salvation, but the other way around.

Räisänen takes a similar line. However, he is considerably more radical than Sanders. He claims that 'contradictions and tensions have

1. Hübner 1986: 148-49.
2. Wilckens 1982a: 154-90; Wilckens 1982b: 17-26.
3. Sanders 1983: 74-75.
4. Sanders 1983: 150; cf. Sanders 1977: 442-47.

to be *accepted* as *constant* features of Paul's theology of the law'; they are 'pointers to Paul's *personal theological problems*'.[1] The main areas in which inconsistency is perceived are as follows: the concept, continuing validity, fulfillability, origin, and function of the law. Räisänen attributes Paul's inconsistent view of the law to his internalization of the Gentile point of view on the law in the course of his missionary work.

4. Dunn, using arguments advanced by himself in a previous article,[2] finds the above interpretations of Sanders and Räisänen unsatisfactory, maintaining that they have both failed to enter sufficiently into the social context of Paul's writings and to understand the full significance of the social function of the law at that time. For Dunn, Paul does not disparage the law as such. What he attacks, however, is the law 'in its social function as distinguishing Jew from Gentile'.[3] The peculiar phrase 'the works of the law' does not refer to good works in general but 'particularly to those requirements which bring to sharp focus the distinctiveness of Israel's identity'.[4] This is the reason why circumcision, food laws and Sabbath observance feature so prominently in the discussion of the phrase. Divorced from this excessively narrow view of the law, the law continues to play a positive role, to be fulfilled in love.

5. Against all the above-mentioned new approaches to Paul's view of the law, Westerholm attempts to rehabilitate Luther's understanding of Paul. In his opinion, the law in Paul most frequently refers to 'the sum of specific divine requirements given to Israel through Moses'.[5] This Mosaic law requires 'doing' for life (Gal. 3.12; Rom. 10.5), and thus obedience to it is 'regarded as Israel's path to life'.[6] Paul, however, contrasts 'the works of the law' with faith in Christ because of human inability to keep the law perfectly. Westerholm goes on to argue that the law is completely superseded by Christ. The Christians are no longer obligated to adhere to the precepts of the law but to follow the all-sufficient guidance of the indwelling Spirit.

1. Räisänen 1983: 11, 12, italics his.
2. Dunn 1983a.
3. Dunn 1985: 531.
4. Dunn 1985: 531; cf. Dunn 1983a: 107-11; Wright 1978: 61-88.
5. Westerholm 1988: 108.
6. Westerholm 1988: 142.

To my mind, none of the above solutions is satisfactory. The topic of Paul and the law still remains a problem which requires further scientific investigation in search of a reasonable solution. This has challenged me to launch a fresh approach to the theme in the light of recent hermeneutical developments. It is my conviction that a comprehensive treatment of Paul's view of the law must be based on a full and thorough examination of his remarks on the subject in each of his letters. For each letter is addressed to a specific rhetorical and social situation and must thus be understood on its own terms. Because of the complexity of the problem, my research will be limited to the letter to the Galatians in which the issue of the law is dealt with for the first time.[1] In my opinion, no one has thus far made a serious attempt to penetrate deeply Paul's understanding of the law as expressed in this letter.

The present work is divided into seven chapters. Chapter 1 analyses the surface structure of Galatians. The main tool employed here is discourse analysis; however, the ancient epistolary form and the rhetorical structure are also taken into account. Chapter 2 examines pivotal statements revealed by the structural analysis with a view to grasping the perspective of Paul in the letter. Chapter 3 attempts to reconstruct the argument and identity of the opponents. The implications deduced from the structure of Galatians and from the perspective of Paul are utilized as criteria for this attempt. These three chapters form the first part of the work. On the basis of these preliminary considerations, Part II deals with Paul's treatment of the law in Galatians. This consists of four chapters. In Chapter 4 I briefly argue that νόμος in Galatians, with a few exceptions (3.21b; 4.21b), refers to the Mosaic Torah, given to Israel on Mount Sinai, which is regarded as a complete unit. Chapter 5 considers the law as the obligation of the Sinai covenant, not as a requirement for entering the covenant community of God. Chapter 6 investigates the function of the law in God's plan of salvation. Chapter 7 treats the law and the Christian life. In conclusion, the main results of my discussion of the law in Galatians are brought together in summary form, and thereafter some implications which have a bearing on the current debate on Paul and the law are drawn from my research. In this way I hope to contribute some clarification to understanding Paul's various statements about the law.

1. Cf. Cranfield 1964: 62.

Part I

PRELIMINARY CONSIDERATIONS

Chapter 1

THE STRUCTURE OF GALATIANS

1. *Methodological Considerations*

My investigation of Paul's view of the law in Galatians begins with an analysis of the surface structure of the letter. There are two reasons for such a procedure. On the one hand, the structure of the entire text determines the function and meaning of its parts. Words, phrases and sentences are not taken arbitrarily but are selected and arranged according to the premeditated structure in which an author tries to communicate his thought to his readers. The components do not govern the structure, but the structure governs the components. This means that the parts are to be understood in the light of the total structure.[1]

On the other hand, the exploration of the surface structure is a preliminary step to the analysis of the deep structure. Since the surface structure is a form chosen by the writer to shape his ideas, a careful examination of the form reveals some important clues to the perspective(s) from which the author develops his argument, though it does not answer all the critical questions.[2] Thus following the course of the argument in the surface structure is an important step towards grasping the purport of the author.

a. *Discourse Analysis*
The surface structure of Galatians will be analysed mainly by means of discourse analysis based on colon structure, an approach which has been developed in South Africa.[3] The merit of discourse analysis lies in the fact that it forces us to treat intensively the text as it stands.

1. Cf. Louw 1973: 101-102; Du Toit 1974: 55-56.
2. Cf. Lategan 1978: 345; Combrink 1979: 3; Louw 1982: 94-95.
3. See Louw 1973: 101-18; Louw 1982; Nida *et al.* 1983.

Discourse analysis uses the colon as the unit of analysis.[1] A colon can be defined in syntactic terms, whereas the ancient Greek grammarians understood it semantically as a thought unit.[2] The typical colon is a single, independent grammatical structure consisting of a subjective, nominal element and a predicate, verbal element, both of which may have some embedded subordinate phrases or clauses.[3] The identification of a colon therefore involves syntactic analysis. This analysis exhibits the syntactic relationships of the constituents of the colon, which serve to point clearly to the semantic content of the colon. Thus from a semantic point of view the colon can be seen as containing a relatively coherent piece of information, that is, a kind of proposition. 'Both semantically and syntactically, therefore, the colon is a single integrated structure.'[4] This is the reason why the colon is employed as the basic unit in the present discourse analysis.

The first step in the discourse analysis is to subdivide the text into cola. Next, the cola are to be grouped into colon clusters, colon clusters into paragraphs, and paragraphs into pericopae. Finally, grouping pericopae will expose the macro-structure of the text of Galatians as a whole.

This process of grouping and demarcating will be controlled largely by identifying semantic relations between individual cola and between various groups. According to Nida and others, the semantic relations may be classified and illustrated as follows:

I. Coordinate
    A. Additive
        1. Equivalent: John is stupid; he is dumb.
        2. Different
            a. Consequential: John stopped reading and looked up. Dick approached the lions and one of them charged (an 'unfolding' structure).
            b. Nonconsequential: John was reading and Mary was sewing.

---

1. Thus it is also called 'colon analysis'.
2. Louw 1973: 104; Louw 1982: 95, 106.
3. For fuller explanations, see Du Toit 1977: (1)-(10); Combrink 1979: 4-6; Louw 1982: 95-113.
4. Louw 1982: 106.

B. Dyadic

    1. Alternative: John will do it or die in the attempt.

    2. Contrastive: He came but did not stay.

    3. Comparative: She is more intelligent than Jane.
    He did as fine a job as Bill did.

II. Subordinate

  A. Qualificational

    1. Substance

      a. Content: He said he would go. He yelled, 'Stop!'

      b. Generic–Specific: John travels a lot; each year he goes to the Orient; he's in Europe each summer; and is now in South America.

    2. Character

      a. Characterization: Working for John is terrible.

      b. Manner: He came to town riding on a horse.

      c. Setting:

        1'. Time: When he came, we left.

        2'. Place: Being in the house, he noticed a strange noise.

        3'. Circumstance: As Jim turned, Alice disappeared.

  B. Logical

    1. Cause–Effect: John's leaving made Mary despondent.

    2. Reason–Result: Because John left, he did not see Mary.

    3. Means–Result: By coming, John saw Mary.

    4. Means–Purpose: John came in order to see Mary.

    5. Condition–Result: If John comes, he will see Mary.

    6. Basis–Inference: Since John came, he must have seen Mary.

    7. Concession–Result: Though John came, he did not see Mary.[1]

Within the above framework of analysis the various literary stylistic devices which function on the micro-structural level will also be taken into consideration, because they are often used in the structuring of thematic argument.[2] The most remarkable stylistic feature in Galatians seems to be the various techniques of repetition: repetition of words or phrases, parallelism, chiasmus and antithesis. These usually serve to give emphasis and distinction to various themes, and to reinforce a thematic unity. We should, however, keep in mind that discourse

   1. Nida *et al.* 1983: 102-103; for further explanation, see Nida 1975: 51-54; Nida *et al.* 1983: 103-104.

   2. For detail, see Combrink 1982: 6-10; Nida *et al.* 1983: 22-55.

analysis is not thoroughly objective. Grouping and demarcating are often determined by a theological insight.

b. *Epistolary Form and Rhetorical Structure*
The discourse analysis explained above is not the exclusive key to the examination of the surface structure of the letter to the Galatians. Sometimes the method fails to offer an adequate explanation of the semantic meaning and function of certain parts in relation to others, largely because Galatians is not a systematic theological treatise but is stylistically rather like a speech. As such it displays the influences of rhetorical and epistolary traditions exerted upon its structure. Accordingly one must also take into account these epistolary and rhetorical structures for the analysis of the structure of the letter. This complementary approach to the discourse analysis will significantly enhance our understanding of the surface structure of Galatians.

It is well known that the letter was a popular means of communication employed by government officials and ordinary people in the Graeco-Roman world.[1] Many of the early Christian leaders also utilized the letter form to guide and instruct their young churches in specific situations. Generally speaking, the letter is a written communication between people separated from each other by distance. So it is, in a certain sense, a substitute for oral communication. Ignatius, bishop of Antioch, depicted his letter to the Magnesians as an 'address'.[2] This description is equally appropriate to the Pauline letters, which are also very much like speeches. Their style reveals on every page the marks of oral expression: imagined dialogue, accusation and defence, questions, exclamations, the challenge to listen and so on.[3] Thus, the letter can be roughly defined as a written form of speech, functioning as an oral speech in many significant ways.

This conversational nature of the letter left the door open to a strong influence of rhetoric, a device which originated from speech. By the first century BCE, rhetoric had, in fact, come to have a profound effect on the composition of letters.[4] It is well known that rhetoric was the core subject of ancient education in the Roman

1. See Deissmann 1911: 143-246; Stowers 1986: 49-173.
2. Lightfoot [1891] 1980: 69.
3. Funk 1966: 248.
4. Aune 1987: 160.

Empire. According to Kennedy, it 'represented approximately the level of high-school education today and was, indeed, the exclusive subject of secondary education'.[1] The theory of rhetoric was widely practised in almost every form of communication, written as well as oral.[2] Hence, we can say that Paul could hardly escape this pervasive influence of rhetoric,[3] though whether he received a formal Hellenistic education is a matter of debate.[4] In fact, his letters display rhetorical characteristics on both the macro-structural and the micro-structural levels.[5] It is therefore natural that the letter addressed to people under the influence of this culture served not only as a means of communication but also as a sophisticated means of persuasion.[6]

According to Aristotle and subsequent rhetorical theorists such as Cicero and Quintilian, Graeco-Roman rhetoric is classified into three types: judicial (or forensic), deliberative, and epideictic (or demonstrative). Judicial speech is the speech of the court of law. Its intention is to persuade the hearer to make a judgment about events which took place in the past. Deliberative speech is political speech delivered to persuade the public assembly to take a particular course of action in the future, usually in the immediate future. Epideictic speech is commemorative speech persuading the audience to maintain common values in the present. Each type has two basic forms, depending upon whether the intention of the author is positive or negative. Judicial speech can take the form of accusation or defence; deliberative is concerned with persuasion or dissuasion; and epideictic is characterized as praise or blame.[7]

Here we should raise the question: to which type of rhetorical speech does the letter to the Galatians belong? According to Betz followed by Brinsmead and Hester,[8] Galatians is an apologetic letter and

1.   Kennedy 1984: 9.
2.   Cf. Stowers 1986: 51.
3.   Selby 1962: 124-25; Kennedy 1984: 9-10.
4.   See van Unnik 1973: 259-320; Bornkamm 1975: 3ff.; Kim 1984: 32ff.
5.   See e.g. Betz 1975: 353-79; Betz 1979; Betz 1985; Bultmann [1910] 1984; Kennedy 1984: 141-56; Hester 1984: 223-33; Hester 1986: 386-408.
6.   Aristotle defines rhetoric as the art of persuasion.
7.   Kennedy 1963: 87; Kennedy 1984: 19-20; Stowers 1986: 51; Aune 1987: 198.
8.   Betz 1975: 353-79; Betz 1976: 99-113; Betz 1979: 14-25; Brinsmead 1982: 42-55; Hester 1984: 223-33; cf. Hester 1986: 386-408.

thus belongs to the category of judicial rhetoric. It seems that the direct references to the opponents, the apparent statements of defence and the existence of a narrative led Betz to that classification. But Aune criticizes Betz for his failure to account for the eclectic combination of different kinds of rhetoric in Galatians. After pointing out that the role of the paraenesis in Galatians 5–6, which is part of so-called 'philosophical rhetoric', does not fit into the rhetorical analysis of Betz, Aune argues that Paul combines forensic rhetoric with deliberative oratory in Galatians 1–4: Galatians 1–2 is a forensic speech which contains Paul's defence against false accusations, while Galatian 3–4 is a deliberative rhetoric which persuades the Galatians to follow a different course of action from that which they are presently considering taking.[1] This interpretation is endorsed by Hübner.[2]

Kennedy, a leading historian of Graeco-Roman rhetoric, goes one step further in his critique of Betz. He rightly points out that Betz overemphasizes the presence of narrative and underestimates the presence of exhortation, and thereby distorts the interpretation of Galatians. The narrative in Galatians 1–2 is not concerned with an account of the facts at issue, which is necessary in the case of judicial rhetoric, but with establishing Paul's ethos, that is, Paul's moral credibility required for deliberative rhetoric, thus supporting his claim that his gospel is not from man, but from God (Gal. 1.11-12). The exhortation in Gal. 5.1–6.10 furnishes further strong evidence that Galatians is a deliberative letter, in which Paul persuades the Galatians, on the basis of his argument in Galatians 3–4, to take quite specific actions, in particular to reject the practice of circumcision. Kennedy concludes, therefore, that the letter is not an apology but an attempt to persuade the Galatians to live in accordance with the gospel of Christ and is thus probably best viewed as deliberative rhetoric.[3] Recently Aune appears to have modified his position and to agree basically with Kennedy, saying 'Galatians can be read as a deliberative letter with some apologetic features'.[4] More recently Hall and Smit

1. Aune 1981: 324-26; cf. Harnisch 1987: 286-87.
2. Hübner 1984: 243-45.
3. Kennedy 1984: 144-52.
4. Aune 1987: 207.

also arrived at the same conclusion as Kennedy with their own detailed rhetorical analyses of Galatians.[1]

I have argued, thus far, that the letter to the Galatians was structured under the influence of ancient rhetorical principles. This does not necessarily suggest that Paul ignored formal letter-elements in structuring his argument. It has been convincingly proved that Paul made use of many formal features of Hellenistic letters in writing his letters. The comparison of the Pauline letters with the ancient Greek letters led scholars to discover striking formal similarities: (1) opening (sender, recipient, greeting); (2) thanksgiving; (3) body; (4) closing.[2] This does not mean that Paul slavishly imitated the Greek letter models. Paul, as a Christian theologian, modified the traditional letter forms for his own purposes in specific circumstances. The basic form of his letters, as Funk discovered in spite of Deissmann's thesis that the letters are chaotic due to their spontaneous arrangement,[3] is as follows: (1) salutation (sender, receiver, greeting); (2) thanksgiving; (3) body consisting of a formal opening, connective and transitional formulae, concluding 'eschatological climax' and travelogue; (4) paraenesis; (5) closing elements (greetings, doxology, benediction).[4] Paul's letter to the Galatians with which we are concerned in this study includes all these elements except for the thanksgiving section. Apart from such obvious epistolary elements as greeting, closing, body-opening formulae and paraenesis, Funk identifies the section Gal. 4.12-20 with a travelogue-surrogate and Gal. 6.7-10 with the eschatological climax.[5]

At this point we encounter the problem of the relationship between letter form and rhetorical structure, since Galatians exhibits the influences of both ancient rhetoric and epistolography. Brinsmead deals with this problem critically. For him, the epistolary nature of Galatians has little consequence for understanding the structure of its contents, because the letter form suggested by Funk above is not fixed enough to be the basis of an analysis of structure in any one of the

1. Hall 1987: 277-87; Smit 1989: 1-26.
2. White 1972: 93ff.; Roetzel [1975] 1983: 30-31; Du Toit 1985: 5-9; cf. Doty 1973: 27.
3. See Deissmann 1909: 3-59.
4. Funk 1966: 263-74, especially 270.
5. Funk 1966: 271; cf. White 1971: 93-97; White 1972: 49-52, 54-56, 59-69; Tolmie 1986a: 22-33.

Pauline letters. Thus Galatians, as Brinsmead contends,[1] is to be analysed according to the rhetorical structure alone.[2] This solution
offered by Brinsmead is not totally acceptable. To be sure, the simple
identification of scattered formal letter-elements does not provide substantial assistance in grasping the flow of the argument,[3] though their
presence does indicate that Paul did not stand outside the epistolary
tradition. This does not mean, however, that the letter-elements are
used pointlessly. Rather, they seem to be employed for various
rhetorical purposes, being fused into the rhetorical arrangement. But
in the cases of the opening (1.1-5) and the closing (6.11-18) the
epistolary nature is more prominent. They belong to the epistolary
framework rather than the rhetorical structure. Their basic elements
are clearly derived from ancient epistolary conventions, though
modified for Christian purposes and influenced by rhetorical strat-
egies. Thus Betz[4] asserts that the opening and the closing serve as a
kind of external bracket for the rhetorical speech presented in the
central part of the letter (1.6–6.10).[5]

Finally let me emphasize that one should be careful not to impose a
preconceived rhetorical structure on the text of Galatians by
attempting to push Galatians too far into a specific rhetorical framework.[6] Because we do not know exactly how far rhetoric exerted an
influence upon the structuring of the letter, we have first to make a
serious attempt to follow the flow of the argument of Galatians as it
stands, by means of discourse analysis. We should then examine the
rhetorical approach to see whether it throws further light on our
understanding of the structure of Galatians. In doing so I will not
proceed in two separate steps but will treat the results in an integrated
manner. In this way I hope to do justice to the text of Galatians as such.

1.   Brinsmead 1982: 37-55.
2.   Brinsmead adopts Betz's view that Galatians is an apologetic letter.
3.   Cf. Aune 1987: 188-91.
4.   Betz 1975: 355; Betz 1979: 15.
5.   Here I should admit that a further clarification of the relationship between
epistolography and rhetoric is worthy of investigation, as demonstrated in Petersen's
epistolary argument (1987: 6-34) against Wuellner's rhetorical approach to Rom. 16
(1977: 162-68).
6.   Cf. Betz 1975: 353-79; Betz 1979.

2. *Analysis of the Structure of Galatians*

On the basis of the discussion above, I will now undertake an analysis of the structure of Galatians. As mentioned already, the entire text of Galatians will, in the first place, be divided into cola. Next, the cola are to be grouped together on various levels up to the level of pericopae by identifying semantic relationships between individual cola and between larger units such as clusters and paragraphs. Finally, grouping pericopae according to their semantic relations will unfold the structure of Galatians in its entirety. In this whole course of grouping, the various stylistic devices, rhetorical arrangement and epistolary form, which exercised a considerable effect upon the structuring of Galatians, will also be taken into account. In particular, the important stylistic devices will be identified and marked as follows:

chiasmus

contrast

parallelism

pivotal colon

correspondence

recurring words

retrospection

anticipation

This formalization will be kept to a minimum.

a. *Grouping of Cola up to the Level of Pericopae*
i. *Pericope 1: Cola 1-2 (Galatians 1.1-5)*

```
┌─ 1   ¹Παῦλος ἀπόστολος
│         οὐκ ἀπ' ἀνθρώπων οὐδὲ δι' ἀνθρώπου
│         ἀλλὰ διὰ Ἰησοῦ Χριστοῦ καὶ θεοῦ πατρὸς
│            τοῦ ἐγείραντος αὐτὸν ἐκ νεκρῶν,
│         ²καὶ οἱ σὺν ἐμοὶ πάντες ἀδελφοὶ
│            ταῖς ἐκκλησίαις τῆς Γαλατίας,
└─ 2   ³χάρις ὑμῖν καὶ εἰρήνη
```

ἀπὸ θεοῦ πατρὸς ἡμῶν καὶ κυρίου Ἰησοῦ Χριστοῦ
⁴τοῦ δόντος ἑαυτὸν ὑπὲρ τῶν ἁμαρτιῶν ἡμῶν,
  ὅπως ἐξέληται ἡμᾶς ἐκ τοῦ αἰῶνος τοῦ ἐνεστῶτος πονηροῦ
  κατὰ τὸ θέλημα τοῦ θεοῦ καὶ πατρὸς ἡμῶν,
⁵ᾧ ἡ δόξα εἰς τοὺς αἰῶνας τῶν αἰώνων, ἀμήν.

Cola 1[1.1-2]-2[1.3-5]: additive consequential. This pericope is the
salutation of the letter, containing the three conventional elements of
the ancient epistolary prescript: sender, recipient and greeting. It is
remarkable that the first and the third elements are considerably
amplified. The element of the sender is expanded into an emphatic
statement of the divine origin of Paul's apostleship with the combination of οὐκ-οὐδέ-ἀλλά: Παῦλος ἀπόστολος οὐκ ἀπ' ἀνθρώπων
οὐδὲ δι' ἀνθρώπου ἀλλὰ διὰ Ἰησοῦ Χριστοῦ καὶ θεοῦ
πατρὸς... This statement is closely related to the narrative section in
Gal. 1.13–2.21, whose function is to establish Paul's ethos.[1] It is
interesting to note in the extension the contrast between God (or
Christ) and man (cf. 1.10-12).

The element of greeting is also enlarged: χάρις ὑμῖν καὶ εἰρήνη
ἀπό...κυρίου Ἰησοῦ Χριστοῦ τοῦ δόντος ἑαυτὸν ὑπὲρ τῶν
ἁμαρτιῶν ἡμῶν, ὅπως ἐξέληται ἡμᾶς ἐκ τοῦ αἰῶνος τοῦ
ἐνεστῶτος πονηροῦ... This understanding of the salvific significance
of Jesus' death in terms of eschatological deliverance functions as the
pivot of the argumentative section in Galatians: the argument of justification by faith versus justification by the works of the law (3.1-14)
and of sonship in Christ versus slavery under the law (3.23-29; 4.1-7;
cf. 4.21-31) hinges on this understanding (3.13-14; 3.25; 4.4-5).[2] This
also applies to the paraenetic section: the exhortation not to accept circumcision (5.1-12) and to walk by the Spirit (5.13-6.10) is based on
the same ground (5.1a, 13a; cf. 5.24).[3] Thus, the prescript, especially
the two expanded elements of sender and greeting, hints at the two
trains of thought in Galatians (cf. Rom. 1.2-6; 1 Cor. 1.2).

1. Cf. Kennedy 1984: 147-48; Ebeling 1985: 11; Hall 1987: 280, 284ff.
2. See below Ch. 1.2.a.vii, ix.
3. See below Ch. 1.2.a.xiii, xiv.

ii. *Pericope 2: Cola 3-8 (Galatians 1.6-10)*

```
┌─3  ⁶θαυμάζω ὅτι οὕτως ταχέως μετατίθεσθε
│       ἀπὸ τοῦ καλέσαντος ὑμᾶς ἐν χάριτι [Χριστοῦ]
│       εἰς ἕτερον εὐαγγέλιον,
│       ⁷ὃ οὐκ ἔστιν ἄλλο,
│       εἰ μή τινές εἰσιν
│       οἱ ταράσσοντες ὑμᾶς
│       καὶ θέλοντες μεταστρέψαι τὸ εὐαγγέλιον τοῦ Χριστοῦ.
├─4  ⁸ἀλλὰ καὶ ἐὰν ἡμεῖς ἢ ἄγγελος ἐξ οὐρανοῦ εὐαγγελίζηται [ὑμῖν]
│       παρ' ὃ εὐηγγελισάμεθα ὑμῖν,
│       ἀνάθεμα ἔστω.
└─5  ⁹ὡς προειρήκαμεν
        καὶ ἄρτι πάλιν λέγω,
        εἴ τις ὑμᾶς εὐαγγελίζεται παρ' ὃ παρελάβετε,
        ἀνάθεμα ἔστω.
┌─6  ¹⁰ἄρτι γὰρ ἀνθρώπους πείθω ἢ τὸν θεόν;
├─7    ἢ ζητῶ ἀνθρώποις ἀρέσκειν;
└─8    εἰ ἔτι ἀνθρώποις ἤρεσκον,
        Χριστοῦ δοῦλος οὐκ ἂν ἤμην.
```

Cola 4[1.8]-5[1.9]: additive equivalent. These two statements are basically the same pronouncement of ἀνάθεμα against those who preach a gospel contrary to Paul's gospel, namely the gospel of Christ. Note the repetition of ἀνάθεμα ἔστω.

Cola 6[1.10a]-7[1.10b]: additive equivalent. These two rhetorical questions are parallel, equally denying that Paul is seeking to please men. According to Burton, ζητῶ ἀρέσκειν in 1.10b takes the place of πείθω in 1.10a and expresses its idea more definitely.[1]

Cola (6[1.10a]-7[1.10b])-8[1.10c]: result–reason. Paul does not seek to please men but God (1.10a-10b), because he is a servant of Christ (1.10c). Gal. 1.10c is a 'contrary to fact' sentence. This cluster strongly asserts Paul's ethos.

Cola (4[1.8]-5[1.9])-(6[1.10a]-8[1.10c]): result–reason. Paul's strong pronouncements of ἀνάθεμα are justified (1.8-9), because he is not a pleaser of men but a true servant of Christ (1.10a-10c). The ἄρτι in

---

1.   Burton 1921: 32; cf. Bultmann 1968: 2; Betz 1979: 54-56.

1.10a, which repeats the ἄρτι in 1.9, limits us to the thought of 1.9.[1] The particle γάρ in 1.10a has a causal-defensive force, justifying the preceding harsh verdicts in 1.8-9.[2]

Cola 3[1.6-7]-(4[1.8]-8[1.10c]): reason–result. Because some preach to the Galatians a different gospel (1.6-7), they are accursed (1.8-10c). What Paul actually stresses by calling down a curse upon the false preachers is that there is no other gospel, that is, there is only one true gospel, the gospel of Christ. Note the antithesis between a different gospel and the gospel of Christ in 1.6-7. There are various opinions about the function of this pericope. Burton and Schlier view it as the occasion for Galatians,[3] Brinsmead as the cause of the letter,[4] and Petersen as an anti-thanksgiving.[5] It seems to me, however, that Kennedy is right in seeing it as the *proposition* of the letter as a whole.[6] This view will be supported by my further analysis of the structure of Galatians.

iii. *Pericope 3: Cola 9-12 (Galatians 1.11-12)*

```
┌─9   ¹¹γνωρίζω γὰρ ὑμῖν, ἀδελφοί, τὸ εὐαγγέλιον τὸ εὐαγγελισθὲν
│       ὑπ' ἐμοῦ ὅτι οὐκ ἔστιν κατὰ ἄνθρωπον·
│  ┌─10 ¹²οὐδὲ γὰρ ἐγὼ παρὰ ἀνθρώπου παρέλαβον αὐτὸ
│  └─11   οὔτε ἐδιδάχθην
└──12   ἀλλὰ δι' ἀποκαλύψεως Ἰησοῦ Χριστοῦ.
```

Cola 10[1.12a]-11[1.12b]: additive equivalent. Paul neither received his gospel from man (1.12a), nor was he taught it (1.12b). The two negative statements equally deny the human origin of Paul's gospel.

Cola (10[1.12a]-11[1.12b])-12[1.12c]: dyadic contrastive. Paul did not receive his gospel by human tradition or by human instruction (1.12a-12b); on the contrary, he received it through the revelation of Jesus Christ (1.12c). Admittedly, the actual content of 1.12a-12b is equivalent to that of 1.12c. On the surface level, however, Paul here

---

1. Lenski [1937] 1961: 43.
2. Burton 1921: 31; cf. Lenski [1937] 1961: 43; Schlier 1971: 41; Mussner 1974: 63.
3. Burton 1921: 18; Schlier 1971: 8.
4. Brinsmead 1982: 49; cf. Betz 1975: 359-62; Betz 1979: 44-46.
5. Petersen 1987: 24.
6. Kennedy 1984: 148; cf. Hall 1987: 283-84.

intentionally contrasts man with Christ. The revelation clearly refers to the Damascus event.

Cola 9[1.11]-(10[1.12a]-12[1.12c]): result–reason. Paul's gospel is not according to man (1.11), because he received it through the revelation of Christ (1.12a-12c). The γάρ in 1.12a explains 1.11. On the other hand, the γάρ in 1.11 marks the beginning of a new argument.[1] This pericope is the *thesis* of the narrative section in 1.13-2.21.[2] Note the contrast between man and Christ. By this contrast Paul puts emphasis upon the divine origin of his gospel. It is very interesting to observe the correspondence between the *divine origin* of Paul's apostleship in 1.1-2 and the *divine origin* of Paul's gospel here. This suggests that they are closely related (cf. 1.15, 16).

iv. *Pericope 4: Cola 13-25 (Galatians 1.13-24)*

13 ¹³ἠκούσατε γὰρ τὴν ἐμὴν ἀναστροφήν ποτε ἐν τῷ Ἰουδαϊσμῷ,
         ὅτι καθ' ὑπερβολὴν ἐδίωκον τὴν ἐκκλησίαν τοῦ θεοῦ
         καὶ ἐπόρθουν αὐτήν,
    ¹⁴καὶ προέκοπτον ἐν τῷ Ἰουδαϊσμῷ
         ὑπὲρ πολλοὺς συνηλικιώτας ἐν τῷ γένει μου,
         περισσοτέρως ζηλωτὴς ὑπάρχων
         τῶν πατρικῶν μου παραδόσεων.
14 ¹⁵ὅτε δὲ εὐδόκησεν [ὁ θεὸς]
         ὁ ἀφορίσας με ἐκ κοιλίας μητρός μου
         καὶ καλέσας διὰ τῆς χάριτος αὐτοῦ
         ¹⁶ἀποκαλύψαι τὸν υἱὸν αὐτοῦ ἐν ἐμοί,
         ἵνα εὐαγγελίζωμαι αὐτὸν ἐν τοῖς ἔθνεσιν,
         εὐθέως οὐ προσανεθέμην σαρκὶ καὶ αἵματι
15 ¹⁷οὐδὲ ἀνῆλθον εἰς Ἰεροσόλυμα πρὸς τοὺς πρὸ ἐμοῦ
         ἀποστόλους,
16 ἀλλὰ ἀπῆλθον εἰς Ἀραβίαν
17 καὶ πάλιν ὑπέστρεψα εἰς Δαμασκόν.
18 ¹⁸ἔπειτα μετὰ ἔτη τρία ἀνῆλθον εἰς Ἰεροσόλυμα ἱστορῆσαι
         Κηφᾶν
19 καὶ ἐπέμεινα πρὸς αὐτὸν ἡμέρας δεκαπέντε,

---

1. Bauer 1979: s.v. 4.
2. Burton 1921: 35; Schlier 1971: 43; Betz 1979: 61; Hester 1984: 233; Kennedy 1984: 148; Ebeling 1985: 73; Hall 1987: 285; Lategan 1988: 419.

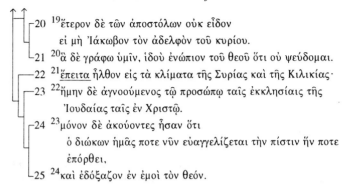

-20 ¹⁹ἕτερον δὲ τῶν ἀποστόλων οὐκ εἶδον
εἰ μὴ Ἰάκωβον τὸν ἀδελφὸν τοῦ κυρίου.

-21 ²⁰ἃ δὲ γράφω ὑμῖν, ἰδοὺ ἐνώπιον τοῦ θεοῦ ὅτι οὐ ψεύδομαι.

-22 ²¹ἔπειτα ἦλθον εἰς τὰ κλίματα τῆς Συρίας καὶ τῆς Κιλικίας·

-23 ²²ἤμην δὲ ἀγνοούμενος τῷ προσώπῳ ταῖς ἐκκλησίαις τῆς
Ἰουδαίας ταῖς ἐν Χριστῷ.

-24 ²³μόνον δὲ ἀκούοντες ἦσαν ὅτι
ὁ διώκων ἡμᾶς ποτε νῦν εὐαγγελίζεται τὴν πίστιν ἥν ποτε
ἐπόρθει,

-25 ²⁴καὶ ἐδόξαζον ἐν ἐμοὶ τὸν θεόν.

Cola 14[1.15-16]-15[1.17a]: additive equivalent. The main clause of 1.15-16 and that of 1.17a equally mean that after the revelation of the Son of God Paul did not turn immediately to men for counsel.

Cola 16[1.17b]-17[1.17c]: additive consequential. In response to the revelation Paul immediately went to Arabia (1.17b), and returned again to Damascus (1.17c).

Cola (14[1.15-16]-15[1.17a])-(16[1.17b]-17[1.17c]): dyadic contrastive. When God revealed his Son in Paul in order that he might preach the Son among the Gentiles, Paul did not seek human counsel (1.15-17a), but immediately went to Arabia to fulfil his commission to preach the Son and returned again to Damascus (1.17b-17c). In my opinion, the adverb εὐθέως in 1.16 qualifies not only προσανεθέμην in 1.16 and ἀνῆλθον in 1.17a but also ἀπῆλθον in 1.17b. The point here is that, in starting to carry out the commission, Paul did not depend on men but took an independent position.

Cola 18[1.18a]-19[1.18b]: additive consequential. Then three years later Paul went up to Jerusalem to visit Cephas (1.18a), and stayed with him fifteen days (1.18b).

Cola 20[1.19]-21[1.20]: purpose–means. The solemn oath (1.20) is made in order to affirm the truthfulness of the negative assertion (1.19). The words ἃ δὲ γράφω ὑμῖν in 1.20 refer to what immediately precedes.[1]

Cola (18[1.18a]-19[1.18b])-(20[1.19]-21[1.20]): dyadic contrastive. Three years later Paul visited Cephas in Jerusalem for fifteen days (1.18a-18b), but did not see any other apostles except James (1.19-20). Paul's denial of contact with any apostles other than James in his visit

1. Cf. Schlier 1971: 62; Sampley 1976–77: 479-82; Bruce 1982a: 102.

with Cephas is to stress that he did not receive any collective, official and apostolic seal of approval from Jerusalem.[1] Thus he asserts the independence of his apostleship and his gospel.

Cola 24[1.23]-25[1.24]: additive consequential. The Judaean churches heard of Paul's conversion and preaching (1.23), and glorified God because of him (1.24). The subject of the words ἀκούοντες ἦσαν in 1.23 refers to ταῖς ἐκκλησίαις in 1.22. 'Feminine or neuter personal collectives standing in the plural may be continued by a masculine plural.'[2]

Cola 23[1.22]-(24[1.23]-25[1.24]): dyadic contrastive. The Judaean churches did not know Paul personally (1.22), but only heard accounts of his preaching and glorified God (1.23-24). The word μόνον in 1.23 indicates the only exception to the ignorance mentioned in 1.22.

Cola 22[1.21]-(23[1.22]-25[1.24]): additive consequential. After a short visit to Jerusalem Paul went to the regions of Syria and Cilicia (1.21), and remained personally unknown to the Judaean churches, which only heard of his conversion and mission (1.22-24). Gal. 1.22-24 is an implied result of 1.21. So the δέ in 1.22 should be taken to be continuative, not contrastive. Paul's intention here is to show that he carried on an independent mission, not placing himself under the direction of the Jerusalem authorities.

Cola (14[1.15-16]-17[1.17c])-(18[1.18a]-21[1.20])-(22[1.21]-25[1.24]): additive consequential. When God revealed his Son in Paul that he might preach the Son to the Gentiles, Paul did not go to anyone for advice but at once went to Arabia to preach him and thereafter returned to Damascus (1.15-17c). Three years later he went up to Jerusalem to visit Cephas for fifteen days, but did not come into contact with any apostles other than James (1.18a-20). Then Paul went to Syria and Cilicia, remaining personally unknown to the Judaean churches (1.21-24). The main thrust here is that when he received the revelation of the Son of God and the commission to preach him, he did not seek any human advice or approval, but immediately took an independent position to fulfil the commission.

Cola 13[1.13-14]-(14[1.15-16]-25[1.24]): dyadic contrastive. Before his conversion Paul persecuted the church and was extremely zealous for his ancestral traditions (1.13-14). However, on receiving the

1.   Sampley 1976: 482.
2.   Blass and Debrunner 1961: §133.2.

revelation of the Son of God and the commission to preach him, he at once launched an independent mission without seeking any human counsel or authorization (1.15-24). Here Paul's former conduct in Judaism is in contrast to his immediate obedience to the revelation of the Son of God. This sharp contrast shows that his sudden, radical change is the result of the revelation of the Son and thereby underscores the divine origin of Paul's gospel and apostleship.

v. *Pericope 5: Cola 26-32 (Galatians 2.1-10)*

26 ¹<u>ἔπειτα</u> διὰ δεκατεσσάρων ἐτῶν πάλιν ἀνέβην εἰς Ἱεροσόλυμα

μετὰ Βαρναβᾶ συμπαραλαβὼν καὶ Τίτον·

27 ²ἀνέβην δὲ κατὰ ἀποκάλυψιν·

28 καὶ ἀνεθέμην αὐτοῖς τὸ εὐαγγέλιον

ὃ κηρύσσω ἐν τοῖς ἔθνεσιν,

κατ' ἰδίαν δὲ τοῖς δοκοῦσιν,

μή πως εἰς κενὸν τρέχω ἢ ἔδραμον.

29 ³ἀλλ' οὐδὲ Τίτος ὁ σὺν ἐμοί, Ἕλλην ὤν, ἠναγκάσθη

<u>περιτμηθῆναι</u>·

30 ⁴διὰ δὲ τοὺς παρεισάκτους ψευδαδέλφους,

οἵτινες παρεισῆλθον κατασκοπῆσαι τὴν <u>ἐλευθερίαν ἡμῶν</u>

ἣν ἔχομεν ἐν Χριστῷ Ἰησοῦ,

ἵνα ἡμᾶς <u>καταδουλώσουσιν</u>,

⁵οἷς οὐδὲ πρὸς ὥραν εἴξαμεν τῇ ὑποταγῇ,

ἵνα ἡ <u>ἀλήθεια τοῦ εὐαγγελίου</u> διαμείνῃ πρὸς ὑμᾶς.

31 ⁶ἀπὸ δὲ τῶν δοκούντων εἶναί τι,

—ὁποῖοί ποτε ἦσαν οὐδέν μοι διαφέρει·

πρόσωπον [ὁ] θεὸς ἀνθρώπου οὐ λαμβάνει—

ἐμοὶ γὰρ οἱ δοκοῦντες οὐδὲν προσανέθεντο,

32 ⁷ἀλλὰ τοὐναντίον ἰδόντες

ὅτι πεπίστευμαι τὸ εὐαγγέλιον τῆς ἀκροβυστίας

καθὼς Πέτρος τῆς περιτομῆς,

⁸ὁ γὰρ ἐνεργήσας Πέτρῳ εἰς ἀποστολὴν τῆς περιτομῆς

ἐνήργησεν καὶ ἐμοὶ εἰς τὰ ἔθνη,

⁹καὶ γνόντες τὴν χάριν τὴν δοθεῖσάν μοι,

Ἰάκωβος καὶ Κηφᾶς καὶ Ἰωάννης,

οἱ δοκοῦντες στῦλοι εἶναι,

δεξιὰς ἔδωκαν ἐμοὶ καὶ Βαρναβᾷ κοινωνίας,
ἵνα ἡμεῖς εἰς τὰ ἔθνη, αὐτοὶ δὲ εἰς τὴν περιτομήν·
[10]μόνον τῶν πτωχῶν ἵνα μνημονεύωμεν,
ὃ καὶ ἐσπούδασα αὐτὸ τοῦτο ποιῆσαι.

Cola 26[2.1]-27[2.2a]: means–purpose. Fourteen years later Paul returned to Jerusalem with Barnabas and Titus (2.1) in order to defend the revelation (2.2a). Hester defines the meaning of κατά in 2.2a as 'in defence of' or 'in behalf of'.[1] The revelation here points to the revelation of Christ mentioned in 1.12c and 1.15-16.[2]

Cola (26[2.1]-27[2.2a])-28[2.2b]: additive consequential. Paul went up to Jerusalem in order to defend the revelation (2.1-2a), and laid before those of reputation his gospel for fear that he might be running or had run in vain (2.2b).

Cola 29[2.3]-30[2.4-5]: result–reason. Not even Titus, a Greek, was compelled to be circumcised (2.3), because of the false brethren who tried to enslave those who had liberty in Christ and to whom Paul did not yield in subjection for the sake of the truth of the gospel (2.4-5). Gal. 2.4-5, whose main clause is missing, is an anacoluthon. Note the correspondence between circumcision and enslavement and between liberty in Christ and the truth of the gospel, and also the contrast between these two groups.

Cola 31[2.6]-32[2.7-10]: dyadic contrastive. Those of reputation added nothing to Paul (2.6), but acknowledged the validity of his gospel and his commission to preach to the Gentiles (2.7-10).

Cola (29[2.3]-30[2.4-5])-(31[2.6]-32[2.7-10]): dyadic contrastive. Not even Titus was forced to be circumcised (2.3-5). But the validity of Paul's gospel and his commission was recognized (2.6-10).

Cola (26[2.1]-28[2.2b])-(29[2.3]-32[2.7-10]): additive consequential. Fourteen years later Paul went back to Jerusalem and set his gospel before those of reputation (2.1-2b), and the validity of his gospel and his apostleship was fully recognized (2.3-10).

---

1.   Hester 1984: 231; Hester 1986: 397; cf. Howard 1979: 37-38.
2.   Lührmann 1965: 41, 80; Howard 1979: 38; Hester 1984: 231; Hester 1986: 397.

vi. *Pericope 6: Cola 33-37.12 (Galatians 2.11-21)*

33 ¹¹ὅτε δὲ ἦλθεν Κηφᾶς εἰς Ἀντιόχειαν,
  κατὰ πρόσωπον αὐτῷ ἀντέστην, ὅτι κατεγνωσμένος ἦν.

34 ¹²πρὸ τοῦ γὰρ ἐλθεῖν τινας ἀπὸ Ἰακώβου
  μετὰ τῶν ἐθνῶν συνήσθιεν·

35 ὅτε δὲ ἦλθον,
  ὑπέστελλεν καὶ ἀφώριζεν ἑαυτὸν
  φοβούμενος τοὺς ἐκ περιτομῆς.

36 ¹³καὶ συνυπεκρίθησαν αὐτῷ [καὶ] οἱ λοιποὶ Ἰουδαῖοι,
  ὥστε καὶ Βαρναβᾶς συναπήχθη αὐτῶν τῇ ὑποκρίσει.

37.0 ¹⁴ἀλλ᾽ ὅτε εἶδον
  ὅτι οὐκ ὀρθοποδοῦσιν πρὸς τὴν ἀλήθειαν τοῦ εὐαγγελίου,
  εἶπον τῷ Κηφᾷ ἔμπροσθεν πάντων,

37.1 εἰ σὺ Ἰουδαῖος ὑπάρχων ἐθνικῶς καὶ οὐχὶ Ἰουδαϊκῶς ζῇς,
  πῶς τὰ ἔθνη ἀναγκάζεις Ἰουδαΐζειν;

37.2 ¹⁵ἡμεῖς φύσει Ἰουδαῖοι καὶ οὐκ ἐξ ἐθνῶν ἁμαρτωλοί·
  ¹⁶εἰδότες [δὲ] ὅτι οὐ δικαιοῦται ἄνθρωπος
    ἐξ ἔργων νόμου
    ⟶
    ἐὰν μὴ διὰ πίστεως Ἰησοῦ Χριστοῦ,
    ⟵
  καὶ ἡμεῖς εἰς Χριστὸν Ἰησοῦν ἐπιστεύσαμεν,
    ἵνα δικαιωθῶμεν ἐκ πίστεως Χριστοῦ
    ⟶
  καὶ οὐκ ἐξ ἔργων νόμου,
    ὅτι ἐξ ἔργων νόμου οὐ δικαιωθήσεται πᾶσα σάρξ.

37.3 ¹⁷εἰ δὲ ζητοῦντες δικαιωθῆναι ἐν Χριστῷ
  εὑρέθημεν καὶ αὐτοὶ ἁμαρτωλοί,
  ἆρα Χριστὸς ἁμαρτίας διάκονος;

37.4 μὴ γένοιτο.

37.5 ¹⁸εἰ γὰρ ἃ κατέλυσα ταῦτα πάλιν οἰκοδομῶ,
  παραβάτην ἐμαυτὸν συνιστάνω.

37.6 ¹⁹ἐγὼ γὰρ διὰ νόμου νόμῳ ἀπέθανον, ἵνα θεῷ ζήσω.
  ⟶   ⟵

37.7 Χριστῷ συνεσταύρωμαι·

37.8 ²⁰ζῶ δὲ οὐκέτι ἐγώ,
  ⟶

37.9 ζῇ δὲ ἐν ἐμοὶ Χριστός·
  ⟵

37.10 ὃ δὲ νῦν ζῶ ἐν σαρκί,
  ἐν πίστει ζῶ τῇ τοῦ υἱοῦ τοῦ θεοῦ
    τοῦ ἀγαπήσαντός με
    καὶ παραδόντος ἑαυτὸν ὑπὲρ ἐμοῦ.

┌─37.11 ²¹οὐκ ἀθετῶ τὴν χάριν τοῦ θεοῦ·
└─37.12   εἰ γὰρ διὰ νόμου δικαιοσύνη,
        ἄρα Χριστὸς δωρεὰν ἀπέθανεν.

Cola 35[2.12b]-36[2.13]: reason–result. Because Cephas withdrew from eating with the Gentiles when certain men from James came (2.12b), the rest of the Jews and even Barnabas were led astray by Cephas's hypocrisy (2.13).

Cola 34[2.12a]-(35[2.12b]-36[2.13]): dyadic contrastive. Before certain men from James came, Cephas was eating together with the Gentiles (2.12a). But, when they came, he separated himself from them (2.12b-13).

Cola 37.3[2.17a]-37.4[2.17b]: additive equivalent. The expression μὴ γένοιτο in 2.17b reinforces the negative answer implied in the rhetorical question of 2.17a. The actual meaning of this question is that even if the Jews, seeking to be justified in Christ, have also been found sinners, Christ is not a minister of sin. I consider the protasis in 2.17a as a realis.[1]

Cola 37.2[2.15-16]-(37.3[2.17a]-37.4[2.17b]): concession–result. Although even the Jews have believed in Christ in order to be justified, realizing that no one is justified by the works of the law but by faith in Jesus Christ (2.15-16), it does not follow that Christ is a minister of sin (2.17a-b). It seems that the interrogative particle ἆρα in 2.17a is to be replaced by the inferential particle ἄρα, since the former appears nowhere else in Paul.[2] Even in this case, the ἄρα clause in 2.17a still remains a question. Note the antithesis between ἐξ ἔργων νόμου and διὰ (or ἐκ) πίστεως ('Ιησοῦ) Χριστοῦ in 2.15-16 and their chiastic arrangement. Note also that the verb δικαιόω occurs four times in this cluster.

Cola 37.1[2.14b]-(37.2[2.15-16]-37.4[2.17b]): dyadic contrastive. Cephas tries to Judaize the Gentiles (2.14b). But even the Jews, like the Gentile sinners, are justified by faith in Jesus Christ, not by the works of the law (2.15-17b). The point of this contrast is that Cephas's act of Judaizing the Gentiles opposes God's act of justifying all mankind in Christ, the Jews as well as the Gentiles. It is significant

1. Lambrecht 1977–78: 490.
2. Moule 1944–45: 223; Moule 1963: 196; Lambrecht 1977–78: 489-90; Bruce 1982a: 141.

that Cephas's act of withdrawing from eating with the Gentiles in 2.12a-13 is described as the act of 'Judaizing' in 2.14b.

Cola 37.6[2.19a]-37.7[2.19b]: result–means. Death in relation to the law in order to live in relation to God has taken place (2.19a) by participation in Christ's death (2.19b). The datives of νόμῳ and θεῷ are to be taken in a relational sense.[1] Note the antithesis between the law and God.

Cola 37.8[2.20a]-37.9[2.20b]: dyadic contrastive. It is no longer 'I' who live (2.20a), but it is Christ who lives in the believer (2.20b). Note the antithesis between 'I' and Christ.

Cola (37.8[2.20a]-37.9[2.20b])-37.10[2.20c]: additive equivalent. The life controlled by Christ (2.20a-b) is equivalent to the life of faith, that is, the life of dependence on the Son of God (2.20c).

Cola (37.6[2.19a]-37.7[2.19b])-(37.8[2.20a]-37.10[2.20c]): additive equivalent. The believer's death in relation to the law, that is, his life in relation to God (2.19a-b), is equivalent to his life controlled by Christ, namely the life of faith in Christ (2.20a-c). The particle δέ in 2.20a is continuative, expressing another aspect of the same fact presented in 2.19a-b.[2] Note the repeated occurrences of the verb ζάω.

Cola 37.11[2.21a]-37.12[2.21b]: result–reason. Paul does not nullify the grace of God (2.21a), because he does not rely on the law for righteousness but on Christ who died for him (2.21b). 'God's grace is forever established by Christ's death.'[3]

Cola (37.6[2.19a]-37.10[2.20c])-(37.11[2.21a]-37.12[2.21b]): reason–result. Because the believer lives in relation to God by faith in Christ (2.19a-20c), he does not nullify the grace of God (2.21a-b).

Cola 37.5[2.18]-(37.6[2.19a]-37.12[2.21b]): dyadic contrastive. As a result of his behaviour at Antioch (2.12) Cephas restored the prescriptions of the law which forbade eating with the Gentiles, thereby paradoxically proving himself to be a transgressor of the prescriptions, and thus returning to his former status of a slave of the law (2.18). The believer, however, died in relation to the law by participation in Christ's death, and now lives in relation to God (2.19a-21b). The 'I' in 2.18 obviously refers to Cephas. The γάρ in 2.19a is not

1. Bruce 1982a: 143.
2. Burton 1921: 137.
3. Lenski [1937] 1961: 120.

causal, but serves to introduce a new idea.[1]

Cola (37.1[2.14b]-37.4[2.17b])-(37.5[2.18]-37.12[2.21b]): additive consequential. Cephas's act of Judaizing the Gentiles opposes God's act of justifying all mankind in Christ (2.14b-17b). Further, his act of restoring the law and thereby returning to the slavery of the law contradicts Christ's act of liberating men from the slavery of the law for the new life in relation to God (2.18-21b). The γάρ in 2.18 is continuative, introducing a new start.[2] Note the shift from the first person plural in 2.15-17a to the first person singular in 2.18-21b. Note also the change of the main verb: from δικαιόω in 2.15-17a to ζάω in 2.19a-20c. This cluster serves as a summary of the argumentative section in 3.1-4.31 and the paraenetic section in 5.1-6.10.[3] I will return to this later on.[4]

Cola 37.0[2.14a]-(37.1[2.14b]-37.12[2.21b]): substance content. The long speech against Cephas (2.14b-21b) gives the content of Paul's criticism of Cephas whose conduct contradicts the truth of the gospel (2.14a). In my opinion, the speech in 2.14b-21b is a reconstruction of Paul's rebuke to Cephas at Antioch with a view to clarifying the Galatians' problems.[5] This section functions not only as the conclusion of the narrative section, but also as a transition to the argumentative section.

Cola (34[2.12a]-36[2.13])-(37.0[2.14a]-37.12[2.21b]): reason–result. Because Cephas withdrew from eating with the Gentiles (2.12a-13), Paul rebuked him (2.14a-21b).

Cola 33[2.11]-(34[2.12a]-37.12[2.21b]): generic–specific. Paul's opposition to Cephas (2.11) is fully specified in 2.12a-21b.

vii. *Pericope 7: Cola 38-54 (Galatians 3.1-14)*

38 [1]ὦ ἀνόητοι Γαλάται, τίς ὑμᾶς ἐβάσκανεν,
οἷς κατ᾽ ὀφθαλμοὺς Ἰησοῦς Χριστὸς
προεγράφη ἐσταυρωμένος;
39 [2]τοῦτο μόνον θέλω μαθεῖν ἀφ᾽ ὑμῶν·
ἐξ ἔργων νόμου τὸ πνεῦμα ἐλάβετε ἢ ἐξ ἀκοῆς πίστεως;

1. Cf. Lambrecht 1977–78: 493.
2. Lambrecht 1977–78: 493.
3. Cf. Betz 1975: 367-68; Betz 1979: 113-27; Brinsmead 1982: 51-52, 69-78.
4. See below Ch. 1.2.b.ii.
5. Cf. Schlier 1971: 87; Mussner 1974: 178; Lambrecht 1977–78: 484.

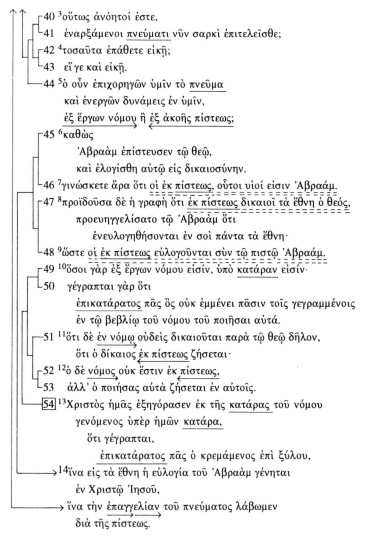

40 ³οὕτως ἀνόητοί ἐστε,
41 ἐναρξάμενοι πνεύματι νῦν σαρκὶ ἐπιτελεῖσθε;
42 ⁴τοσαῦτα ἐπάθετε εἰκῇ;
43 εἴ γε καὶ εἰκῇ.
44 ⁵ὁ οὖν ἐπιχορηγῶν ὑμῖν τὸ πνεῦμα
καὶ ἐνεργῶν δυνάμεις ἐν ὑμῖν,
ἐξ ἔργων νόμου ἢ ἐξ ἀκοῆς πίστεως;
45 ⁶καθὼς
Ἀβραὰμ ἐπίστευσεν τῷ θεῷ,
καὶ ἐλογίσθη αὐτῷ εἰς δικαιοσύνην.
46 ⁷γινώσκετε ἄρα ὅτι οἱ ἐκ πίστεως, οὗτοι υἱοί εἰσιν Ἀβραάμ.
47 ⁸προϊδοῦσα δὲ ἡ γραφὴ ὅτι ἐκ πίστεως δικαιοῖ τὰ ἔθνη ὁ θεός,
προευηγγελίσατο τῷ Ἀβραὰμ ὅτι
ἐνευλογηθήσονται ἐν σοὶ πάντα τὰ ἔθνη·
48 ⁹ὥστε οἱ ἐκ πίστεως εὐλογοῦνται σὺν τῷ πιστῷ Ἀβραάμ.
49 ¹⁰ὅσοι γὰρ ἐξ ἔργων νόμου εἰσίν, ὑπὸ κατάραν εἰσίν·
50 γέγραπται γὰρ ὅτι
ἐπικατάρατος πᾶς ὃς οὐκ ἐμμένει πᾶσιν τοῖς γεγραμμένοις
ἐν τῷ βεβλίῳ τοῦ νόμου τοῦ ποιῆσαι αὐτά.
51 ¹¹ὅτι δὲ ἐν νόμῳ οὐδεὶς δικαιοῦται παρὰ τῷ θεῷ δῆλον,
ὅτι ὁ δίκαιος ἐκ πίστεως ζήσεται·
52 ¹²ὁ δὲ νόμος οὐκ ἔστιν ἐκ πίστεως,
53 ἀλλ᾽ ὁ ποιήσας αὐτὰ ζήσεται ἐν αὐτοῖς.
54 ¹³Χριστὸς ἡμᾶς ἐξηγόρασεν ἐκ τῆς κατάρας τοῦ νόμου
γενόμενος ὑπὲρ ἡμῶν κατάρα,
ὅτι γέγραπται,
ἐπικατάρατος πᾶς ὁ κρεμάμενος ἐπὶ ξύλου,
¹⁴ἵνα εἰς τὰ ἔθνη ἡ εὐλογία τοῦ Ἀβραὰμ γένηται
ἐν Χριστῷ Ἰησοῦ,
ἵνα τὴν ἐπαγγελίαν τοῦ πνεύματος λάβωμεν
διὰ τῆς πίστεως.

Cola 40[3.3a]-41[3.3b]: result–reason. The Galatians are foolish (3.3a), because they began by the Spirit but are now trying to be perfected by the flesh (3.3b). Paul here is not asking a question, but is making a forceful statement by means of a rhetorical question.[1] This

1. Cronje 1986: 218-19.

is true of the other questions in 3.1, 2, 4, 5; 4.9, 15, 21; 5.7.

Cola 42[3.4a]-43[3.4b]: additive equivalent. These two statements both underscore Paul's point that the Galatians' experiences of the Spirit were not in vain. It is extremely difficult to translate precisely the second statement in 3.4b: εἴ γε καὶ εἰκῇ. But it doubtless strengthens the force of the preceding rhetorical question. According to the context, the word ἐπάθετε in 3.4a seems to refer to the experiences connected with the Spirit,[1] but not to the persecutions of the Galatians.[2]

Cola (40[3.3a]-41[3.3b])-(42[3.4a]-43[3.4b]): dyadic contrastive. The Galatians are foolishly trying to be perfected by the flesh, having begun by the Spirit (3.3a-b). However, their experiences of the Spirit have not been in vain (3.4a-b).

Cola (40[3.3a]-43[3.4b])-44[3.5]: cause–effect. Paul's conviction that the Galatians' experiences of the Spirit were not in vain in spite of their present backsliding (3.3a-4b) causes him to reaffirm the statement made in 3.5.

Cola 39[3.2]-(40[3.3a]-44[3.5]): additive equivalent. Gal. 3.5 is a repetition of 3.2. Although their subjects are different, both of these statements forcefully underline the fact that the gift of the Spirit was given to the Galatians on the basis of the hearing of faith, not on the basis of the works of the law. Note the opposition between ἐξ ἔργων νόμου and ἐξ ἀκοῆς πίστεως in 3.2 and 5. The οὖν in 3.5 connects 3.5 with 3.2.[3] The present participles of ἐπιχορηγῶν and ἐνεργῶν in 3.5 point to the initial spiritual experiences of the Galatians extended enough to be thought of as in progress.[4]

Cola 38[3.1]-(39[3.2]-44[3.5]): cause–effect. The fact that the Galatians have foolishly been bewitched (3.1) causes Paul to stress the fundamental fact that the Spirit had not been bestowed to them on the basis of the works of the law, but on the basis of the hearing of faith (3.2-5). The focus of the rhetorical question in 3.1 is on the condition of the Galatians, not on the trouble-maker(s). Note the repeated appearances of the key word πνεῦμα in 3.2, 3b and 5.

Cola 45[3.6]-46[3.7]: basis–inference. Since Abraham believed in

1. Schlier 1971: 124; Mussner 1974: 209-10; Betz 1979: 134.
2. Cf. Lightfoot 1880: 135; Zahn 1907: 144-45.
3. Schlier 1971: 125 n. 2.
4. Burton 1921: 152; cf. Betz 1979: 135.

God and obtained righteousness (3.6), those who are of faith are sons of Abraham (3.7). The ἄρα in 3.7 is an inferential particle. The καθώς in 3.6 is to be taken as introducing a new point, though it closely links receiving the Spirit by faith in 3.1-5 with being justified by faith in 3.6ff.[1]

Cola 47[3.8]-48[3.9]: basis–inference. Since the Scripture promised that all the nations would be blessed in Abraham, that is, be justified by faith as Abraham was (3.8), the men of faith, Gentiles as well as Jews, are blessed together with Abraham (3.9). The ὥστε in 3.9 is an inferential particle.

Cola (45[3.6]-46[3.7])-(47[3.8]-48[3.9]): additive equivalent. The statement in 3.7, deduced from God's acceptance of Abraham on the grounds of his belief (3.6), is identical to the statement in 3.9, inferred from God's promise to justify the nations as he justified Abraham (3.8). Becoming a son of Abraham by faith (3.7) actually means the same thing as being blessed with Abraham by faith (3.9).

Cola 49[3.10a]-50[3.10b]: result–reason. All who are of the works of the law are under a curse (3.10a), because they fail to obey everything that is written in the book of the law (3.10b). Gal. 3.10b implies the conviction of the universal failure to keep the law perfectly.

Cola 52[3.12a]-53[3.12b]: result–reason. The law has nothing to do with faith (3.12a), because the perfect obedience of the law promises life (3.12b). This life is life within the covenant, since in the original context of Lev. 18.5 cited in Gal. 3.12b the promise was given to Israel who had already become the covenant people of God.

Cola 51[3.11]-(52[3.12a]-53[3.12b]): basis–inference. Since no one is justified by the law but by faith (3.11), the law has nothing to do with faith (3.12a-b). Note the antithesis between νόμος and πίστις.

Cola (49[3.10a]-50[3.10b])-(51[3.11]-53[3.12b]): additive consequential. All who are of the works of the law are under a curse due to their transgression of the law (3.10a-b), and no one is justified by the law but by faith (3.11-12b). In my opinion, the δέ in 3.11 is continuative.

Cola (49[3.10a]-53[3.12b])-54[3.13-14]: reason–result. Because all who are of the works of the law fail to keep every precept in the law and are thus under the curse of the law (3.10a-12b), Christ redeemed them from the curse by his substitutionary death on the cross in order

1. Cf. Bruce 1982a: 152.

that the Gentiles might share in the blessing of Abraham, namely justification by faith, and in order that the believers might receive the promised Spirit (3.13-14). Gal. 3.13 takes up 3.10a-b, answering the problem of the curse of the law. Note the occurrences of κατάρα and ἐπικατάρατος in 3.10a-b and 3.13. The two coordinate ἵνα clauses in 3.14 are closely related to the preceding arguments: the first ἵνα clause shows that the promise of the Gentiles' participation in the blessing of Abraham, occasioned by Abraham's believing God in 3.6-9, found fulfilment through Christ's redemption; the second clause demonstrates that the Galatians' reception of the Spirit in 3.1-5 is a result of the redemption.[1] This makes it clear that 3.13-14 (colon 54) is the *pivotal point* of Paul's argument in this pericope (cf. Ch. 1.2.a.i). To be justified before God, to become a son of Abraham and to receive the Spirit all depend upon faith in Christ who carried away the curse of the law on behalf of all mankind. Note the sudden appearance of the word ἐπαγγελία in 3.14, which is picked up for further consideration in the next pericope.

viii. *Pericope 8: Cola 55-68 (Galatians 3.15-22)*

55 ¹⁵ἀδελφοί, κατὰ ἄνθρωπον λέγω·
    ὅμως ἀνθρώπου κεκυρωμένην διαθήκην
    οὐδεὶς ἀθετεῖ ἢ ἐπιδιατάσσεται.
56 ¹⁶τῷ δὲ Ἀβραὰμ ἐρρέθησαν αἱ ἐπαγγελίαι
    καὶ τῷ σπέρματι αὐτοῦ.
57 οὐ λέγει,
    καὶ τοῖς σπέρμασιν, ὡς ἐπὶ πολλῶν
    ἀλλ’ ὡς ἐφ’ ἑνός, καὶ τῷ σπέρματί σου,
    ὅς ἐστιν Χριστός.
58 ¹⁷τοῦτο δὲ λέγω·
    διαθήκην προκεκυρωμένην ὑπὸ τοῦ θεοῦ
    ὁ μετὰ τετρακόσια καὶ τριάκοντα ἔτη γεγονὼς νόμος
    οὐκ ἀκυροῖ εἰς τὸ καταργῆσαι τὴν ἐπαγγελίαν.
59 ¹⁸εἰ γὰρ ἐκ νόμου ἡ κληρονομία,
    οὐκέτι ἐξ ἐπαγγελίας·
60 τῷ δὲ Ἀβραὰμ δι’ ἐπαγγελίας κεχάρισται ὁ θεός.

1.   Cf. Betz 1979: 138-39; Tolmie 1986b: 40-42.

┌─61 [19]τί οὖν ὁ νόμος;
└─62 τῶν παραβάσεων χάριν προσετέθη,
      ἄχρις οὖ ἔλθῃ τὸ σπέρμα ᾧ ἐπήγγελται,
      διαταγεὶς δι᾽ ἀγγέλων ἐν χειρὶ μεσίτου.
┌─63 [20]ὁ δὲ μεσίτης ἑνὸς οὐκ ἔστιν,
└─64 ὁ δὲ θεὸς εἷς ἐστιν.
┌─65 [21]ὁ οὖν νόμος κατὰ τῶν ἐπαγγελιῶν [τοῦ θεοῦ];
└─66 μὴ γένοιτο.
┌─67 εἰ γὰρ ἐδόθη νόμος
      ὁ δυνάμενος ζῳοποιῆσαι,
      ὄντως ἐκ νόμου ἂν ἦν ἡ δικαιοσύνη·
└─68 [22]ἀλλὰ συνέκλεισεν ἡ γραφὴ τὰ πάντα ὑπὸ ἁμαρτίαν,
      ἵνα ἡ ἐπαγγελία ἐκ πίστεως Ἰησοῦ Χριστοῦ δοθῇ
      τοῖς πιστεύουσιν.

Cola 56[3.16a]-57[3.16b]: result–reason. The promises were made to Abraham and his seed (3.16a), because the Scripture does not say 'and to seeds', but 'and to your seed', namely Christ (3.16b). This cluster is parenthetical, because the phrase τοῦτο δὲ λέγω in 3.17 directly takes up 3.15 for comparison.[1] But the cluster is related to 3.17, because both of them speak of God's covenant with Abraham.

Cola 55[3.15], 58[3.17]: dyadic comparative. Just as no one can annul or add to a man's covenant (or will) (3.15), so the law given 430 years later cannot invalidate God's covenant with Abraham so as to nullify the promise (3.17).

Cola 59[3.18a]-60[3.18b]: result–reason. The inheritance is not of the law but of a promise (3.18a), because God granted it to Abraham by a promise (3.18b). Note the contrast between ἐκ νόμου and ἐξ ἐπαγγελίας.

Cola (55[3.15]-58[3.17])-(59[3.18a]-60[3.18b]): result–reason. The law cannot abolish the promise of the covenant (3.15-17), because the inheritance is not of the law but of the promise (3.18a-b). The particle γάρ in 3.18a is explicative, explaining further the point made in the preceding cluster of 3.15-17.[2]

Cola 61[3.19a]-62[3.19b]: substance content. What is the purpose of the law (3.19a)? It was added for the sake of transgressions until the

1. Cf. Burton 1921: 180-82.
2. Mussner 1974: 242; cf. Lenski [1937] 1961: 164.

seed should come, to whom the promise had been made (3.19b). The context seems to suggest that the χάριν in 3.19b is to be taken in a final sense.[1]

Cola 63[3.20a]-64[3.20b]: dyadic contrastive. A mediator is not for one party (3.20a); however, God is one (3.20b). The meaning of this enigmatic statement has been sufficiently clarified: in the giving of the law, a mediator was employed; however, in the bestowing of the promise, God acted alone. What is intended here is to contrast the *indirect* character of the law with the *direct* character of the promise, and thereby to emphasize the *inferiority* of the law to the promise.[2]

Cola (61[3.19a]-62[3.19b])-(63[3.20a]-64[3.20b]): additive consequential. The law was added for the sake of transgressions until the seed of the promise should come (3.19a-b), and it was indirectly enacted and is thus inferior to the promise given directly by God (3.20a-b).

Cola 65[3.21a]-66[3.21b]: additive equivalent. The implied negative answer of the rhetorical question that the law is not against the promises of God (3.21a) is reinforced by the expression μὴ γένοιτο (3.21b).

Cola (61[3.19a]-64[3.20b])-(65[3.21a]-66[3.21b]): dyadic contrastive. The law was added to produce transgressions until the coming of the seed of the promise and it was indirectly ordained (3.19a-20b); however, it is not contrary to the promises of God (3.21a-b). The rhetorical question of 3.21a is an illegitimate inference deduced from 3.19a-20b, especially from the assertion τῶν παραβάσεων χάριν προσετέθη in 3.19b which cannot but provoke the Jews.[3] The inference is immediately rejected by μὴ γένοιτο.

Cola 67[3.21c]-68[3.22]: dyadic contrastive. The law was not given as a basis of righteousness (3.21c); however, the Scripture shut up all men under sin that the promise by faith in Jesus Christ might be given to the believers (3.22). The singular γραφή in 3.22 does not refer to a particular passage of the Scripture[4] but to the entire Scripture whose verdict includes the verdict of the law.[5] Note that the γραφή stands

---

1.   See below Ch. 6.1.
2.   Cf. Howard 1979: 77.
3.   Lambrecht 1977–78: 492.
4.   Cf. Burton 1921: 195-96; Ridderbos 1953: 141 n. 28.
5.   Guthrie 1973: 107; Ebeling 1985: 192-93; Fung 1988: 164.

alone without any accompanying OT passage (cf. 3.8; 4.30; Rom. 4.3;
9.17; 10.11; 11.2). The statement in 3.21c is hypothetical.

Cola (61[3.19a]-66[3.21b])-(67[3.21c]-68[3.22]): reason–result.
Because the law was added for the purpose of transgressions and is not
against the promises of God (3.19a-21b), the Scripture confined all men
under sin that the believers might receive the promise by faith in Christ
(3.21c-22). The particle γάρ in 3.21c seems to be continuative rather
than causal,[1] because the γάρ-clause and those clauses which follow do
not simply furnish a reason for the emphatic negation of μὴ γένοιτο
in 3.21b, but lead to a new argument.[2] The idea presented in 3.22,
which is closely connected with 3.21c, is further developed in the
following pericope. Note that the verb συγκλείω is taken up in 3.23.

Cola (55[3.15]-60[3.18b])-(61[3.19a]-68[3.22]): dyadic contrastive.
The law could not invalidate the covenantal promise (3.15-18b). Yet
the law was given to produce transgressions, and in consequence the
Scripture shut up all men under sin that the believers might receive
the promise by faith in Christ (3.19a-22). This radical understanding
of the purpose of the law is very important for interpreting the subsequent statements of the law. This pericope is an excursus, marking a
transition from the preceding argument of justification not by the
works of the law but by faith to the following argument of the two
different modes of existence, namely slavery under the law and sonship in Christ (3.23-4.31). This will become obvious in the broader
context.[3]

ix. *Pericope 9: Cola 69-78 (Galatians 3.23-29)*

69 ²³πρὸ τοῦ δὲ ἐλθεῖν τὴν πίστιν

ὑπὸ νόμον ἐφρουρούμεθα

συγκλειόμενοι εἰς τὴν μέλλουσαν πίστιν ἀποκαλυφθῆναι,

70 ²⁴ὥστε ὁ νόμος παιδαγωγὸς ἡμῶν γέγονεν εἰς Χριστόν,

ἵνα ἐκ πίστεως δικαιωθῶμεν·

71 ²⁵ἐλθούσης δὲ τῆς πίστεως

οὐκέτι ὑπὸ παιδαγωγόν ἐσμεν.

72 ²⁶πάντες γὰρ υἱοὶ θεοῦ ἐστε διὰ τῆς πίστεως ἐν Χριστῷ Ἰησοῦ·

1. Lambrecht 1977–78: 492.
2. Cf. Malherbe 1980: 239.
3. See below Ch. 1.2.b.ii.

46   The Law in Galatians

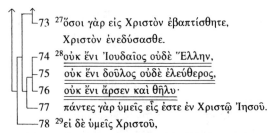

73 ²⁷ὅσοι γὰρ εἰς Χριστὸν ἐβαπτίσθητε,
   Χριστὸν ἐνεδύσασθε.
74 ²⁸οὐκ ἔνι Ἰουδαῖος οὐδὲ Ἕλλην,
75 οὐκ ἔνι δοῦλος οὐδὲ ἐλεύθερος,
76 οὐκ ἔνι ἄρσεν καὶ θῆλυ·
77 πάντες γὰρ ὑμεῖς εἷς ἐστε ἐν Χριστῷ Ἰησοῦ.
78 ²⁹εἰ δὲ ὑμεῖς Χριστοῦ,
   ἄρα τοῦ Ἀβραὰμ σπέρμα ἐστέ, κατ' ἐπαγγελίαν κληρονόμοι.

Cola 69[3.23]-70[3.24]: reason–result. Because all the Jews were confined under the law until faith should be revealed (3.23), the law became their pedagogue till the coming of Christ that they might be justified by faith (3.24). The personal pronoun 'we' of ἐφρουρούμεθα in 3.23 primarily refers to the Jews who have the law, but they represent all the nations.[1] The ὥστε in 3.24 as in 3.9 is inferential.

Cola 72[3.26]-73[3.27]: result–reason. All the believers are sons of God through faith in Christ Jesus (3.26), because all who were baptized into Christ have put on Christ, that is, have been incorporated into Christ who is the Son of God (3.27). The metaphor of 'putting on Christ' in 3.27 presupposes the eschatological idea of Christ as the second Adam.[2]

Cola 74[3.28a]-75[3.28b]-76[3.28c]: additive equivalent. The three statements form a parallelism.

Cola (74[3.28a]-76[3.28c])-77[3.28d]: result–reason. There is neither Jew nor Greek, neither slave nor free man, neither male nor female (3.28a-28c), because all the believers are one in Christ Jesus (3.28d).

Cola (72[3.26]-73[3.27])-(74[3.28a]-77[3.28d]): reason–result. Because all the believers are sons of God by their incorporation into Christ, the Son of God (3.26-27), they are all one without any distinction (3.28a-28d).

Cola (72[3.26]-77[3.28d])-78[3.29]: condition–result. If the believers are sons of God (3.26-28d), then they are Abraham's offspring and heirs according to the promise (3.29). The εἰ-conditional clause in 3.29 summarizes 3.26-28d, especially corresponding to 3.27.[3] The εἰ with the combination of the continuative δέ is used almost in the sense

1. See below Ch. 2.2.b.
2. Oepke 1937: 320.
3. Cf. Mussner 1974: 266; Betz 1979: 201.

of causal 'since'.[1] The word σπέρμα in 3.29 calls our attention back
to the argument about the identity of 'sons of Abraham' in 3.7-9.
Note also the emergence of κληρονόμος in 3.29 which is picked up as a
key word in the next pericope.

Cola 71[3.25]-(72[3.26]-78[3.29]): result–reason. In the time of faith
the believers are no longer under a pedagogue (3.25), because they
are sons of God, Abraham's offspring and heirs of God (3.26-29).

Cola (69[3.23]-70[3.24])-(71[3.25]-78[3.29]): dyadic contrastive.
Before the coming of faith all the Jews were confined under the law as
a pedagogue (3.23-24). In the time of faith, however, the believers are
no longer under the law but are God's sons and heirs (3.25-29).

x. *Pericope 10: Cola 79-84 (Galatians 4.1-7)*

```
┌79  ¹λέγω δέ,
│        ἐφ’ ὅσον χρόνον ὁ κληρονόμος νήπιός ἐστιν,
│        οὐδὲν διαφέρει δούλου
│            κύριος πάντων ὤν,
│        ²ἀλλὰ ὑπὸ ἐπιτρόπους ἐστὶν καὶ οἰκονόμους
│        ἄχρι τῆς προθεσμίας τοῦ πατρός.
└80  ³οὕτως καὶ ἡμεῖς, ὅτε ἦμεν νήπιοι,
        ὑπὸ τὰ στοιχεῖα τοῦ κόσμου ἤμεθα δεδουλωμένοι·
┌81  ⁴ὅτε δὲ ἦλθεν τὸ πλήρωμα τοῦ χρόνου,
│        ἐξαπέστειλεν ὁ θεὸς τὸν υἱὸν αὐτοῦ,
│            γενόμενον ἐκ γυναικός,
│            γενόμενον ὑπὸ νόμον,
│        ⁵ἵνα τοὺς ὑπὸ νόμον ἐξαγοράσῃ,
│        ἵνα τὴν υἱοθεσίαν ἀπολάβωμεν.
└82  ⁶ὅτι δέ ἐστε υἱοί,
        ἐξαπέστειλεν ὁ θεὸς τὸ πνεῦμα τοῦ υἱοῦ αὐτοῦ
            εἰς τὰς καρδίας ἡμῶν
            κρᾶζο⸱, αββα ὁ πατήρ.
┌83  ⁷ὥστε οὐκέτι εἶ δοῦλος ἀλλὰ υἱός·  ⟶  ⟵
└84  εἰ δὲ υἱός,
        καὶ κληρονόμος διὰ θεοῦ.
```

---

1. Blass and Debrunner 1961: §372.1; Mussner 1974: 266.

Cola 79[4.1-2]-80[4.3]: dyadic comparative. The heir, as long as he
is a child, does not differ from a slave and is under guardians and
stewards until the time set by the father (4.1-2). Similarly, the
believers, when they were children, were enslaved under the elements
of the world (4.3).

Cola 81[4.4-5]-82[4.6]: additive consequential. God sent his Son that
he might redeem those who were under the law and that the believers
might receive the adoption as sons (4.4-5), and he sent the Spirit of his
Son into the hearts of the believers to prove that the believers are sons
(4.6). Moule suggests that the ὅτι in 4.6 does not mean 'since', but
'that' which indicates a sense of *proof* (cf. Rom. 8.16).[1] NEB and TEV
reflect this suggestion. Note the close parallel between the two main
clauses.

Cola 83[4.7a]-84[4.7b]: condition–result. If the believer is a son
(4.7a), then he is an heir through God (4.7b). The εἰ-clause in 4.7b
takes up 4.7a. The εἰ in 4.7b is almost equivalent to 'since' (cf. 3.29).

Cola (81[4.4-5]-82[4.6])-(83[4.7a]-84[4.7b]): reason-result. Because
God sent his Son that the believers might become God's sons and then
sent the Spirit of his Son into the believers' hearts to show that they
are sons (4.4-6), the believers are not slaves but sons and heirs of God
(4.7a-7b). It appears that the inferential ὥστε in 4.7a links 4.7a with
4.6 together with 4.4-5, since God's sending of the Spirit of his Son
(4.6) is the consequent event of his sending of his Son (4.4-5). Note
the contrast between δοῦλος and υἱός in 4.7a.

Cola (79[4.1-2]-80[4.3])-(81[4.4-5]-84[4.7b]): dyadic contrastive.
When the believers were minors they were slaves under the elements
of the world (4.1-3). But by the great saving work of God they are no
longer slaves but sons of God (4.4-7b). It is noteworthy that existence
ὑπὸ τὰ στοιχεῖα τοῦ κόσμου in 4.3 is equated with existence ὑπὸ
νόμον in 4.4-5.

xi. *Pericope 11: Cola 85-98 (Galatians 4.8-20)*

85 ⁸ἀλλὰ τότε μὲν οὐκ εἰδότες θεὸν
   ἐδουλεύσατε τοῖς φύσει μὴ οὖσιν θεοῖς·
86a ⁹νῦν δὲ γνόντες θεόν, μᾶλλον δὲ γνωσθέντες ὑπὸ θεοῦ,
86b πῶς ἐπιστρέφετε πάλιν ἐπὶ τὰ ἀσθενῆ καὶ πτωχὰ στοιχεῖα

1.   Moule 1963: 147.

1. The Structure of Galatians 49

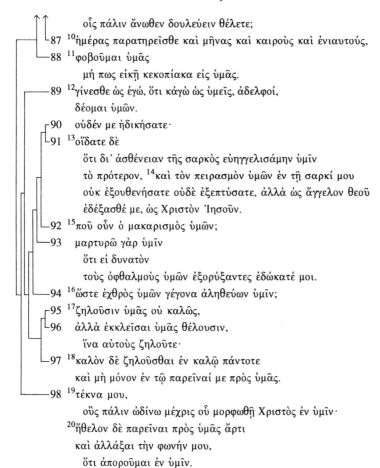

οἷς πάλιν ἄνωθεν δουλεύειν θέλετε;
87 10ἡμέρας παρατηρεῖσθε καὶ μῆνας καὶ καιροὺς καὶ ἐνιαυτούς,
88 11φοβοῦμαι ὑμᾶς
μή πως εἰκῇ κεκοπίακα εἰς ὑμᾶς.
89 12γίνεσθε ὡς ἐγώ, ὅτι κἀγὼ ὡς ὑμεῖς, ἀδελφοί,
δέομαι ὑμῶν.
90 οὐδέν με ἠδικήσατε·
91 13οἴδατε δὲ
ὅτι δι' ἀσθένειαν τῆς σαρκὸς εὐηγγελισάμην ὑμῖν
τὸ πρότερον, 14καὶ τὸν πειρασμὸν ὑμῶν ἐν τῇ σαρκί μου
οὐκ ἐξουθενήσατε οὐδὲ ἐξεπτύσατε, ἀλλὰ ὡς ἄγγελον θεοῦ
ἐδέξασθέ με, ὡς Χριστὸν Ἰησοῦν.
92 15ποῦ οὖν ὁ μακαρισμὸς ὑμῶν;
93 μαρτυρῶ γὰρ ὑμῖν
ὅτι εἰ δυνατὸν
τοὺς ὀφθαλμοὺς ὑμῶν ἐξορύξαντες ἐδώκατέ μοι.
94 16ὥστε ἐχθρὸς ὑμῶν γέγονα ἀληθεύων ὑμῖν;
95 17ζηλοῦσιν ὑμᾶς οὐ καλῶς,
96 ἀλλὰ ἐκκλεῖσαι ὑμᾶς θέλουσιν,
ἵνα αὐτοὺς ζηλοῦτε·
97 18καλὸν δὲ ζηλοῦσθαι ἐν καλῷ πάντοτε
καὶ μὴ μόνον ἐν τῷ παρεῖναί με πρὸς ὑμᾶς.
98 19τέκνα μου,
οὓς πάλιν ὠδίνω μέχρις οὗ μορφωθῇ Χριστὸς ἐν ὑμῖν·
20ἤθελον δὲ παρεῖναι πρὸς ὑμᾶς ἄρτι
καὶ ἀλλάξαι τὴν φωνήν μου,
ὅτι ἀποροῦμαι ἐν ὑμῖν.

Cola 85[4.8]-86a[4.9a]: dyadic contrastive. Then the Galatians did not know God and were slaves to those who by nature are no gods (4.8). But now they have come to be known by God (4.9a). Note the opposition between τότε and νῦν.

Cola 86b[4.9b]-87[4.10]: inference–basis. That the Galatians turn back again to the weak and worthless elements to become their slaves (4.9b) is evident from their observance of days, months, seasons, and years (4.10). The rhetorical question of 4.9b is a form of forceful statement (cf. 3.1-5).

Cola (85[4.8]-86a[4.9a])-(86b[4.9b]-87[4.10]): dyadic contrastive.

The Galatians have come to be known by God (4.8-9a); however, they turn back again to the bondage of the weak and worthless elements by observing the cultic calendar (4.9b-10).

Cola   (85[4.8]-87[4.10])-88[4.11]: cause–effect. The Galatians' returning to their old bondage (4.8-10) makes Paul fear for them that all his work on them has been done in vain (4.11).

Cola 90[4.12b]-91[4.13-14]: dyadic contrastive. The Galatians did Paul no wrong (4.12b), but in spite of his bodily illness they received him as an angel of God, as Christ Jesus, when he came to preach the gospel (4.13-14).

Cola (90[4.12b]-91[4.13-14])-92[4.15a]: additive consequential. The Galatians welcomed Paul as an angel of God (4.12b-14), and considered themselves as happy (4.15a). The οὖν relates 4.15a to 4.12b-14. The rhetorical question in 4.15a presupposes the previous happiness of the Galatians in accepting Paul. The ὑμῶν after the μακαρισμός is possibly a subjective genitive as well as an objective genitive,[1] in view of the fact that the term μακαρισμός is a substantive stemming from the verb μακαρίζω which means 'consider blessed, happy or fortunate'.[2]

Cola (90[4.12b]-92[4.15a])-93[4.15b]: result–reason. It is true that the Galatians regarded themselves happy in receiving Paul as a messenger of God (4.12b-15a), for they would, if possible, have given their eyes to Paul (4.15b). Paul's testimony of 4.15b confirms the genuine happiness of the Galatians. The εἰ-sentence in 4.15b is contrary to fact.

Cola (90[4.12b]-93[4.15b])-94[4.16]: basis–inference. Since the Galatians considered themselves blessed in accepting Paul as a messenger of God and were willing to sacrifice their eyes for Paul (4.12b-15b), it is unthinkable that Paul had become their enemy by preaching the truth, in other words Paul had become their true friend by his proclamation of the gospel (4.16). The ὥστε in 4.16 is an inferential particle. The rhetorical question in 4.16 implies a strong negative answer.[3] The perfect tense of γέγονα in this question seems to suggest that Paul's telling of the truth refers to his first proclamation of the

1   Ridderbos 1953: 167 n. 10; cf. Burton 1921: 243; Mussner 1974: 309 n. 82; Betz 1979: 226-27.
2.   Bauer 1979: s.v.
3.   Mussner 1974: 309.

gospel to the Galatians, mentioned in 4.13-14.[1]

Cola 95[4.17a]-96[4.17b]: result–reason. It is certain that those other people (the agitators) do not zealously court the Galatians in a good manner (4.17a), for they desire to exclude the Galatians in order that the Galatians may court them (4.17b). The ἀλλά-clause in 4.17b actually gives a reason for the statement οὐ καλῶς ζηλοῦσιν in 4.17a.[2] It is interesting to note that here, for the first time, Paul explicitly mentions a dishonourable motive in his opponents.

Cola (95[4.17a]-96[4.17b])-97[4.18]: dyadic contrastive. The agitators do not eagerly court the Galatians in a commendable manner (4.17a-b). It is always good, however, to be courted eagerly in a commendable manner (4.18). This contrast is devised to discredit the opponents, and thus implies that they are false teachers and bad friends.

Cola (90[4.12b]-94[4.16])-(95[4.17a]-97[4.18]): dyadic contrastive. Since the Galatians regarded themselves happy in welcoming Paul as a messenger of God and were willing to give one of their most precious possessions to Paul, it is evident that Paul has become their true friend by preaching the truth of the gospel (4.12b-16). But, since the agitators zealously court the Galatians with the bad intention of excluding them, it is evident that they are false friends (4.17a-18). In this connection Betz's relation of this section to the theme of 'friendship', an important ancient epistolary topos, is quite illuminating.[3]

Cola 89[4.12a]-(90[4.12b]-97[4.18]): purpose–means. Paul appeals to the Galatians to become like him, that is, to remain free from the bondage of the law (4.12a), by reminding them of their good friendship with him (4.12b-18).

Cola (89[4.12a]-97[4.18])-98[4.19-20]: additive consequential. Paul appeals to the Galatians to become like him in remaining free from the law (4.12a-18). And he wishes he were now with the Galatians, his spiritual children, to change his voice, because he is perplexed about them (4.19-20). Mussner views the particle δέ in 4.20 as copulative, assuming a dash or colon after 4.19.[4] The imperfect tense of ἤθελον before the δέ denotes the impossibility of realizing the wish.[5] The

1. Cf. Betz 1979: 229.
2. Schlier 1971: 212.
3. Betz 1979: 221-33.
4. Mussner 1974: 313; cf. Betz 1979: 236.
5. Burton 1894: §33; cf. Blass and Debrunner 1961: §359.2; Moule 1963: 9.

52   *The Law in Galatians*

wish to be present with the readers instead of resorting to a letter is
recognized as the so-called 'yearning' (πόθος) motif as an epistolary
topos.[1] Betz understands Paul's confession of perplexity in the ὅτι-
clause in 4.20 as a rhetorical strategy leading to the next pericope
which invites the Galatians to discover the truth by themselves.[2]
        Cola (85[4.8]-88[4.11])-(89[4.12a]-98[4.19-20]): reason–result.
Because the Galatians are reverting to the slavery of the elements of
the world (4.8-11), Paul appeals to them to follow him in remaining
free from the bondage of the law (4.12a-20).

xii. *Pericope 12: Cola 99-114 (Galatians 4.21-31)*

```
┌────99   ²¹λέγετέ μοι,
│                   οἱ ὑπὸ νόμον θέλοντες εἶναι, τὸν νόμον οὐκ ἀκούετε;
│  ┌ 100  ²²γέγραπται γὰρ ὅτι
│  │                   Ἀβραὰμ δύο υἱοὺς ἔσχεν,
│  │                   ἕνα ἐκ τῆς παιδίσκης καὶ ἕνα ἐκ τῆς ἐλευθέρας.
│  ├ 101  ²³ἀλλ' ὁ μὲν ἐκ τῆς παιδίσκης κατὰ σάρκα γεγέννηται,
│  └ 102   ὁ δὲ ἐκ τῆς ἐλευθέρας δι' ἐπαγγελίας.
├──103  ²⁴ἅτινά ἐστιν ἀλληγορούμενα·
├──104   αὗται γάρ εἰσιν δύο διαθῆκαι,
├┌ 105   μία μὲν ἀπὸ ὄρους Σινᾶ εἰς δουλείαν γεννῶσα,
││                   ἥτις ἐστὶν Ἁγάρ.
│├ 106  ²⁵τὸ δὲ Ἁγὰρ Σινᾶ ὄρος ἐστὶν ἐν τῇ Ἀραβίᾳ·
│├ 107   συστοιχεῖ δὲ τῇ νῦν Ἰερουσαλήμ,
│└ 108   δουλεύει γὰρ μετὰ τῶν τέκνων αὐτῆς.
├┌ 109  ²⁶ἡ δὲ ἄνω Ἰερουσαλὴμ ἐλευθέρα ἐστίν,
││                   ἥτις ἐστὶν μήτηρ ἡμῶν·
│└ 110  ²⁷γέγραπται γάρ,
│                   εὐφράνθητι, στεῖρα ἡ οὐ τίκτουσα, ῥῆξον καὶ βόησον,
│                   ἡ οὐκ ὠδίνουσα·
│                   ὅτι πολλὰ τὰ τέκνα τῆς ἐρήμου μᾶλλον
│                   ἢ τῆς ἐχούσης τὸν ἄνδρα.
└──111  ²⁸ὑμεῖς δέ, ἀδελφοί, κατὰ Ἰσαὰκ ἐπαγγελίας τέκνα ἐστέ.
```

1. Mussner 1974: 313 n. 110; Betz 1979: 236.
2. Betz 1979: 236-37, 240.

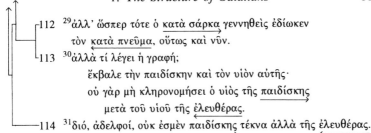

112 ²⁹ἀλλ' ὥσπερ τότε ὁ κατὰ σάρκα γεννηθεὶς ἐδίωκεν
τὸν κατὰ πνεῦμα, οὕτως καὶ νῦν.

113 ³⁰ἀλλὰ τί λέγει ἡ γραφή;
ἔκβαλε τὴν παιδίσκην καὶ τὸν υἱὸν αὐτῆς·
οὐ γὰρ μὴ κληρονομήσει ὁ υἱὸς τῆς παιδίσκης
μετὰ τοῦ υἱοῦ τῆς ἐλευθέρας.

114 ³¹διό, ἀδελφοί, οὐκ ἐσμὲν παιδίσκης τέκνα ἀλλὰ τῆς ἐλευθέρας.

Cola 101[4.23a]-102[4.23b]: dyadic contrastive. The son by the slave
woman was born according to the flesh (4.23a); however, the son by
the free woman was born through the promise (4.23b).

Cola 100[4.22]-(101[4.23a]-102[4.23b]): additive consequential.
Abraham had two sons, one by the slave woman and one by the free
woman (4.22). The former was born according to the flesh, the latter
through the promise (4.23a-b). The ἀλλά in 4.23a marks a pro-
gression of argument.[1] With this particle Paul underlines a further
point of difference between the two sons who have different mothers,
namely the different manner of their birth. Note the antithesis
between παιδίσκης and ἐλευθέρας. Note also the opposition
between κατὰ σάρκα and δι' ἐπαγγελίας. It is significant that δι'
ἐπαγγελίας is equated to κατὰ πνεῦμα in 4.29.

Cola 107[4.25b]-108[4.25c]: result–reason. Hagar corresponds to
the present Jerusalem (4.25b), because she (Jerusalem), like Hagar, is
in slavery with her children (4.25c). The subject of δουλεύει in
4.25c is best understood as τῇ νῦν Ἰερουσαλήμ in 4.25b, as
indicated
by the contrast in 4.25b-26 between the present Jerusalem and the
Jerusalem above which is free.[2] Furthermore, the chiastic arrangement of Hagar–the present Jerusalem–the Jerusalem above–our
mother in 4.25a-26 suggests that Hagar is to be taken as the subject of
συστοιχεῖ in 4.25b.

Cola 106[4.25a]-(107[4.25b]-108[4.25c]): additive consequential.
Hagar stands for Mount Sinai in Arabia (4.25a), and she corresponds
to the present Jerusalem in slavery with her children (4.25b-25c). The
τὸ Ἀγάρ in 4.25a refers back to the slave woman Hagar mentioned in
4.24c, since the neuter article τό is used to quote simply a preceding

1. Cf. Betz 1979: 242.
2. Cosgrove 1987: 228-29.

54   *The Law in Galatians*

word or words.[1] Some old manuscripts ($\mathfrak{P}$[46] C G 1241 1739 Origen[lat] Ambrosiaster[txt] al) omit Hagar in 4.25a. It seems that this omission is an attempt to correct the apparently awkward text.[2]

Cola 105[4.24c]-(106[4.25a]-108[4.25c]): additive consequential. The one covenant from Mount Sinai, bearing children for slavery, is Hagar (4.24c), and Hagar who represents Mount Sinai corresponds to the present Jerusalem which is in slavery with her children (4.25a-25c). The δέ in 4.25a is continuative, as the development of the comparisons indicates. Here another textual problem is involved. Some feel that γάρ may be preferred to the δέ, reasoning that 4.25a-25c justifies the thesis 4.24c.[3] But δέ is better attested than γάρ: δέ $\mathfrak{P}$[46] A B D[gr] syr[hmg,pal] cop[sa,bo] Ambrosiaster al; γάρ ℵ C G K P byz al.

Cola 109[4.26]-110[4.27]: result–reason. The Jerusalem above which is free is the mother of the believers, Sarah (4.26), because the prophet Isaiah connects the eschatological Jerusalem with Sarah (4.27).

Cola (105[4.24c]-108[4.25c])-(109[4.26]-110[4.27]): dyadic contrastive. Hagar, who stands for the Sinai covenant, corresponds to the present Jerusalem which is in slavery with her children (4.24c-25c). In contrast, the Jerusalem above which is free is the believers' mother, Sarah (4.26-27). Note the correspondences and antitheses.

Cola 104[4.24b]-(105[4.24c]-110[4.27]): substance content. These are two covenants (4.24b): Hagar, a symbol of the Sinai covenant, represents the present Jerusalem, whereas Sarah stands for the Jerusalem above (4.24c-27). It is interesting to observe that the Hagar-side of the comparison is given greater prominence than the Sarah-side (cf. 4.21).

Cola 103[4.24a]-(104[4.24b]-110[4.27]): result–reason. These things have an allegorical meaning (4.24a), because the two women represent two covenants (4.24b-27). The ἅτινά in 4.24a refers to the content of 4.22-23b.

Cola (100[4.22]-102[4.23b])-(103[4.24a]-110[4.27]): dyadic comparative. Abraham had two sons: the son by the slave woman was born according to the flesh; however, the other son by the free woman was born through the promise (4.22-23b). Allegorically speaking, the

1.   Bauer 1979: s.v., ὁ II.8.b; cf. Robertson 1919: 411.
2.   For fuller discussions, see Zahn 1907: 230ff.; Burton 1921: 258-61; Schlier 1971: 219-20; Mussner 1974: 322ff.; Cosgrove 1987: 227ff.
3.   Barrett 1976: 12; Cosgrove 1987: 227.

two women stand for two covenants: Hagar, who symbolizes the Sinai covenant, corresponds to the present Jerusalem, whereas Sarah corresponds to the Jerusalem above (4.24a-27).

Cola (100[4.22]-110[4.27])-111[4.28]: reason–result. Because the believers do not belong to the present Jerusalem which is the slave woman Hagar but to the Jerusalem above which is Sarah (4.22-27), they are children of promise, like Isaac born by the free woman, Sarah (4.28). Mussner sees the particle δέ in 4.28 as copulative, and he goes on to say: 'The apostle thus presents the conclusion of his "allegory" for the Galatians not formally as such, but rather as an apodictic-sounding sentence...'[1]

Cola 112[4.29]-113[4.30]: dyadic contrastive. The son born according to the flesh persecuted the son born according to the Spirit (4.29). However, the son of the slave woman was rejected, because he was not an heir along with the son of the free woman (4.30).

Cola (100[4.22]-111[4.28])-(112[4.29]-113[4.30]): dyadic contrastive. The believers are children of promise, like Isaac born by the free woman, Sarah (4.22-28). But the son born according to the flesh is rejected (4.29-30). The cluster of 4.29-30 is an additional interpretation of the Scripture to confirm the basic truth of 4.28.[2]

Cola (100[4.22]-113[4.30])-114[4.31]: reason–result. Because the believers are not included in the present Jerusalem, which is Hagar, but in the Jerusalem above, which is Sarah, and because they do not correspond to the son of the slave woman but to the son of the free woman (4.22-30), they are not children of a slave woman but of the free woman (4.31). According to Betz, the διό in 4.31 which occurs only here in this letter may be an indication that the argumentative section (3.1–4.31) is brought to an end at this point.[3]

Cola 99[4.21]-(100[4.22]-114[4.31]): substance content. The foregoing consideration of 4.22-31 is the content of Paul's allegorical interpretation of the law which he invites the Galatians to hear (4.21). Note the correspondence between the existence ὑπὸ νόμον in 4.21 and the Hagar side of the allegory in 4.22ff. Note also the repetition of the antithesis between παιδίσκης and ἐλευθέρας in 4.22, 23, 30 and 31 (cf. 4.25a-26, 29), which strengthens the coherence of this pericope.

1.   Mussner 1974: 328; cf. Cosgrove 1987: 222.
2.   Cf. Schlier 1971: 228; Mussner 1974: 333; Betz 1979: 249.
3.   Betz 1979: 251; cf. Cosgrove 1987: 232-33.

xiii. *Pericope 13: Cola 115-131 (Galatians 5.1-12)*

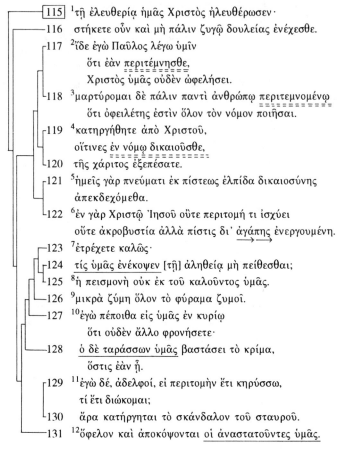

```
┌──── 115  ¹τῇ ἐλευθερίᾳ ἡμᾶς Χριστὸς ἠλευθέρωσεν·
├──── 116  στήκετε οὖν καὶ μὴ πάλιν ζυγῷ δουλείας ἐνέχεσθε.
├─ 117  ²ἴδε ἐγὼ Παῦλος λέγω ὑμῖν
│          ὅτι ἐὰν περιτέμνησθε,
│          Χριστὸς ὑμᾶς οὐδὲν ὠφελήσει.
└─ 118  ³μαρτύρομαι δὲ πάλιν παντὶ ἀνθρώπῳ περιτεμνομένῳ
           ὅτι ὀφειλέτης ἐστὶν ὅλον τὸν νόμον ποιῆσαι.
├─ 119  ⁴κατηργήθητε ἀπὸ Χριστοῦ,
│          οἵτινες ἐν νόμῳ δικαιοῦσθε,
└─ 120  τῆς χάριτος ἐξεπέσατε.
├─ 121  ⁵ἡμεῖς γὰρ πνεύματι ἐκ πίστεως ἐλπίδα δικαιοσύνης
│          ἀπεκδεχόμεθα.
└─ 122  ⁶ἐν γὰρ Χριστῷ Ἰησοῦ οὔτε περιτομή τι ἰσχύει
           οὔτε ἀκροβυστία ἀλλὰ πίστις δι' ἀγάπης ἐνεργουμένη.
├─ 123  ⁷ἐτρέχετε καλῶς·
├─ 124  τίς ὑμᾶς ἐνέκοψεν [τῇ] ἀληθείᾳ μὴ πείθεσθαι;
└─ 125  ⁸ἡ πεισμονὴ οὐκ ἐκ τοῦ καλοῦντος ὑμᾶς.
├─ 126  ⁹μικρὰ ζύμη ὅλον τὸ φύραμα ζυμοῖ.
├─ 127  ¹⁰ἐγὼ πέποιθα εἰς ὑμᾶς ἐν κυρίῳ
│          ὅτι οὐδὲν ἄλλο φρονήσετε·
└─ 128  ὁ δὲ ταράσσων ὑμᾶς βαστάσει τὸ κρίμα,
           ὅστις ἐὰν ᾖ.
├─ 129  ¹¹ἐγὼ δέ, ἀδελφοί, εἰ περιτομὴν ἔτι κηρύσσω,
│          τί ἔτι διώκομαι;
└─ 130  ἄρα κατήργηται τὸ σκάνδαλον τοῦ σταυροῦ.
└─ 131  ¹²ὄφελον καὶ ἀποκόψονται οἱ ἀναστατοῦντες ὑμᾶς.
```

Cola 117[5.2]-118[5.3]: result–reason. If the Galatians receive circumcision, Christ will be of no benefit to them (5.2), because everyone who receives circumcision is obliged to keep the whole law (5.3). Mussner thinks that the δέ in 5.3 has an explanatory function, but not an adversative one.[1]

Cola 119[5.4a]-120[5.4b]: additive equivalent. The Galatians who are seeking to be justified by the law have been severed from Christ

---

1. Mussner 1974: 347; cf. Ridderbos 1953: 187.

(5.4a); they have fallen away from grace (5.4b).

Cola   (117[5.2]-118[5.3])-(119[5.4a]-120[5.4b])):   reason–result.
Because the Galatians who allow themselves to be circumcised are
under obligation to obey the whole law and do not receive any benefit
from Christ (5.2-3), the Gentiles who are seeking to be justified by the
law have been separated from Christ and fallen away from grace
(5.4a-4b). It is remarkable that Paul equates 'to be circumcised' with
'to be justified by the law'.

Cola 121[5.5]-122[5.6]: result–reason. The believers through the
Spirit, by faith, are waiting for the hope of righteousness (5.5),
because in Christ Jesus what matters is faith working through love,
not circumcision (5.6). The concept of ἀγάπη introduced here will be
taken up as a dominant theme in the following paraenetical pericopae.

Cola (117[5.2]-120[5.4b])-(121[5.5]-122[5.6]): dyadic contrastive.
The Galatians, who receive circumcision and are thereby seeking to be
justified by the law, have been severed from Christ and fallen away
from grace (5.2-4b). But the believers through the Spirit, by faith in
Christ, are waiting for the hope of righteousness (5.5-6). In this
contrast the shift of personal pronoun from 'you' to 'we' is striking.
The γάρ in 5.5 'indicates that Paul here presents an argument which
in a sense explains the previous verse by pointing up the contrasts
involved'.[1]

Cola 124[5.7b]-125[5.8]: dyadic contrastive. The Galatians are hindered from obeying the truth (5.7b). But the persuasion is not from
God who calls them (5.8). The rhetorical question of 5.7b is regarded
as an emphatic statement like those in 3.1-5 and 4.9.

Cola   123[5.7a]-(124[5.7b]-125[5.8]):   dyadic contrastive. The
Galatians were running well (5.7a), but they are hindered from
obeying the truth (5.7b-8).

Cola (123[5.7a]-125[5.8])-126[5.9]: reason–result. Because the
Galatians have been persuaded not to obey the truth (5.7a-8), Paul, in
the form of a proverb, warns them of the serious consequence of
submitting to the persuasion (5.9).

Cola (123[5.7a]-126[5.9])-127[5.10a]: dyadic contrastive. The
Galatians are hindered from obeying the gospel and could, in the end,
be seriously harmed (5.7a-9). But Paul has confidence in them in the
Lord that they will take no other view than his (5.10a). White labels

1.   Arichea and Nida 1976: 123; cf. Mussner 1974: 349-50.

5.10a as a 'confidence formula', an epistolary topos[1] (cf. Rom. 15.14-15; Philemon 21).

Cola (123[5.7a]-127[5.10a])-128[5.10b]: dyadic contrastive. Paul has confidence in the Lord that the Galatians will adopt no other view (5.7a-10a). He believes, however, that the one who disturbs them will bear the judgment of God, whoever he is (5.10b).

Cola 129[5.11a]-130[5.11b]: condition–result. If Paul were still preaching circumcision (5.11a), then the cross of Christ would no longer be a stumbling block (5.11b). Betz's interpretation that the statement of 5.11b can best be taken as the conclusion to the discussion on circumcision in 5.2-12[2] is hardly natural and reasonable. For this abrupt cluster of 5.11a-b does not have an immediate connection with what precedes or what follows in the paragraph of 5.7a-12.

Cola (123[5.7a]-128[5.10b])-131[5.12]: additive consequential. In spite of his confidence that the Galatians will take no other view, Paul believes that the one who disturbs them will be punished by God (5.7a-10b), and he wishes that those who stir them up would castrate themselves and thereby exclude themselves from the church of God (cf. Deut. 23.1) (5.12). Note the three references to the agitators in 5.7b, 10b and 12.

Cola (117[5.2]-122[5.6])-(123[5.7a]-131[5.12]): additive consequential. The Galatians who, by receiving circumcision, try to be justified by the law have been cut off from Christ and have fallen away from grace (5.2-6). And the agitators who hinder them from obeying the truth will be judged by God (5.7a-12).

Cola 116[5.1b]-(117[5.2]-131[5.12]): purpose–means. Paul exhorts the Galatians to stand firm and not to subject themselves again to a yoke of slavery (5.1b), by pointing out the christological and soteriological implications of their submission to circumcision and by pronouncing the future judgment of God on the agitators (5.2-12).

Cola 115[5.1a]-(116[5.1b]-131[5.12]): basis–inference. Since Christ has set the believers free for freedom (5.1a), Paul admonishes the Galatians to preserve their freedom and to reject a yoke of slavery, particularly not to accept circumcision for justification (5.1b-12). The typical structure of Pauline paraenesis is unfolded here. The *imperative* to keep freedom in 5.1b is grounded on the *indicative* of Christ's

1. White 1972: 61, 64-65.
2. Betz 1979: 269.

redemption in 5.1a. This relationship between indicative and imperative also determines the structure of subsequent pericopae.[1]

xiv. *Pericope 14: Cola 132-145 (Galatians 5.13-24)*

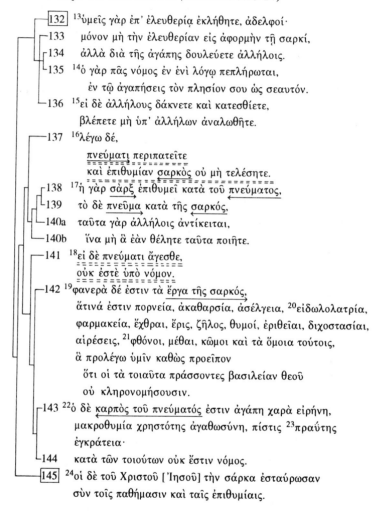

|132| ¹³ὑμεῖς γὰρ ἐπ᾿ ἐλευθερίᾳ ἐκλήθητε, ἀδελφοί·

133　μόνον μὴ τὴν ἐλευθερίαν εἰς ἀφορμὴν τῇ σαρκί,

134　ἀλλὰ διὰ τῆς ἀγάπης δουλεύετε ἀλλήλοις.

135　¹⁴ὁ γὰρ πᾶς νόμος ἐν ἑνὶ λόγῳ πεπλήρωται,
　　　　ἐν τῷ ἀγαπήσεις τὸν πλησίον σου ὡς σεαυτόν.

136　¹⁵εἰ δὲ ἀλλήλους δάκνετε καὶ κατεσθίετε,
　　　　βλέπετε μὴ ὑπ᾿ ἀλλήλων ἀναλωθῆτε.

137　¹⁶λέγω δέ,
　　　　πνεύματι περιπατεῖτε
　　　　καὶ ἐπιθυμίαν σαρκὸς οὐ μὴ τελέσητε.

138　¹⁷ἡ γὰρ σὰρξ ἐπιθυμεῖ κατὰ τοῦ πνεύματος,

139　τὸ δὲ πνεῦμα κατὰ τῆς σαρκός,

140a　ταῦτα γὰρ ἀλλήλοις ἀντίκειται,

140b　ἵνα μὴ ἃ ἐὰν θέλητε ταῦτα ποιῆτε.

141　¹⁸εἰ δὲ πνεύματι ἄγεσθε,
　　　　οὐκ ἐστὲ ὑπὸ νόμον.

142　¹⁹φανερὰ δέ ἐστιν τὰ ἔργα τῆς σαρκός,
　　　　ἅτινά ἐστιν πορνεία, ἀκαθαρσία, ἀσέλγεια, ²⁰εἰδωλολατρία,
　　　　φαρμακεία, ἔχθραι, ἔρις, ζῆλος, θυμοί, ἐριθεῖαι, διχοστασίαι,
　　　　αἱρέσεις, ²¹φθόνοι, μέθαι, κῶμοι καὶ τὰ ὅμοια τούτοις,
　　　　ἃ προλέγω ὑμῖν καθὼς προεῖπον
　　　　ὅτι οἱ τὰ τοιαῦτα πράσσοντες βασιλείαν θεοῦ
　　　　οὐ κληρονομήσουσιν.

143　²²ὁ δὲ καρπὸς τοῦ πνεύματός ἐστιν ἀγάπη χαρὰ εἰρήνη,
　　　　μακροθυμία χρηστότης ἀγαθωσύνη, πίστις ²³πραΰτης
　　　　ἐγκράτεια·

144　κατὰ τῶν τοιούτων οὐκ ἔστιν νόμος.

|145|　²⁴οἱ δὲ τοῦ Χριστοῦ [Ἰησοῦ] τὴν σάρκα ἐσταύρωσαν
　　　　σὺν τοῖς παθήμασιν καὶ ταῖς ἐπιθυμίαις.

1.　Cf. Betz 1979: 254-55; Ebeling 1985: 241-42.

Cola 134[5.13c]-135[5.14]: result–reason. The Galatian believers are exhorted to serve one another through love (5.13c), because the whole law is fulfilled in love (5.14).

Cola 133[5.13b],136[5.15]: generic–specific. The Galatians should not use their freedom as an opportunity for the flesh (5.13b); specifically, they should take heed not to destroy one another by biting and devouring one another (5.15).

Cola (133[5.13b],136[5.15])-(134[5.13c]-135[5.14]): dyadic contrastive. It is interesting to note that this colon group is built up in a chiastic way.

Cola 132[5.13a]-(133[5.13b]-136[5.15]): basis–inference. Since the Galatian believers were called to freedom (5.13a), they are urged not to turn their freedom into an opportunity for the flesh, but to serve one another through love (5.13b-15). The γάρ in 5.13a, as in 1.11, expresses transitional continuation.[1]

Cola 138[5.17a]-139[5.17b]: additive consequential. The flesh sets its desire against the Spirit (5.17a), and the Spirit against the flesh (5.17b). Note the antithesis between the flesh and the Spirit which repeatedly occurs in the section of 5.13–6.10 (5.16, 17, 19-22; 6.8; cf. 5.13, 24-25). This reinforces the coherence of the section.

Cola (138[5.17a]-139[5.17b])-140a[5.17c]: result–reason. The flesh desires against the Spirit, and the Spirit against the flesh (5.17a-b), because these are in opposition to each other (5.17c).

Cola (138[5.17a]-140a[5.17c])-140b[5.17d]: reason–result. Because the flesh and the Spirit oppose each other (5.17a-c), the Galatians cannot do whatever they want (5.17d). The ἵνα in 5.17d is to be taken as consecutive rather than final, because it fits neatly in the context.[2] The verb θέλητε in the ἵνα clause in 5.17d refers to the human free will, not the will of the flesh or of the Spirit.[3]

Cola 137[5.16]-(138[5.17a]-140b[5.17d]): result–reason. The Galatians are exhorted to walk by the Spirit and thereby not to carry out the desire of the flesh (5.16), because the mutual opposition between the flesh and the Spirit frustrates the Galatians' free will (5.17a-d). The believers are not autonomous in their moral action.

---

1. Bauer 1979: s.v., 4; Betz 1979: 272; cf. Burton 1921: 291; Schlier 1971: 241; Mussner 1974: 366.
2. See below Ch. 7.2.
3. Ellicott 1867: 115; Fung 1988: 251.

They must follow the Spirit or the flesh.

Cola 143[5.22-23a]-144[5.23b]: additive consequential. The fruit of the Spirit is love, joy, peace, patience, kindness, goodness, faithfulness, gentleness, self-control (5.22-23a). Against such things the law does not take a stand (5.23b). The context (5.14, 18) seems to require the νόμος in 5.23b to be understood to refer to the Mosaic law, not to any law in general. If this is so, it should be said that the popular translation 'Against such things there is no law' of 5.23b is misleading.

Cola 142[5.19-21]-(143[5.22-23a]-144[5.23b]): dyadic contrastive. The works of the flesh whose practise prevents the evildoers from inheriting the kingdom of God (5.19-21) are set in contrast to the fruit of the Spirit against which the law does not bring a charge (5.22-23b).

Cola 141[5.18]-(142[5.19-21]-144[5.23b]): result–reason. If the Galatians are led by the Spirit, they are not under the law, that is, under the curse of the law (5.18), for those who produce the fruit of the Spirit in contrast to the works of the flesh are free from the charge of the law (5.19-23b).

Cola (137[5.16]-140b[5.17d])-(141[5.18]-144[5.23b]): additive equivalent. The Galatians are urged to walk by the Spirit, and thereby not to satisfy the desire of the flesh (5.16-17d); they are exhorted to allow themselves to be led by the Spirit, and thereby to be free from the slavery of the law (5.18-23b). The correspondence between 5.16 and 5.18 is to be observed, since 'walk by the Spirit' is identical to 'be led by the Spirit'. The εἰ-clause in 5.18 has an imperative force, though weak,[1] as the verb ἄγεσθε implies the voluntary subjection of the will to the Spirit.[2]

Cola (137[5.16]-144[5.23b])-145[5.24]: inference–basis. The two main exhortations in 5.16 and 5.18 are based on the indicative that those who belong to Christ Jesus have crucified the flesh with its passions and desires (5.24). The aorist of ἐσταύρωσαν in 5.24 suggests the believers' participation in the historical crucifixion of Christ.

Cola (132[5.13a]-136[5.15])-(137[5.16]-145[5.24]): additive equivalent. Since the Galatians were called to freedom, they should not use their freedom for the flesh but serve one another through love (5.13a-15); since they have crucified the flesh by participating in the

1. Cf. Ridderbos 1953: 204.
2. Burton 1921: 303.

62   The Law in Galatians

crucifixion of Christ, they should not satisfy the desire of the flesh but
walk by the Spirit whose fruit is essentially love (5.16-24).

xv. *Pericope 15: Cola 146-161 (Galatians 5.25–6.10)*

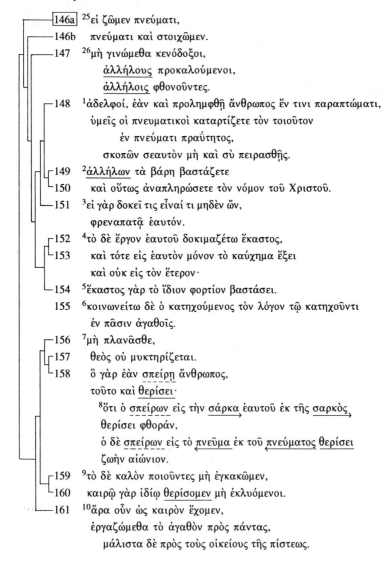

146a ²⁵εἰ ζῶμεν πνεύματι,
146b πνεύματι καὶ στοιχῶμεν.
147 ²⁶μὴ γινώμεθα κενόδοξοι,
      ἀλλήλους προκαλούμενοι,
      ἀλλήλοις φθονοῦντες.
148 ¹ἀδελφοί, ἐὰν καὶ προλημφθῇ ἄνθρωπος ἔν τινι παραπτώματι,
      ὑμεῖς οἱ πνευματικοὶ καταρτίζετε τὸν τοιοῦτον
          ἐν πνεύματι πραΰτητος,
      σκοπῶν σεαυτὸν μὴ καὶ σὺ πειρασθῇς.
149 ²ἀλλήλων τὰ βάρη βαστάζετε
150 καὶ οὕτως ἀναπληρώσετε τὸν νόμον τοῦ Χριστοῦ.
151 ³εἰ γὰρ δοκεῖ τις εἶναί τι μηδὲν ὤν,
      φρεναπατᾷ ἑαυτόν.
152 ⁴τὸ δὲ ἔργον ἑαυτοῦ δοκιμαζέτω ἕκαστος,
153 καὶ τότε εἰς ἑαυτὸν μόνον τὸ καύχημα ἕξει
      καὶ οὐκ εἰς τὸν ἕτερον·
154 ⁵ἕκαστος γὰρ τὸ ἴδιον φορτίον βαστάσει.
155 ⁶κοινωνείτω δὲ ὁ κατηχούμενος τὸν λόγον τῷ κατηχοῦντι
      ἐν πᾶσιν ἀγαθοῖς.
156 ⁷μὴ πλανᾶσθε,
157 θεὸς οὐ μυκτηρίζεται.
158 ὃ γὰρ ἐὰν σπείρῃ ἄνθρωπος,
      τοῦτο καὶ θερίσει·
          ⁸ὅτι ὁ σπείρων εἰς τὴν σάρκα ἑαυτοῦ ἐκ τῆς σαρκὸς
          θερίσει φθοράν,
          ὁ δὲ σπείρων εἰς τὸ πνεῦμα ἐκ τοῦ πνεύματος θερίσει
          ζωὴν αἰώνιον.
159 ⁹τὸ δὲ καλὸν ποιοῦντες μὴ ἐγκακῶμεν,
160 καιρῷ γὰρ ἰδίῳ θερίσομεν μὴ ἐκλυόμενοι.
161 ¹⁰ἄρα οὖν ὡς καιρὸν ἔχομεν,
      ἐργαζώμεθα τὸ ἀγαθὸν πρὸς πάντας,
      μάλιστα δὲ πρὸς τοὺς οἰκείους τῆς πίστεως.

Cola 149[6.2a]-150[6.2b]: condition–result. If the Galatians bear one
another's burdens (6.2a), they will fulfil the law of Christ (6.2b). Here
we have a textual problem. According to Metzger, the reading
ἀναπληρώσετε ([𝔓⁴⁶] B G and most ancient versions) is slightly
preferable to the alternative reading ἀναπληρώσατε (ℵ A C Dᵍʳ K P
al).[1] In fact, the future indicative fits in the context.[2]

   Cola 148[6.1]-(149[6.2a]-150[6.2b]): specific–generic. The specific
injunction to restore one who is caught in any trespass (6.1) is
included in the more general exhortation to bear one another's
burdens (6.2a-2b).

   Cola (148[6.1]-150[6.2b])-151[6.3]: result–reason. The Galatians
should bear one another's burdens (6.1-2b), because no one is actually
of importance (6.3). This implies that the self-inflated man finds it
difficult to share another's burden.[3]

   Cola 152[6.4a]-153[6.4b]: condition–result. If each one examines his
own work (6.4a), then he will have reason for boasting in regard to
himself alone and not in regard to another (6.4b). Gal. 6.4b implicitly
gives a reason for the admonition of 6.4a.[4]

   Cola (152[6.4a]-153[6.4b])-154[6.5]: result–reason. Each one should
examine his own work (6.4a-b), because he shall bear his own load
(6.5). Gal. 6.5 probably refers to the final judgment.[5] This smooths
the transition to the eschatological exhortation in 6.7a-10.

   Cola (148[6.1]-151[6.3])-(152[6.4a]-154[6.5]): dyadic contrastive.
The Galatians should carry one another's burdens with humility (6.1-
3); however, each of them should examine his own work with awareness of the eschatological judgment (6.4a-5). It is to be noted that both
of the two main cola 149 (6.2a) and 152 (6.4a) are imperatives.

   Cola 147[5.26]-(148[6.1]-154[6.5]): dyadic contrastive. The Galatians
should not become boastful, challenging one another, envying one
another (5.26); however, they should bear one another's burdens with
self-examination of their own works (6.1-5). Note the repetition of
the word ἀλλήλων in 5.26 and 6.2a.

1. Metzger 1971: 598.
2. See below Ch. 7.1.
3. Burton 1921: 330; cf. Arichea and Nida 1976: 147.
4. Betz 1979: 302.
5. Lenski [1937] 1961: 301; Mussner 1974: 401-402.

Cola 146b[5.25b]-(147[5.26]-154[6.5]): generic–specific. The Galatians are urged to walk by the Spirit (5.25b), and specifically not to become vainglorious but to bear one another's burdens (5.26–6.5).

Cola 146a[5.25a]-(146b[5.25b]-154[6.5]): basis–inference. Since the Galatians live by the Spirit (5.25a), they should walk by the Spirit, and specifically carry one another's burdens (5.25b–6.5). The εἰ in 5.25a would be better translated as 'since', because its clause refers to something that exists at present.[1]

Cola 157[6.7b]-158[6.7c-8]: result–reason. God is not mocked (6.7b), for his verdict in the final judgment (harvesting) will correspond to the deeds of everyone (sowing): he who sows to his own flesh shall from the flesh reap corruption; however, he who sows to the Spirit shall from the Spirit reap eternal life (6.7c-8). The metaphor θερίζω clearly refers to the last judgment of God (cf. Mt. 3.12; Lk. 3.17; Mt. 13.30; Rev. 14.15ff.). Note that the antithesis between the Spirit and the flesh in 5.16-25 reappears here. The link between the flesh and corruption is in line with the eschatological warning in 5.21b; the link between the Spirit and eternal life in line with the assertions in 5.18 and 23b.

Cola 156[6.7a]-(157[6.7b]-158[6.7c-8]): result–reason. The Galatians are exhorted not to be deceived (6.7a), because God's verdict in the last judgment will correspond to the deeds of everyone (6.7b-8).

Cola 159[6.9a]-160[6.9b]: result–reason. The Galatians should not become weary in doing good (6.9a), because in due time they shall reap, if they do not give up (6.9b). Note that the *eschatological* metaphor of θερίζω is again employed in 6.9b as in 6.7c-8.

Cola (156[6.7a]-158[6.7c-8])-(159[6.9a]-160[6.9b]): additive consequential. The Galatians should not be deceived, because every one of them shall be judged according to his deeds (6.7a-8). And they should not grow weary in doing good, because they shall be rewarded at the time of the final judgment (6.9a-b).

Cola (156[6.7a]-160[6.9b])-161[6.10]: reason–result. Because it is certain that God will judge (reward or punish) everyone according to his deeds (6.7a-9b), the Galatians are exhorted to do good towards all, especially towards the fellow believers, whenever they have opportunity (6.10). Note the combination of ἄρα οὖν in 6.10.[2]

1. Arichea and Nida 1976: 142.
2. Cf. Thrall 1962: 10-11.

1. The Structure of Galatians   65

Surprisingly, the exhortations in this colon cluster are grounded on
the coming judgment of God (cf. 5.21), while the preceding admonitions are based on the indicative of salvation accomplished already by
the redemptive work of Christ (5.1a, 13a, 24, 25a).
Colon 155[6.6] is a separate injunction without any obvious connection with what precedes or with what follows.[1]
Cola (146a[5.25a]-154[6.5])-(156[6.7a]-161[6.10]): additive consequential. Since the Galatians live by the Spirit, they should not become
vainglorious but bear one another's burdens (5.25a-6.5). Further,
since they will be judged according to their deeds, they should do
good towards all men (6.7a-10). It now becomes obvious that Paul's
injunction is not only grounded on the indicative of salvation (i.e.
possessing the Spirit), but also on the eschatological judgment of God.
This shows that Paul's ethic is not simply actualization of the
indicative but an 'interim ethic'.[2]

xvi. *Pericope 16: Cola 162-172 (Galatians 6.11-18)*

```
┌──162 ¹¹ἴδετε πηλίκοις ὑμῖν γράμμασιν ἔγραψα τῇ ἐμῇ χειρί.
│ ┌─163 ¹²ὅσοι θέλουσιν εὐπροσωπῆσαι ἐν σαρκί,
│ │      οὗτοι ἀναγκάζουσιν ὑμᾶς περιτέμνεσθαι,
│ │      μόνον ἵνα τῷ σταυρῷ τοῦ Χριστοῦ μὴ διώκωνται.
│ ├─164 ¹³οὐδὲ γὰρ οἱ περιτεμνόμενοι αὐτοὶ νόμον φυλάσσουσιν
│ └─165   ἀλλὰ θέλουσιν ὑμᾶς περιτέμνεσθαι,
│         ἵνα ἐν τῇ ὑμετέρᾳ σαρκὶ καυχήσωνται.
│ ┌─166 ¹⁴ἐμοὶ δὲ μὴ γένοιτο καυχᾶσθαι
│ │      εἰ μὴ ἐν τῷ σταυρῷ τοῦ κυρίου ἡμῶν Ἰησοῦ Χριστοῦ,
│ │      δι' οὗ ἐμοὶ κόσμος ἐσταύρωται κἀγὼ κόσμῳ.
│ ┌─167 ¹⁵οὔτε γὰρ περιτομή τί ἐστιν οὔτε ἀκροβυστία
│ │      ἀλλὰ καινὴ κτίσις.
│ └─168 ¹⁶καὶ ὅσοι τῷ κανόνι τούτῳ στοιχήσουσιν,
│         εἰρήνη ἐπ' αὐτοὺς καὶ ἔλεος καὶ ἐπὶ τὸν Ἰσραὴλ τοῦ θεοῦ.
│ ┌─169 ¹⁷τοῦ λοιποῦ κόπους μοι μηδεὶς παρεχέτω·
↓ └─170   ἐγὼ γὰρ τὰ στίγματα τοῦ Ἰησοῦ ἐν τῷ σώματί μου βαστάζω.
```

1. Cf. Burton 1921: 335; Bruce 1982a: 263; Ebeling 1985: 261.
2. Beker 1980: 275ff.

┌─171 ¹⁸ἡ χάρις τοῦ κυρίου ἡμῶν Ἰησοῦ Χριστοῦ
│   μετὰ τοῦ πνεύματος ὑμῶν, ἀδελφοί·
└─172 ἀμήν.

Cola 164[6.13a]-165[6.13b]: dyadic contrastive. The circumcised people themselves do not keep the law (6.13a), but want the Galatians to be circumcised in order that they may boast in their flesh (6.13b). The sentence construction requires that the subject of 6.13a and 6.13b be the same. Note that the two cola form one sentence.

Cola 163[6.12]-(164[6.13a]-165[6.13b]): result–reason. Paul's own conclusion that those who want to make a good showing in the flesh compel the Galatians to be circumcised simply that they may not be persecuted for the cross of Christ (6.12) is motivated by his judgment that they themselves do not obey the law but desire to boast in the circumcision of the Galatians (6.13a-13b). It is noteworthy that 6.13b is almost a reiteration of the ὅσοι clause of 6.12.

Cola 167[6.15]-168[6.16]: condition–result. If the Galatians live by the principle set forth in 6.15, there shall be peace and mercy upon them (6.16). The κανών in 6.16 refers to the statement in 6.15, as the combination of ὁ and οὗτος suggests. This conditional blessing implies a curse on those who continually insist on the validity of circumcision.[1]

Cola 166[6.14]-(167[6.15]-168[6.16]): result–reason. Paul boasts only about the cross of Christ through which the world has been crucified to him and he to the world (6.14), because what matters is not circumcision or uncircumcision but a new creation brought about by the cross (6.15-16).

Cola (163[6.12]-165[6.13b])-(166[6.14]-168[6.16]): dyadic contrastive. The circumcised desire to boast of the circumcision of the Galatians to escape persecution due to the cross of Christ (6.12-13b). In contrast, Paul boasts only of the cross of Christ which has brought about a new creation (6.14-16). Note the contrast between ἐν τῇ ὑμετέρᾳ σαρκί in 6.13b and ἐν τῷ σταυρῷ τοῦ κυρίου ἡμῶν Ἰησοῦ Χριστοῦ in 6.14. This section serves to recapitulate the main points of the entire letter. It starkly discloses the central issue: circumcision versus the cross of Christ. In this sense it contains an important clue to Paul's perspective in the letter. This summary

1. Cf. Betz 1979: 321.

can be regarded as epistolary[1] or rhetorical.[2]

Cola 169[6.17a]-170[6.17b]: result–reason. Paul asks the Galatians not to give him any more trouble (6.17a), because he bears on his body the marks of Jesus (6.17b). This is a sort of appeal, asking the Galatians to remain faithful to the gospel of Christ which Paul, as a slave of Christ, has preached.[3] τὰ στίγματα τοῦ 'Ιησοῦ on Paul's body undoubtedly show, whatever they refer to, that he is a slave of Jesus Christ.

Cola (163[6.12]-168[6.16])-(169[6.17a]-170[6.17b]): additive consequential. Paul states that unlike the circumcised he boasts only of the cross which has invalidated circumcision and brought about a new creation (6.12-16), and he asks the Galatians to remain loyal to his gospel (6.17a-17b).

Cola 171[6.18a]-172[6.18b]: additive consequential. The benediction of 6.18a is followed by the ἀμήν of 6.18b. This acclamation is not merely a confirmation from Paul's side, but expresses a hope for a response from the congregation.[4]

Cola (163[6.12]-170[6.17b])-(171[6.18a]-172[6.18b]): additive non-consequential. Both the final benediction and the 'amen' of 6.18a-18b are a form of Paul's letter-closing (cf. Rom. 16.24; 1 Cor. 16.23, 24), and do not logically relate to what immediately precedes.

Cola 162[6.11]-(163[6.12]-172[6.18b]): means–purpose. Paul asks the Galatians to pay attention to the large letters with which he is writing to them (6.11) in order to emphasize the main points which are about to be made (6.12-18b). Most interpreters view the aorist ἔγραψα in 6.11 as an epistolary aorist[5] (cf. 1 Cor. 5.11; 9.15; Philemon 19, 21).

b. *Grouping of Pericopae*
i. *Summary of Each Pericope.* Thus far the demarcation of various pericopae and the description of the structure of individual pericope have been done. The remaining work is to group many different

1. Bahr 1968: 35; White 1972: 47.
2. Betz 1975: 356ff.; Betz 1979: 312-13; Brinsmead 1982: 63ff.; Kennedy 1984: 151.
3. Cf. Betz 1975: 358; Betz 1979: 323ff.
4. Ridderbos 1953: 230; Mussner 1974: 421.
5. Robertson 1919: 846; Burton 1921: 348-49; Moule 1963: 12 n. 1; Schlier 1971: 279; Mussner 1974: 410; Betz 1979: 314; Bruce 1982a: 268.

pericopae according to their semantic relations and thereby to describe
the macro-structure of the letter to the Galatians as a whole. For this
task I will first summarize briefly the main point(s) of each pericope.

1. *1.1-5*

> Prescript. This introduces two lines of thought: the divine origin of
> Paul's apostleship and the eschatological character of the redemption
> of Christ.

2. *1.6-10*

> Paul asserts, by pronouncing a curse upon the false preachers, that
> there is no other gospel than the gospel of Christ.

3. *1.11-12*

> Paul's gospel is not according to man, but was received through the
> revelation of Jesus Christ.

4. *1.13-24*

> When receiving the revelation of the Son of God and the commission
> to preach him among the Gentiles, Paul immediately launched an
> independent mission, not seeking any human advice or authorization.

5. *2.1-10*

> Fourteen years later Paul went up to Jerusalem and laid his gospel
> before those of reputation. The validity of Paul's gospel and
> apostleship was acknowledged.

6. *2.11-21*

> Paul spoke against Cephas who separated himself from eating with
> the Gentiles due to his fear of the people of circumcision:
> a) Cephas's act of Judaizing the Gentiles opposed God's act of
> justifying all mankind in Christ;
> b) Cephas's act of restoring the law contradicted Christ's act of
> liberating his people from the law for the new life to God.

7. *3.1-14*

> No one is justified by the works of the law, but by faith in Christ who
> has carried away the curse of the law.

8. *3.15-22*

> The law given later could not invalidate the promise. But the law
> served to produce transgressions. In consequence, the Scripture shut
> up all men under sin that the believers might receive the promise by
> faith in Christ.

9. *3.23-29*

> Now that faith (Christ) has come, the believers are no longer slaves
> under the law as a pedagogue but are sons of God.

10. *4.1-7*

> By virtue of the redemption of the Son of God and the receiving of the
> Spirit, the believers are no longer slaves under the elements of the
> world but are sons of God.

11. *4.8-20*

> Paul is concerned for the Galatians who are turning back from God to the elements of the world, and therefore appeals to them to become like him in remaining free from the law.

12. *4.21-31*

> The believers are not children of the slave woman, Hagar, who represents the present Jerusalem, but children of the free woman, Sarah, who stands for the Jerusalem above.

13. *5.1-12*

> Since Christ has set the believers free, the Galatians should not accept circumcision for justification, but live by faith.

14. *5.13-24*

> Since they have been called to freedom, the Galatians should not subject themselves to the flesh, but walk by the Spirit.

15. *5.25–6.10*

> Since they live by the Spirit, the Galatians should not become vainglorious but bear one another's burdens and do good towards all men.

16. *6.11-18*

> Postscript. This contains a summary of the main points of the letter, a final appeal, and a benediction.

ii. *Grouping of Various Pericopae.* Pericopae 4[1.13-24]-5[2.1-10]: additive consequential. Receiving the revelation of the Son of God and the commission to preach him, Paul at once took an independent position in fulfilling the mandate (1.13-24). Later his gospel and apostleship were recognized by the Jerusalem authorities (2.1-10).

Pericopae (4[1.13-24]-5[2.1-10])-6[2.11-21]: additive non-consequential. The pericope of 2.11-21 that Paul opposed Cephas for the sake of the truth of the gospel is materially non-consequential to 1.13–2.10, though it is perhaps chronologically sequential to them. Gal. 1.13–2.21 constitutes the narrative section of the letter, introduced by ἠκούσατε in 1.13.[1] The unity of this section is strengthened by the repeated appearance of ὅτε in 1.15; 2.11 and ἔπειτα in 1.18, 21; 2.1.

Pericopae 3[1.11-12]-(4[1.13-24]-6[2.11-21]): result–reason. Gal. 1.11-12 is the thesis of the narrative section in 1.13–2.21. The divine origin of Paul's gospel (1.11-12) is proved by the following facts: Paul received the revelation of the Son of God and the commission to preach him, and thereafter launched an independent mission (1.13-24);

---

1. Cf. White 1971: 97.

the validity of his gospel and apostleship was recognized by the Jerusalem authorities (2.1-10); and he opposed Cephas for the sake of the truth of the gospel (2.11-21). Interestingly, Paul's gospel here is inseparably tied up with his apostleship.

Pericopae 6a[2.14b-17b]-6b[2.18-21b]: additive consequential. Cephas's act of Judaizing the Gentiles opposes God's act of justifying all mankind in Christ (2.14b-17b), and his act of restoring the law contradicts Christ's act of liberating the believers from the slavery of the law for the new life in relation to God (2.18-21b). Cephas's Judaizing act leads to the restoration of the law, whereas God's justifying act leads to the liberation from the law for the new life to him.

Pericope 8[3.15-22] deals with the salvation-historical purpose of the law in relation to the promise. It functions as an excursus, preparing the way for the following discussion of slavery under the law and sonship in Christ.

Pericopae 9[3.23-29]-10[4.1-7],12[4.21-31]: additive equivalent. All of the three pericopae basically advance the same argument that the believers are not slaves of the law but sons of God in Christ. Slavery under the law, existence under the elements of the world and belonging to the present Jerusalem which Hagar represents are all identical. On the other hand, sons of God are identical to children of Sarah, the free woman (3.26, 29; 4.7, 28, 31).

Pericope 11[4.8-20] is Paul's appeal to the Galatians to become like him in remaining free from the law. It anticipates the paraenetic section in 5.1–6.10.

Pericopae 7[3.1-14]-(9[3.23-29]-12[4.21-31]): additive consequential. The believers are not justified by the works of the law but by faith in Christ (3.1-14), and they are no longer slaves of the law but sons of God (3.23-4.31).

Pericopae 14[5.13-24]-15[5.25-6.10]: generic–specific. The general injunction of 5.13-24 not to submit to the flesh but to walk by the Spirit is specified in the exhortation of 5.25–6.10 not to become vainglorious but to bear one another's burdens and to do good towards all men.

Pericopae 13[5.1-12]-(14[5.13-24]-15[5.25–6.10]): additive consequential. The Galatians should not receive circumcision for justification but live by faith (5.1-12), and they should not live according to the flesh but walk by the Spirit (5.13–6.10).

Pericopae (7[3.1-14]-12[4.21-31])-(13[5.1-12]-15[5.25–6.10]): basis–inference. The argument of justification by faith alone in 3.1-14 (pericope 7) provides the basis of the exhortation to reject circumcision for justification in 5.1-12 (pericope 13). On the other hand, the argument that the believers are not slaves of the law but sons of God in 3.23-4.7 (pericopae 9-10) and in 4.21-31 (pericope 12) gives the basis of the exhortation not to live according to the flesh but to walk by the Spirit in 5.13–6.10 (pericopae 14-15). In this respect it is to be observed that slavery under the law corresponds to existence under the flesh (cf. 5.18). In fact, both the law and the flesh are the old rulers of the present evil age (cf. 1.4). Thus Paul urges the sons of God, who are liberated from the old powers, to walk by the Spirit, the power of the new age.

Pericopae (6a[2.14b-17b]-6b[2.18-21b])-(7[3.1-14]-15[5.25–6.10]): generic–specific. As I have already argued above, Paul's speech against Cephas in Antioch (2.14b-21b), in one way or another, serves as a summary of both the argumentative section in 3.1-4.31 and the paraenetic section in 5.1-6.10. The simple assertion of justification by faith in 2.14b-17b (pericope 6a) is brought into the full argument in 3.1-14 (pericope 7), on the basis of which the exhortation in 5.1-12 (pericope 13) is given, while the brief discussion of the new life to God in 2.18-21b (pericope 6b) is further elaborated on in the arguments of 3.23–4.7 and 4.21-31 (pericopae 9-10, 12) and in the corresponding exhortations of pericopae 5.13-6.10 (pericopae 14-15). These relationships can be described as follows:

Paul's speech against Cephas (2.14b-21)
    A) pericope 6a (2.14b-17b): justification by faith
    B) pericope 6b (2.18-21b): new life to God
Argumentative section (3.1-4.31)
    A') pericope 7 (3.1-14): justification by faith
    B') pericopae 9-10, 12 (3.23–4.7; 4.21-31): sonship in Christ
Paraenetic section (5.1–6.10)
    A″) pericope 13 (5.1-12): no circumcision for justification
    B″) pericope 14-15 (5.13–6.10): walking by the Spirit

This clearly shows that Paul's argument in the letter is developed on the two levels: the first level (A, A', A″) deals with the way of justification; the second level (B, B', B″) with the new existence of the justified believer.

Pericopae (3[1.11-12]-6[2.11-21])-(6a[2.14b-17b]-15[5.25-6.10]): basis–inference. The thesis (1.11-12) of the narrative section (1.13–2.21b) is the basis upon which Paul's whole exposition of the gospel of Christ rests (2.14b–6.10). This implies that his theology of justification by faith and new existence in Christ is derived from his vision of the resurrected Christ on the way to Damascus (1.12, 15-16).

Pericopae 2[1.6-10]-(3[1.11-12]-15[5.25–6.10]): generic–specific. The main thought of 1.6-10 that there is no other gospel than the gospel of Christ is taken up and given specific meanings in 1.11–6.10. As claimed earlier (Ch. 1.2.a.ii), 1.6-10 is the *proposition* of the letter. The whole purpose of the letter is to persuade the Galatians to reject the false gospel and to hold fast to the gospel of Christ, as Hall rightly maintains.[1] The Galatians are urged to choose justification by faith in Christ rather than justification by the works of the law (2.14b-17b; 3.1-14; 5.1-12), sonship in Christ rather than slavery under the law (2.18-21; 3.23–4.7; 4.21-31), and walking by the Spirit rather than subjection to the flesh (5.13–6.10). In the postscript Paul most sharply states what course of action the Galatians should take: to select the cross of Christ rather than circumcision (6.12-16). Such a purpose in the letter exactly conforms to the aim of deliberative rhetoric, that is, to persuade the audience to take some future action. Thus it is proved, as contended earlier (Ch. 1.1.b), that the letter to the Galatians is a deliberative work.

Finally, it remains to show the macro-structure of Galatians. This can be diagrammed as follows:

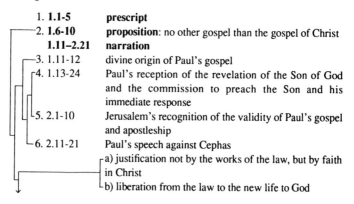

1. **1.1-5**   **prescript**
2. **1.6-10**   **proposition**: no other gospel than the gospel of Christ
   1.11–2.21   **narration**
3. 1.11-12   divine origin of Paul's gospel
4. 1.13-24   Paul's reception of the revelation of the Son of God and the commission to preach the Son and his immediate response
5. 2.1-10   Jerusalem's recognition of the validity of Paul's gospel and apostleship
6. 2.11-21   Paul's speech against Cephas
                      a) justification not by the works of the law, but by faith in Christ
                      b) liberation from the law to the new life to God

---

1. Hall 1987: 279ff.; cf. Smit 1989: 23-24.

	3.1–4.31	**argument**
⌐	7. 3.1-14	justification not by the works of the law, but by faith in Christ
	8. 3.15-22	the law and the promise
⌐	9. 3.23-29	no longer slaves under the law, but sons of God
⌐	10. 4.1-7	no longer slaves under the elements of the world, but sons of God.
	11. 4.8-20	Paul's appeal to remain free from the law
⌐	12. 4.21-31	not children of Hagar, but children of Sarah
	5.1–6.10	**exhortation**
⌐	13. 5.1-12	not circumcision, but faith
⌐	14. 5.13-24	not the flesh, but the Spirit.
⌐	15. 5.25–6.10	not vainglory, but love
	16. **6.11-18**	**postscript**

Chapter 2

The Perspective of Paul

1. *Proceeding from the Structure*

As observed above, Paul characteristically draws many pairs of
antitheses between the false gospel of the opponents and the gospel of
Christ in Galatians: justification by the works of the law versus
justification by faith in Christ (2.15-16; 3.1-14; cf. 5.1-12), the curse
of the law versus the blessing of Abraham (3.6-14), slavery under the
law versus sonship in Christ (3.23–4.7; cf. 2.18-21), children of
Hagar versus children of Sarah (4.21-31), subjection to the flesh
versus walking by the Spirit (5.13–6.10), the works of the flesh versus
the fruit of the Spirit (5.19-23), circumcision versus the cross of
Christ (6.12-14). Between these two different groups of contrasts Paul
urges his readers, the Galatians, to repudiate the first group and to
choose the second one. This is the main purpose of the letter.

In order to penetrate Paul's argument in the letter more deeply
there are now further questions to be raised: from what perspective
does Paul try to persuade the Galatians to make this choice? In other
words, what is his understanding of the gospel of Christ with which he
seeks to combat the gospel of the opponents? More specifically, how
does he grasp the salvific meaning of the cross which is the kernel of
the gospel of Christ (Gal. 6.14)? To answer these questions we need to
look closely at the above analysis of the structure of Galatians. The
body of the letter is composed of four parts: proposition (1.6-10),
narration (1.11–2.21), argument (3.1–4.31), and exhortation (5.1–
6.10). While the narrative section deals with the origin of the gospel
of Christ, the proposition that there is no other gospel than the gospel
of Christ is fully discussed in the argumentative and exhortative
sections. The argumentative section contains two basic arguments:
justification by faith versus justification by the works of the law (3.1-
14), and sonship in Christ versus slavery under the law (3.23–4.7).

Pericope 3.15-22 which treats the salvation-historical function of the law in relation to the promise is a transitional excursus. Pericope 4.8-20 is an appeal, anticipating the exhortative section in 5.1–6.10. And pericope 4.21-31 is the allegory of Hagar and Sarah which is, in its nature, a supplementary argument.[1]

The two main arguments in 3.1-14 and 3.23–4.7, which are closely linked by an additive consequential relationship,[2] hinge upon the statements concerning the redemption of Christ. The passage of 3.13-14, which speaks of Christ's redeeming work from the curse of the law (v. 13) and its results (v. 14), functions as the pivot of the argument in 3.1-14. Verse 13 is the conclusion of vv. 10-12, answering the problem of the curse of the law raised in v. 10. Verse 14a takes up the passage 3.6-9, showing that the promise of the Gentiles' participation in the blessing of Abraham which was occasioned by Abraham's believing response to God found fulfilment through Christ's redemption. Verse 14b indicates that the Galatians' reception of the Spirit in 3.1-5 is the outcome of that redemption.[3]

The argument in 3.23–4.7 consists of two pericopae: 3.23-29 and 4.1-7. Although employing different images, they essentially address the same issue, namely the radical change of the believer's existence from slavery under the law to sonship in Christ. This change has been brought about by the coming of Christ mentioned in 3.25 (the coming of faith = the coming of Christ) and in 4.4-5. This suggests the hinge function of these two statements in the pericopae of 3.23-29 and 4.1-7 respectively.[4]

The same can be said of the exhortative section. The statements concerning the liberation of Christ in 5.1a and 13a are the foundation of the two exhortations:[5] to reject circumcision in 5.1-12 and to walk by the Spirit in 5.13–6.10.[6]

The fundamental ground of Paul's argument in Galatians, namely the redemption of Christ, is first introduced in 1.4 in the prescript and finally restated in 6.14-15 in the postscript, though expressed by

1.   Burton 1921: 251; Longenecker 1975: 127-28.
2.   See above Ch. 1.2.b.ii.
3.   See above Ch. 1.2.a.vii.
4.   See above Ch. 1.2.a.ix, x.
5.   See above Ch. 1.2.xiii, xv.
6.   The general injunction of pericope 5.13-24 is specified in pericope 5.25–6.10. See above Ch. 1.2.b.ii.

means of different metaphors. It is therefore my contention that a close study of the pivotal statements will lead to a clearer understanding of the underlying perspective of Paul.

2. *Pivotal Statements*

a. *Galatians 1.4*

Gal. 1.1-5 is the epistolary prescript, separated from the body of the letter. It exhibits conventional elements: sender (1.1-2a), addressees (1.2b), and salutation (1.3-5). It is interesting to observe that the first and last elements are considerably expanded. What is particularly important here is that the christological formula attached to the salutation in 1.4 uncovers the basic premise of the main line of argument in the body of the letter.[1]

Gal. 1.4 speaks of the self-sacrifice of Jesus Christ and its purpose. 1.4a describes the atoning death of Christ: ['Ιησοῦ Χριστοῦ] τοῦ δόντος ἑαυτὸν ὑπὲρ τῶν ἁμαρτιῶν ἡμῶν. The phrase δίδωμι ἑαυτόν, which implies service on behalf of someone,[2] refers to Jesus' voluntary self-sacrifice of his life. In this connection it is noteworthy that instead of δίδωμι Paul uses παραδίδωμι in Gal. 2.20,[3] which seems to indicate the influence of the early Christians' christological understanding of the Greek version of Isa. 53.6, 12 (LXX) where the same term is used.[4] The next phrase ὑπὲρ τῶν ἁμαρτιῶν ἡμῶν explains why the self-giving of Jesus was necessitated. Here we have a textual problem. The manuscripts are almost evenly divided between ὑπέρ and περί: ὑπέρ 𝔓51 ℵ1 B H 6 33 81 al; περί Π46 ℵ* A D F G al. It is difficult to decide which version is to be preferred; however, there is no variation in meaning.[5] The preposition ὑπέρ with the genitive is normally used in the sense 'on behalf of' or 'for the sake of'. This implies that a participant is benefited by an event.[6] So the ὑπέρ used here with τῶν ἁμαρτιῶν ἡμῶν naturally adopts the idea of

---

1. See above Ch. 1.2.a.i.
2. Louw and Nida *et al.* 1988: 53.48.
3. See also Rom. 4.25; 8.32; 1 Cor. 11.23; cf. 1 Tim. 2.6; Tit. 2.14.
4. Perrin 1970: 207-12; Schlier 1971: 32; cf. Mussner 1974: 51.
5. Blass and Debrunner 1961: §229.1; Schlier 1971: 32 n. 3; Betz 1979: 42 n. 55; Louw and Nida *et al.* 1988: 90.36, 39.
6. Louw and Nida *et al.* 1988: 90.36.

deliverance.[1] Thus 1.4a means that Jesus Christ voluntarily sacrificed himself in order to deliver us from our sins. Attention should be drawn to the *plural* of the ἁμαρτιῶν. It is well known that in his own theological language Paul almost always uses the word ἁμαρτία in the singular. The plural here indicates a pre-Pauline view of sins as individual transgressions of the law (cf. 1 Cor. 15.3; Isa. 53.5, 11). It must, however, be read in conjunction with Paul's own concept of the demonic power of sin (cf. Gal. 3.22; Rom. 5.12, 21; 6.6, 17; 7.9ff.), as Betz maintains.[2]

1.4b concerns the purpose of the redeeming death of Christ: ὅπως ἐξέληται ἡμᾶς ἐκ τοῦ αἰῶνος τοῦ ἐνεστῶτος πονηροῦ. This subordinate clause offers the idea of ὑπὲρ τῶν ἁμαρτιῶν ἡμῶν from a different angle. The conjunction ὅπως which expresses the purpose of an event is interchangeable with ἵνα.[3] The expression ὁ αἰὼν ὁ ἐνεστώς which appears only here in the NT is equivalent to the more usual ὁ αἰὼν οὗτος.[4] It is distinguished from and set in contrast to ὁ αἰὼν ὁ μέλλων (Eph. 1.21; Heb. 6.5; Mt. 12.32; cf. Eph. 2.7). It is also sometimes used interchangeably with ὁ κόσμος (1 Cor. 1.20; 3.18, 19). The present age is characterized by πονηρός (cf. 1QpHab 5.7-8), for it is dominated by *evil* powers which are, according to Galatians, sin (3.22), law (2.19; 3.13, 23ff.), the elemental spirits (4.3, 9) and flesh (5.16ff.). On the cross Christ has conquered, though not completely eliminated, these powers (cf. 2.19; 5.24; 6.14; Rom. 8.3-4, 31-39; 1 Cor. 15.24-28; Col. 2.15) and has already inaugurated the coming age by his resurrection. This coming age has broken into the present evil age. By virtue of the victory of the cross the believers have been delivered from the control of the evil powers which rule this age. To be sure, the believers still live in this world; nevertheless, they no longer belong to it. In the indwelling Spirit they experience the life of the new age, looking forward to the final, eschatological, consummation. For them the 'not yet' has become the 'already'. Thus it is clear that Paul understands the death of Christ as the event of

---

1. Bauer 1979: s.v.; Burton 1921: 13; Guthrie 1973: 59.
2. Betz 1979: 42.
3. Louw and Nida *et al.* 1988: 89.59 n. 10.
4. Rom. 12.2; 1 Cor. 1.20; 2.6, 8; 3.18; 2 Cor. 4.4; Eph. 1.21; cf. 1 Tim. 6.17; 2 Tim. 4.10; Tit. 2.12.

eschatological salvation.[1] This understanding forms the basic ground
of his argument in Galatians.

b. *Galatians 3.13-14, 25; 4.4-5*

I have noted above that Gal. 3.13-14, 25 and 4.4-5 undergird the
arguments of pericopae 3.1-14; 3.23-29 and 4.1-7 respectively. In
spite of external differences, they are inherently concerned with the
same theme, namely the redemption of Christ.[2] For this reason I will
not treat them separately here. Nevertheless, 3.13-14 will enjoy most
of the attention, while the other two passages will be taken as com-
plements.

Gal. 3.13-14 is a statement of cardinal importance in understanding
Paul's perspective in this letter. But it presents a puzzling problem to
many interpreters. My interpretation of the passage will begin with
the identification of ἡμεῖς mentioned twice in v. 13. Does the pronoun
refer to Jewish Christians exclusively, or to Jewish and Gentile
Christians inclusively? Scholars are divided on this issue. Some argue
that the 'we' in v. 13 is to be determined by the 'we' in v. 14b which
is definitely used in an inclusive sense.[3] I do not find this argument
convincing, chiefly because it simply ignores the apparent contrast
between the 'we' in v. 13 and τὰ ἔθνη in v. 14a. In my opinion, the
specific mention of τὰ ἔθνη in v. 14a in clear distinction from the
'we' in v. 13 creates a strong impression of the antithesis between the
two.[4] This observation also leads me to reject the similar contention
that the alteration of pronouns from 'we' to 'you' in 3.23-29 and 4.3-7
demonstrates the inclusive emphasis of Paul's wording and argument.[5]

Many interpreters attempt to read Rom. 2.12-15 into Galatians,
arguing the universal dominion of the law.[6] But one must not impose
Romans on Galatians without careful qualification. We should bear in
mind that even in Rom. 2.12, 14; 7.1; 9.4 (cf. 1 Cor. 9.20) Paul

1. Cf. Cullmann 1957: 81ff.; Ladd 1974: 38ff., 68-69; Vos 1982: 1-41; Bruce
1982a: 76; Coetzee 1985: 323ff.
2. Cf. Blank 1968: 162-63; Hays 1983: 86-92, 116-21; Donaldson 1986: 95-98.
3. Schlier 1971: 137; Fung 1988: 149.
4. Zahn 1907: 156; Burton 1921: 169; Donaldson 1986: 97.
5. Cf. Howard 1979: 59; Bruce 1982a: 196.
6. Oepke 1937: 57; Büchsel 1964: 450; Schlier 1971: 132; Mussner 1974: 224;
Bruce 1982a: 167; Fung 1988: 148-49; cf. Klein 1969: 206-207.

makes a clear distinction between the Jews who are under the law and
the Gentiles who do not have the law. In fact, the law was originally
given to the Jews only. They are the people who find their identity in
the law (cf. Gal. 2.15).

In support of the inclusive reading of the first person plural in Gal.
3.13 some scholars advance the argument that in Gal. 4.1-11 being
ὑπὸ νόμον is understood as equivalent to being ὑπὸ τὰ στοιχεῖα τοῦ
κόσμου which is characteristic of the universal human (Jewish and
Gentile) plight before Christ.[1] To be sure, the two different existences
correspond. It must also be conceded that the existence ὑπὸ τὰ
στοιχεῖα τοῦ κόσμου represents all human existence apart from
Christ. But this does not necessarily require the existence ὑπὸ νόμον
to be understood in the same inclusive sense. Paul says to the Gentile
Galatians in 4.9 that to surrender to Judaizing pressure is to turn back
not to the law but to the elemental spirits! Donaldson states that
'Bondage to these cosmic powers who rule "this age" in opposition to
God, is the common category under which Jewish and Gentile existence is described. To be ὑπὸ νόμον is just one way—albeit a very
particular and special way—of being ὑπὸ τὰ στοιχεῖα τοῦ κόσμου.'[2]

I conclude, therefore, that the ἡμεῖς in 3.13 is to be taken in the
exclusive sense. This is true of the 'we' of ἐσμεν in 3.25 and those
who are ὑπὸ νόμον in 4.4-5.[3] (This will be substantiated by my
further consideration of Gal. 3.13-14.) If my conclusion is correct
here, one might immediately pose a question: how does Paul conceive
the redemption of Israel as the prerequisite for the blessing of the
Gentiles (3.14)? Instead of attempting a direct answer to this question
at this point, I will first discuss the meaning of the curse of the law
and Christ's redemption from it. In the course of the discussion I will
gradually progress towards an answer to the question.

What is ἡ κατάρα τοῦ νόμου from which Christ redeemed Israel
(3.13)? I think that it is the curse pronounced by the law, taking the
genitive to be a subjective genitive. Why, then, does the law curse?
What is the exact nature of the curse of the law? These questions are
to be answered in context. Here we turn to 3.10, because it raises for
the first time the problem of the curse of the law. Verse 10 speaks of

---

1. Reicke 1951: 259ff.; Schlier 1971: 136-37.
2. Donaldson 1986: 96-97.
3. Betz 1979: 179; Donaldson 1986: 95ff.; cf. Gaston 1979: 62ff.

who are under the curse and *why*. So I hope that a close scrutiny of these issues will lead us to grasp the real meaning of the curse of the law. Verse 10a reads: ὅσοι γὰρ ἐξ ἔργων νόμου εἰσίν, ὑπὸ κατάραν εἰσίν. A satisfactory understanding of this statement requires a correct interpretation of the expression ἔργα νόμου which occurs six times in Galatians, three times in 2.16 and three times in the pericope of 3.1-14. But this is not the place to go into a detailed discussion of 'the works of the law'. For this we will have to wait till Chapter 5. Suffice it to say here that the phrase refers to works done in conformity with the demand of the law,[1] not legalistic observances of the law or particular Jewish observances such as circumcision, food laws and special feast days. Thus I understand v. 10a to mean: all who set their trust in works done in obedience to the law are under a curse.

Why this is the case is explained by the quotation of Deut. 27.26 in Gal. 3.10b: ἐπικατάρατος πᾶς ὃς οὐκ ἐμμένει πᾶσιν τοῖς γεγραμμένοις ἐν τῷ βιβλίῳ τοῦ νόμου τοῦ ποιῆσαι αὐτά. This quotation of Paul does not fully agree with the Septuagint or the MT. The MT reads: אָרוּר אֲשֶׁר לֹא־יָקִים אֶת־דִּבְרֵי הַתּוֹרָה־הַזֹּאת לַעֲשׂוֹת אוֹתָם (Cursed is he who does not keep the words of this law to do them). The Septuagint adds an accent to this Hebrew text by inserting πᾶς before ἄνθρωπος and πᾶσιν before τοῖς λόγοις τοῦ νόμου τούτου: ἐπικατάρατος πᾶς ἄνθρωπος, ὃς οὐκ ἐμμενεῖ ἐν πᾶσιν τοῖς λόγοις τοῦ νόμου τούτου τοῦ ποιῆσαι αὐτούς. Paul replaces the Septuagint phrase πᾶσιν τοῖς λόγοις τοῦ νόμου τούτου by πᾶσιν τοῖς γεγραμμένοις ἐν τῷ βιβλίῳ τοῦ νόμου.

In spite of these variations, in order to comprehend properly Paul's quotation of Deut. 27.26 I think that it is essential to examine the OT text in its original context. Deut. 27.15-26 is concerned with a series of twelve curses, the so-called 'Dodecalogue of Schechem'. The first eleven curses deal with transgressions committed in secret.[2] The last curse of 27.26 which Paul cites in Gal. 3.10b is the generalizing summary of the eleven curses without mentioning any particular crime. But, by substituting 'the book of the law' in Galatians for 'this law' in both the MT and the Septuagint, as observed just above, Paul extends the application of Deut. 27.26 to the whole

1. Moo 1983: 92ff.; Räisänen 1983: 177; Fung 1988: 113; Westerholm 1988: 116-21.
2. Alt 1953: 314; Von Rad 1966: 168.

OT law.[1] For him the failure to obey any prescript of the Torah incurs a curse (cf. Gal. 5.3; Jas 2.10).

What is important to note is that the Dodecalogue was addressed, probably at a ceremony of the renewal of the Sinai covenant,[2] to the community of Israel who had *already* become the people of God (Deut. 27.9). They were the special community who had a *covenant* relationship with God. They declared Yahweh to be their God and Yahweh declared them to be his people (Deut. 26.17-18); this formula often appears in the OT (e.g. Exod. 6.7; Jer. 31.33; Ezek. 36.28) and is called the 'formula of the Sinai Covenant'.[3] Here we see that the law is closely tied up with the covenant. To understand the distinct character of the curse of the law requires a discussion of the peculiar relationship between the law and the covenant.

As is well known, God made Israel as his own people by delivering her from the bondage of Egypt, and then gave her the law in order that she should lead a holy life in response to his saving grace. The most important thing to bear in mind here is that the law is *not* the precondition of Israel's covenant relationship with God; on the contrary, it is the *result* of the relationship. Von Rad, in his very influential work, says that 'Israel was elected by Jahweh before she was given the commandments. As a result of this election she became Jahweh's chosen people, and this, in fact, happened before she had had any opportunity of proving her obedience.'[4] This relationship between the covenant and the law is a kind of *indicative–imperative* relationship (Deut. 27.9-10; cf. Lev. 18.2-5; Exod. 20.2ff.)—there is no legalism implied here! In this respect it is to be noted that in Lev. 18.2-5 the imperative to keep the statutes and ordinances, by doing which a man should live (Lev. 18.5; cf. Gal. 3.12), is based on the indicative that Yahweh is Israel's saving God (Lev. 18.2-4; cf. Exod. 20.2ff.).

Thus it is clear that the obedience to the law is Israel's covenant obligation. It enables her to remain in the covenant relationship and to enjoy all the blessings of God.[5] The transgression of the law,

1. Noth 1966: 119; Edwards 1972: 198-200; Bruce 1982b: 28.
2. Eichrodt 1961: 85; Von Rad 1975a: 192.
3. Von Rad 1966: 161; cf. Smend 1986: 11-39.
4. Von Rad 1975b: 391; cf. Von Rad 1975a: 194.
5. Cf. Noth 1966: 125ff.; Edwards 1972: 206-209.

however, incurs the curse of the law, for it demonstrates the disloyalty to God and the unworthiness of the relationship with him. This curse is actually the curse of God, because the law is his law (cf. Rom. 7.22, 25; 8.7). It brings punishment and death upon unfaithful breakers of the law of the covenant; this is quite evident in the messages of prophets.[1] So to be cursed means to be cut off from God. Now we arrive at the point where we are able to comprehend Gal. 3.10 as a whole in a better light: all the Jews as the covenant people who rely on obedience to the law in order to stay in their covenant relationship with God are under the curse of the law, because they fail to obey all the prescripts of the law of the covenant[2]—the assumption here is the idea of the general non-fulfilment of the law.[3]

It is noteworthy that in 3.13 the curse of the law is depicted as *bondage* under the law. The word ἐξαγοράζω means 'to cause the release or freedom of someone',[4] and thus implies *deliverance* from slavery. So redemption from the curse of the law refers to release from bondage under the law. This becomes more apparent when we turn to 4.5. Here the same Greek word is used again to describe liberation from the slavery under the law. The phrase ὑπὸ νόμον in this verse does not mean 'under obligation to abide by the regulations of the law'[5] but *under the enslaving power of the law*, in view of the fact that the effect of Christ's redemption is the radical change of the status of the believer from being a slave of the law (and also of the elemental spirits of the world in 4.3, 9) to being a son of God (4.5-7).[6] Thus it is obvious that the curse of the law is equivalent to the bondage of the law. To be under the curse of the law means to be under its tyranny. With regard to this it is very interesting to note that the law is described as a custodian who keeps sinners in custody for restraint, not for protection (3.23).

This enslaving power of the law is derived from its new function stated in 3.19b: τῶν παραβάσεων χάριν προσετέθη. Many inter-

---

1. Cf. Fensham 1963: 155-75; Fensham 1966: 220-21; Fensham 1967: 316-17; Fensham 1971: 89; Clements 1965: *passim*.

2. Cf. Lambrecht 1986: 113-16.

3. Cf. Schreiner 1984: 151-60.

4. Louw and Nida *et al.* 1988: 131.

5. Louw and Nida *et al.* 1988: 37.7.

6. Cf. Byrne 1979: 181-82; Van Deventer 1986: 123ff.

preters take χάριν to denote purpose.[1] So the Greek statement can be translated this way: 'It was added for the purpose of transgressions (or for the sake of transgressions).'[2] This means that the law was given not to check or prevent transgressions but to produce them. In other words, the law provokes men to break its prescripts. As a result it brings the transgressors under its curse (cf. Rom. 7.5, 8, 11, 13). For Paul this strange function of the law was somehow added to its original function as the stipulation of the Sinai covenant.[3]

It is very significant that Paul closely relates the Jewish plight under the law to the universal plight ὑπὸ ἁμαρτίαν and ὑπὸ τὰ στοιχεῖα τοῦ κόσμου. These two different plights are put side by side: in 3.22-23 being 'under sin'[4] and being 'under the law' are parallel; in 4.3-9 being 'under the elemental spirits of the world'[5] corresponds to being 'under the law'. In this regard, Donaldson says, 'Israel's plight is a special form of the universal plight'.[6]

In order to understand this, we once again return to 3.19b: τῶν παραβάσεων χάριν προσετέθη. The παράβασις is a technical term, denoting 'sin in its relation to law'.[7] More precisely, it means the concrete breach of a specific commandment. Before the introduction of the law there was sin (ἁμαρτία) but no transgression (παράβασις). Rom. 4.15 says, 'where there is no law, there is no transgression'. This absence of the definite form of violation of the divine will kept people from realizing fully their imprisonment under the power of sin. But the law was given in order to produce transgressions (cf. Rom. 5.20), and thereby has revealed that all people without exception are confined under sin (cf. Gal. 3.22; Rom. 3.20). In fact, the coming of the law is to shed light on the universal human plight under sin. If this is the case, it can be said that Israel, the people of the law, serve

1. Ridderbos 1953: 137-38; Schlier 1971: 152; Betz 1979: 165; Bruce 1982a: 175; Donaldson 1986: 104; cf. Burton 1921: 188; Mussner 1974: 245-46.
2. This is Paul's radical reinterpretation of the law in the light of the Christ event.
3. I will discuss this matter in Ch. 6.
4. The Greek words τὰ πάντα in front of 'under sin' in 3.22 refer to all people.
5. Gal. 4.3 speaks of the Jews under the elemental spirits, while 4.9 speaks of the Gentiles under them.
6. Donaldson 1986: 103.
7. Schneider 1967: 739.

as a kind of *representative sample* for the whole of humankind. 'Within Israel's experience, the nature of the universal human plight—bondage to sin and to the powers of this age—is thrown into sharp relief through the functioning of the law', as Donaldson maintains.[1] It then follows that the particular redemption of Israel from the curse of the law can bring about universal consequences.

Thus far, it has been argued that Christ redeemed Israel from the curse of the covenant law, and that the slavery under the law is representative of universal slavery under sin and under the elemental spirits of the world. Gal. 3.13 goes on to say how Christ accomplished the redemption from the curse of the law: γενόμενος ὑπὲρ ἡμῶν κατάρα. The participle γενόμενος expresses means, and so the phrase means 'by becoming a curse for "us"'. When and how did Christ become a curse for Israel? Does the phrase speak of the crucifixion or of the incarnation? Both the immediate context, that is, the citation of Deut. 21.23 which follows, and the larger context (2.20-21; 3.1; 6.12, 14; cf. 5.24) might be taken to suggest that the death of Christ on the cross is in view. At this point, however, Hooker wisely gives a word of caution that we should be careful of driving a wedge between the incarnation and the crucifixion in Paul's thought.[2] Interestingly enough, Gal. 4.4, which corresponds to 3.13,[3] states that Christ was 'born under the law'. If, as argued just above, we are correct in viewing 'under the law' here as identical with 'under the curse of the law', not with 'under the obligation to keep the law', the expression 'born under the law' can be understood this way: by the deep humiliation of his incarnation Christ voluntarily took on himself the curse which the Jews had incurred because of their violation of the covenant law.[4] This condescension led him to undergo temptation, misunderstanding, contempt and rejection for his accursed people during his earthly life.[5] Finally, through his identification with them on the cross Christ completely removed the curse of the law from them; this is the culmination of his redemptive work.[6] Therefore they

---

1. Donaldson 1986: 105-106.
2. Hooker 1971: 351.
3. Cf. Schweizer 1972: 383.
4. Cf. Whiteley 1957: 246; Berkouwer 1965: 323; Kertelge 1967: 211; Hooker 1971: 351-52; Käsemann 1971: 43; Bruce 1982a: 196; Bruce 1982b: 34.
5. Cf. Whiteley 1957: 244-45.
6. Cf. Gaston 1979: 66.

are no longer under the curse of the law (cf. 3.25). In reaching this conclusion I reject the misleading contention that Jesus was killed for his alleged criticism against the law.[1]

This view that Christ first became a curse and was then crucified is confirmed by the quotation of Deut. 21.23b in Gal. 3.13b: ἐπικατάρατος πᾶς ὁ κρεμάμενος ἐπὶ ξύλου. This statement does not fully correspond to the Septuagint or to the MT. The MT reads: קִלְלַת אֱלֹהִים תָּלוּי (he who is hanged is a curse of God). This Hebrew text is ambiguous, because the phrase קִלְלַת אֱלֹהִים can be taken as an objective or subjective genitive. According to Billerbeck, the rabbinical literature generally understands the expression as an objective genitive.[2] But the Septuagint decidedly opts for the alternative of a subjective genitive and renders the text: κεκατηραμένος ὑπὸ θεοῦ πᾶς κρεμάμενος ἐπὶ ξύλου. Paul adopts the decision of the Septuagint. But he changes the perfect, passive participle κεκατηραμένος for the adjective ἐπικατάρατος, probably to make the wording agree with that of his quotation of Deut. 27.26 in 3.10.[3] Consequently he omits ὑπὸ θεοῦ, because the grammatical construction of the adjective ἐπικατάρατος with the words ὑπὸ θεοῦ would be extremely awkward.[4] Some interpreters contend, however, that the reason for the omission is that Christ was not cursed by God but by the law. For them, it is absurd to think that God cursed Christ who died in obedience to his will.[5] This idea is unacceptable. I believe that in Paul's view Christ was indeed cursed by God, though in a substitutional manner (cf. Mk 15.34). The curse of the law is the curse of God, because the law is the covenant law of God. If not, what else? At any rate, in spite of the changes of his rendering Paul does not misuse Deut. 21.23b. Deut. 21.22-23 speaks of the regulation of hanging a criminal on a tree. If a man had broken certain laws of the covenant community,[6] he was executed and hanged on a tree in order to show that he was cursed by God. Then the corpse was removed and buried at sunset so as not to defile the land. What is important to note here is

---

1. Cf. Edwards 1972: 266ff.; Hamerton-Kelly 1990a: 113ff.
2. Billerbeck 1926: 544-45.
3. Edwards 1972: 262; Wilcox 1977: 87; Bruce 1982a: 165.
4. Edwards 1972: 263.
5. Denney 1905: 160; Mussner 1974: 233; Bruce 1982a: 165; Bruce 1982b: 32; cf. Burton 1921: 168.
6. Craigie 1976: 285.

the relationship between cursing and hanging: the criminal was not cursed because he had been hanged on a tree; rather, he was hanged because he had already been cursed on account of his heinous offence.[1] In other words, hanging was to show a curse, not to make a curse. Thus for Paul the crucifixion of Christ is a strong evidence of his curse. That Christ was crucified means that he had *already* been cursed by God. It should be emphasized, however, that this curse of Christ was not for his own sin but for the sins of his people (cf. 2 Cor. 5.21).

Now it becomes clear that Paul comprehends the Christ event as the eschatological redemption of the Jews who were brought under the curse of the covenant because of their breaking of the law.[2] Christ redeemed them by becoming a curse for them. This redemption of the Jews is *at the same time* and *on equal terms* the redemption of the Gentiles, because the Jews serve as the representative of all the nations. In his humiliating incarnation and suffering, Christ fully identified himself not only with Israel under the curse of the law but also with the Gentiles under sin and under the demonic forces. Especially on the cross, Christ substituted for all the sinners as their representative.[3] In fact, he is the substitute and representative of all humankind! Thus 'in Christ' the Gentiles, along with the Jews, can receive the blessing of Abraham, that is, justification by faith (3.8-9, 14), sonship (3.26; 4.5), and the Spirit (3.14; 4.6). 'In Christ' the old distinction between Jews and Gentiles which existed under the Sinai covenant administration is demolished (3.26-29; cf. Eph. 2.14-16). Through him the new covenant between God and all humankind is now established (cf. 4.21-31; 6.15).

c. *Galatians 5.1a, 13a*

The redemption of Christ furnishes the ground for the exhortation in 5.1–6.10. This paraenetical section is subdivided into three pericopae: 5.1-12; 5.13-24 and 5.25–6.10. The latter two pericopae 5.13-24 and 5.25–6.10 are bound together by a generic–specific relationship.[4] So it can be said that 5.1-12 and 5.13–6.10 are two basic parts of the

---

1. Lindars 1961: 233; Craigie 1976: 285; Caneday 1989: 199-200.
2. Cf. Fensham 1966: 222-23; Fensham 1967: 320; Fensham 1971: 92.
3. Cf. Kim 1984: 276 n. 3.
4. See above Ch. 1.2.b.ii.

paraenetical section. Interestingly, each of them begins with the restatement of Christ's redemption, which functions as the *indicative* of the two particular admonitions. 5.1a says: τῇ ἐλευθερίᾳ ἡμᾶς Χριστὸς ἠλευθέρωσεν. The dative τῇ ἐλευθερίᾳ seems to be a dative of purpose.[1] The freedom is the result of Christ's redemptive work, as discussed above, 'but this result is stated as a goal, purpose, and direction for the life of the Christian'.[2] Thus, on the basis of the redemption of Christ, Paul urges the Galatians not to accept circumcision, which leads to the slavery of the law (5.1-12). In Paul's opinion, any Gentile who becomes a Jew by receiving circumcision shares the Jewish plight under the curse of the law (cf. 5.3).

There is another reference to Christian freedom at the beginning of the second main part 5.13–6.10: ὑμεῖς γὰρ ἐπ' ἐλευθερίᾳ ἐκλήθητε, ἀδελφοί (5.13a). This sentence is reminiscent of 5.1a. Like 5.1a it is also a summary of the whole preceding argument of Christ's redemption, though focusing on God's salvation in Christ (the subject of the 'calling' is God).[3] The preposition ἐπί with the dative ἐλευθερίᾳ expresses purpose.[4] The *indicative* statement of 5.13a is the foundation of Paul's exhortation in 5.13–6.10 that the Galatians should not submit to the influence of the flesh but walk by the Spirit. The flesh here appears to be a personified power that works against the Spirit (5.16-17). As a subject of action it carries out its 'deeds' in opposition to the fruit of the Spirit (5.19-23). It has its own 'passions and desires' (5.24), which are stimulated by the commandment of the law (cf. 3.19; Rom. 7.5). For Paul, existence under the flesh is compatible with existence under the law (5.16-18), for subjection to the flesh causes man to break the law and thereby brings him under the bondage of the law. The flesh, like the law, is an evil power of the old age (1.4). But the believers who belong to Christ have crucified the flesh by their participation in Christ's crucifixion (5.24; cf. 2.19-20). For this reason they should walk by the Spirit, the power of the new age.

1.   Ridderbos 1953: 186; Mussner 1974: 342-43; Betz 1979: 255.
2.   Betz 1979: 256.
3.   Burton 1921: 291; Betz 1979: 271-72; cf. Schlier 1971: 242; Mussner 1974: 366-67.
4.   Blass and Debrunner 1961: §235.4; Moule 1963: 50; Bauer 1979: s.v., II.1.b.e.

Here it is interesting to see another aspect of Christ's redemption: the liberation from the dominion of the flesh.

d. *Galatians 6.14*

In the postscript, the keynote of which is the recapitulation of the major points in Galatians,[1] Paul restates his own theological stand advocated throughout the letter. After sharply attacking the opponents who have compelled the Galatians to be circumcised (6.12-13), Paul in 6.14 speaks of the grounds for and object of his boasting, namely the cross of Christ through which the world has been crucified to him and he to the world: ἐμοὶ δὲ μὴ γένοιτο καυχᾶσθαι εἰ μὴ ἐν τῷ σταυρῷ τοῦ κυρίου ἡμῶν Ἰησοῦ Χριστοῦ, δι' οὗ ἐμοὶ κόσμος ἐσταύρωται κἀγὼ κόσμῳ. Here we find three different crucifixions: the crucifixion of Christ, the crucifixion of the world to the believer[2] and the crucifixion of the believer to the world. The latter two crucifixions are dependent upon the first one. This means that in the cross of Christ the world has been condemned for the believer and that the believer therefore no longer exists or lives for the world (cf. 2.19). By virtue of the cross of Christ the believer has been completely separated from the world. The key to understanding this assertion is the term 'world'.

The κόσμος in 6.14 is a very difficult term to define, because it is used in so many different ways in the Scripture. But the context of 6.14 is decisive in determining its precise meaning. 6.15 says, 'For neither is circumcision anything, nor uncircumcision, but a new creation.' This statement can be seen as the consequence of v. 14, though the former motivates the latter as the γάρ indicates.[3] From this relationship it becomes apparent that the crucifixion of the world is an event that has made the distinction between circumcision and uncircumcision totally irrelevant. It follows that the *kosmos* is the domain in which people put their trust in circumcision for relationship with God.[4] It is with the crucifixion of this world that καινὴ κτίσις comes up. This implies that the world stands in contrast to the new creation. This nature of the world is further reflected in

1. Betz 1979: 313.
2. In Gal. 6.14 Paul speaks for the believer in general.
3. Betz 1979: 319 n. 76.
4. Cf. Minear 1979: 397.

vv. 12-13. The people who belong to the world still hold the earlier significance of circumcision as the sign of the old covenant (cf. Gen. 17.11), and therefore boast in the circumcised flesh, not in the cross of Christ. For Paul it is they who are under the slavery of the law, flesh, sin and the demonic spirits. Thus I agree with Ridderbos that the world means the 'life-context before and outside Christ',[1] that is, the domain dominated by the old powers. Although it is a space-concept, the world essentially corresponds to the idea of 'this age' (1.4). These two ideas are interchangeable (1 Cor. 1.20; 3.18-19)—so the world, like this age, is an eschatological concept.[2] From this world the believers have been liberated by their participation in Christ's crucifixion, and transferred to the kingdom of the Lord.

Thus far, we have seen that Paul's understanding of the cross of Christ in terms of eschatological redemption undergirds his whole argument in the letter. What, then, is the origin of this understanding? This is the next question to be discussed.

e. *Galatians 1.11-12, 15-16*

It is widely recognized that Gal. 1.11-12 is the thesis of the entire narrative in chs. 1-2.[3] The statement in the passage is supported by the following substantial facts in the narrative which begins from 1.13. The thesis provides the basis for Paul's interpretation of the saving significance of the cross of Christ in chs. 3-4.[4]

Gal. 1.11-12 apparently, if not exclusively, speaks of the *origin* of Paul's gospel,[5] claiming that the gospel of Paul was neither received from humans nor taught by humans but received through the revelation of Jesus Christ (δι' ἀποκαλύψεως 'Ιησοῦ Χριστοῦ). The gospel here refers to the gospel of Christ which Paul preached to the Galatians during his first visit to Galatia (cf. 1.6-9; 3.1; 4.13-14).[6] It provoked a strong anti-Pauline opposition from some antagonists. Against the gospel of Paul these antagonists imposed a different gospel upon the Galatians, insisting on the observance of the law, especially

1. Ridderbos 1975: 91.
2. Bultmann 1951: 256.
3. For references see above Ch. 1.2.a.iii.
4. See above Ch. 1.2.b.ii; cf. Betz 1979: 56, 61; Lategan 1985a: 105; Lategan 1988: 418ff.
5. Cf. Lategan 1988: 418ff.
6. Cf. Chamblin 1977: 115-17; Chamblin 1986: 6-8.

circumcision. This created great confusion among the Galatian
Christians. For Paul the false teaching is a great threat to the very
essence of the Christian message, robbing the death of Christ of its
saving significance and denying the grace of God in Christ (2.21).
This situation of crisis led Paul to remind the Galatians of the gospel
of Christ which he had already proclaimed, and even to clarify the
gospel in contrast to the false gospel of the opponents. This gospel of
Christ, Paul asserts, had been received from the revelation of Jesus
Christ, which clearly refers to the Damascus-road experience
described in 1.15-16.

Before embarking on a discussion of the significance of the
Damascus event for the development of Paul's theological thought, it
is worth considering the reason why he persecuted the Christian
church. Prior to his conversion Paul was a Pharisee, deeply devoted to
Judaism. He was extremely zealous for his ancestral traditions (1.14;
cf. Phil. 3.5-6). This zeal drove him to persecute the church. In Phil.
3.6 Paul comments on his former life in Judaism: 'as to zeal, persecuting the church'. In Acts 22.3-4 we also find the interesting link
between the zeal and his persecution. From this it is clear that Paul's
fervent zeal for the Jewish religion was the driving motive of his
campaign of persecution.[1] What, then, was it that stirred his zeal to
make him a persecutor of the Christians? Some hold that the Christian
proclamation of the crucified Jesus as the messiah provoked Paul's
anger. It is because the proclamation sounded in his ears as blasphemy
against God. For Paul, Jesus of Nazareth who was put to death by
crucifixion certainly died under the curse of God (cf. Deut. 21.23;
4QpNah 3–4; 1.6-8; 11QTemple 64.6-13) and thus could not be
conceived as the messiah of God.[2] We can certainly think
constructively along this line.[3]

We should, however, go one step further. We can find, I believe, a
more important reason for Paul's persecution in the radical nature of
the Hellenistic Jewish Christians' preaching and in their admission
policy towards the Gentiles. The Hellenists were the Christians who
founded the Antioch Church, consisting partly of the Gentile converts

1. Cf. Hultgren 1976: 100-101.
2. Menoud 1953: 133; Jeremias 1963: 14-15; Bruce 1969: 228; Kim 1984:
46-47; cf. Hultgren 1976: 100-103.
3. Cf. Dupont 1970: 187-89; Bornkamm 1975: 15.

won by preaching the Lord Jesus without requiring circumcision and observances of the Jewish law (Acts 11.19ff.). Some scholars assume that the Hellenists had already engaged in the Gentile mission before leaving Jerusalem because of persecution.[1] Unfortunately we do not know exactly what led them to take such a bold new course of action. Yet I presume that the Gentiles' experience of the Spirit in their uncircumcised state (cf. Acts 8.4ff., 25ff.) compelled the Hellenists to abandon the requirements of circumcision and Jewish observances. This thesis is not implausible in view of the fact that the experiential logic is employed by Peter at the Jerusalem council (Acts 15.7-11) and by Paul himself in Gal. 3.1-5.[2] I think that the pneumatic experience of the uncircumcised Gentiles directed the Hellenists to see the Christ event from a completely new perspective: Christ has brought about the universal salvation, breaking down the walls between the Jews and the Gentiles; God has accepted the Gentiles only on the basis of faith in Christ; he has established a new covenant with all mankind in Christ which has superseded his old covenant with Israel; faith is the only condition to become a member of the new Israel of God (cf. Gal. 6.16). This revolutionary message rendered useless the main pillars of Judaism such as circumcision, the Temple cult and other Jewish observances of the Mosaic law. This faith of the Hellenists was probably shared by many of the 'Hebrews'. But these Jews may have been reluctant to admit the Gentiles to their gatherings because of their cultural differences with the Gentiles and other social and political factors.[3] This might be illustrated by Peter's behaviour at Antioch. Before the arrival of certain men from James, Peter used to have table fellowship with the Gentiles without any inner, theological conflict. But, when they came, he irrationally withdrew from the fellowship because of his fear of the party of circumcision (Gal. 2.12). By this *hypocritical* (2.13!) action even Barnabas, a co-worker of Paul, was carried away. At all events, the radical proclamation of the Hellenistic Christians which denied the whole foundation of Judaism aroused the indignation of Paul, the zealous Pharisee, and made him a merciless persecutor.[4] In this connection it is interesting

1. Wedderburn 1985: 620; Räisänen 1987: 406; cf. Hultgren 1976: 99.
2. Cf. Räisänen 1987: 413ff.
3. Cf. Wedderburn 1985: 620-21; Räisänen 1987: 413-15.
4. Cf. Dupont 1970: 189-91; Kim 1984: 44-46; Wedderburn 1985: 621.

to note that after his conversion Paul himself was persecuted because of his preaching of the cross of Christ without circumcision (Gal. 5.11; cf. 6.12).

On the way to Damascus in pursuit of the Hellenists driven out of Jerusalem, however, Paul was forced, by the revelation of Jesus Christ, to stop his persecuting activities. The crucified Jesus whom he persecuted (Acts 9.4-5) was revealed as the Son of God in him.[1] This revelation brought about a complete change in Paul's view of Jesus. According to the pronouncement of the divine curse on the hanged man in the law (Deut. 21.23; Gal. 3.13), he previously thought that Jesus of Nazareth was accursed by God. At the Damascus Christophany, however, Paul perceived that the crucified Jesus was not dead but alive, not condemned but vindicated and exalted by God as the messiah. This led him to realize that Jesus did not die for his own transgressions of the law but for his people who were under the curse of the law (Gal. 3.13; cf. Rom. 8.3; 2 Cor. 5.21), as the early Christians proclaimed. In this respect Paul's introduction of the christological title 'Son of God' in 1.16, which is widely recognized as pre-Pauline, is significant. For the title here does not denote, as usually interpreted, the Risen and Exalted One, but the Son of God sent as man who was made subject to the curse of the law and crucified in order to redeem his people.[2] Note that in Gal. 2.20 Paul describes the 'Son of God' as the one who 'delivered himself up for me'. Moreover, he states in 4.4b-5a that 'God sent forth his Son, born of a woman, born under the law, in order that he might redeem those who were under the law' (cf. Rom. 5.10; 8.3, 32; cf. Rom. 1.3, 4, 9).[3] Furthermore, we should take into consideration the fact that Paul is particularly concerned with the cross of Christ in other places in the letter (1.4; 2.20; 3.1, 13; 5.1, 13, 24; 6.14).

1. Although the prepositional phrase ἐν ἐμοί in Gal. 1.16 could be taken as a simple dative which points to an external vision, it seems to refer to a subjective experience which involves an internal illumination. See my discussion of the implications of the revelation below. It is to be noted, however, that in 1 Cor. 9.1 and 15.8 the revelation of Jesus Christ is perceived as an external vision, as the word ὁράω in those passages suggests. But we should not suppose, as Betz (1979: 71) argues, that for Paul the two forms of visions (external and internal) are as distinct as they may be for some commentators.
2. Cf. Bornkamm 1974: 98.
3. Cf. Schweizer 1972: 382-85; Bornkamm 1974: 97; Lührmann 1976: 356ff.

The revelation further directed Paul to realize that the law completely failed to limit the power of sin and to bring righteousness back into the world.[1] It could not make Israel 'a holy nation' (Exod. 19.6) to guide other nations to acknowledge and worship the holy God. Rather, the law brought Israel under its curse by provoking her to transgress its precepts (Gal. 3.19), and thereby served to throw light on the universal plight under sin and demonic powers. At this point Paul came to understand that the event of Christ was an unprecedented saving act of God which surpassed all his former acts. By his vicarious death on the cross Christ delivered Israel from the curse of the law and all humankind from the slavery of sin, and thus fulfilled the eschatological task of the Servant of Yahweh[2] to bring salvation to the ends of the earth by bearing the sins of the 'many' (Isa. 53.11-12); which without doubt included not only Israel but also the Gentile nations.[3] In consequence, the new era of salvation has been inaugurated. In 'this day of salvation' (2 Cor. 6.2) God accepts all people, the Gentiles as well as the Jews, *only on the grounds of faith in Christ*. Through Christ he has established a new covenant which supersedes the old covenant (cf. Gal. 4.21-31). In Christ he has revealed his righteousness apart from the law (Rom. 3.21). Thus the law as the stipulation of the Sinai covenant (including circumcision as the sign of the old covenant) has been invalidated. Its cursing power has also ceased. In this sense 'Christ is the end of the law' (Rom. 10.4).[4] What counts now is faith in Christ, which constitutes the sole basis for salvation. Therefore Paul declares in connection with all his Jewish covenant privileges such as circumcision, Jewish origin of birth, zeal for the law and so on,[5] 'I...count them but rubbish in order that I may gain Christ' (Phil. 3.8).

Now it becomes clear that Paul's Damascus experience basically

---

1. Cf. Schoeps 1961: 174ff.
2. I assume that before his conversion Paul had already heard the identification of Christ with the Servant of Yahweh from the early Christians, the identification having possibly come from Jesus himself. Cf. Jeremias 1967: 712-17; Jeremias 1971: 286ff.
3. Cf. Odendaal 1970: 184ff.; Von Rad 1975b: 255ff.; Zimmerli 1978: 224.
4. I am not saying here that the law is no longer of any value whatsoever for Christians. I believe that the law as an expression of God's holy will is still in force. This will be treated in detail in Ch. 7.
5. Cf. Watson 1986: 77-80; Räisänen 1987: 408-10.

confirms the truth of the Hellenistic Christians' claims regarding
Christ. This does not mean that Paul had already received the gospel
of Christ before the Damascus event.[1] He strongly denies this in Gal.
1.11-12. As a matter of fact, his previously acquired knowledge about
Jesus did not convince him to believe Jesus to be the promised
messiah. Conversely, God's overwhelming revelation of Jesus Christ
as his Son, the fulfiller of eschatological redemption, led Paul to
realize that the Hellenists' proclamation was true. This revelation
played the major role in the development of his theology. In that light
Paul reinterpreted the kerygmatic traditions concerning Jesus Christ
which he received from the early Christian community.[2] So his gospel
presented to the Galatians is not a simple reproduction of the
traditions; rather, it is his *unique interpretation* of them in the light of
the Damascus revelation.[3] For example, Paul does not understand sin
as the transgression of the law, as usually understood by the early
Christians, but as an eschatological power. Also his interpretation of
the function of the law in Gal. 3.19ff. is unparalleled. Thus I think
that there is no essential conflict between the statement in Gal. 1.11-12
and the statement in 1 Cor. 15.3.[4]

The purpose of God's revelation of his Son, according to Gal.
1.16b, was the apostolic commission to preach the gospel of Christ
among the Gentiles (ἵνα εὐαγγελίζωμαι αὐτὸν ἐν τοῖς ἔθνεσιν).
Here we are not told explicitly that the commission was directly from
Christ at the time of the revelation. Some postulate that Paul's
conviction of the call to the Gentile mission arose, long after his
conversion, from his experience of the successful Gentile mission
following the Jews' rejection of his gospel.[5] But this view cannot
adequately account for the element of compulsion in Paul's
consciousness of the call in 1 Cor. 9.16.[6] Nor can it do justice to the
polemical context of Gal. 1.16: if Paul were not aware of the call
from the beginning, how could he so confidently assert the divine
origin of his apostleship against his opponents' criticism about his

---

1.   Cf. Chamblin 1986: 5-6.
2.   Cf. Betz 1979: 65.
3.   Cf. Lategan 1985a: 198-99.
4.   Cf. Baird 1957: 181-91; Ladd 1970: 223-30; Betz 1979: 64-66; Chamblin
1986: 1-16.
5.   Liechtenhan 1946: 78ff.; Blair 1965: 19-33.
6.   Cf. Munck 1959: 20-24; Kim 1984: 65-66.

apostleship?[1] In fact, Paul constantly maintained that he 'had been entrusted with the gospel to the uncircumcised' (Gal. 2.7; 1 Thess. 2.4; cf. Rom. 1.1, 5; Acts 26.16). It is also significant that he spoke of the Damascus-road vision in terms of a commission rather than a conversion in Gal. 1.15-16. I believe, thus, that the apostolic commission was part of the revelation of the Son of God.[2]

It is interesting that Paul described his call (Gal. 1.15) with an allusion to that of Jeremiah (Jer. 1.5) and that of the Servant of Yahweh (Isa. 49.1, 5), both of whom were sent to the Gentile nations.[3] This means that Paul understood his call in terms of a Jewish eschatological worldwide mission.[4] Very significantly, this understanding corresponds to his perception of Christ as the saviour of *all humankind*.

Paul's immediate reaction to the call was his departure for Arabia to carry out his commission to preach the Son of God to the Gentiles. The adverb εὐθέως in Gal. 1.16c qualifies not only the two negative clauses (οὐ προσανεθέμην...οὐδὲ ἀνῆλθον...) but also the following affirmative clause (ἀλλὰ ἀπῆλθον...).[5] Thereafter, he was continually engaged in the Gentile mission in Syria and Cilicia for a number of years (1.21ff.). Then he went up to Jerusalem with Barnabas and Titus in order to defend the gospel of uncircumcision (2.1ff.) and later opposed Peter to his face for the truth of the gospel at Antioch (2.11ff.). Thus it becomes clear that Paul's gospel originated from his Damascus experience.[6]

3. Conclusion

The pivot of Paul's entire argument in Galatians is his understanding of the cross of Christ as the event of the eschatological redemption. In achieving this redemption there are two logical (not temporal!) steps: first, by becoming a curse for Israel Christ redeemed Israel from the curse of the law; then, the redemption was at the same time and on

---

1. Kim 1984: 58-59.
2. Cf. Dupont 1970: 192-93; Stendahl 1976: 84-85.
3. Cf. Munck 1959: 24ff.
4. Cf. Schoeps 1961: 219ff.
5. Burton 1921: 53-54.; Betz 1979: 72; cf. Bruce 1982a: 94.
6. Cf. Strecker 1976: 479ff.; Räisänen 1983: 229-63; Räisänen 1987: 404ff.

equal terms extended to the Gentiles, because Israel represented all the
nations. Actually the humiliating incarnation, suffering and death of
Christ was for the Gentiles as well as for the Jews. Indeed he is the
substitute and representative of all humankind! In Christ, therefore,
the Gentiles can participate in the blessing of Abraham, namely justification by faith. This is confirmed by the fact that the Gentiles received
the Spirit of the new age on the basis of faith, not 'the works of the
law' (3.1-5). But the people who still put their trust in circumcision
are under the bondage of the law and of all evil forces of this age. The
origin of this understanding is traced back to Paul's vision of Jesus
Christ on the Damascus road. It is my contention, therefore, that we
should adopt this perspective in following Paul's argument in the
letter.

Chapter 3

THE ARGUMENT AND IDENTITY OF THE OPPONENTS

1. *Methodological Considerations*

The analysis of the perspective of Paul in Chapter 2 should, I believe, contribute significantly to following the line of his argument in Galatians. But we will not fully understand the argument until we have reconstructed the message and identity of his opponents. This is because Paul is involved, though indirectly, in a dispute with them through the letter to the Galatians. Unfortunately, however, we have no primary source which independently testifies to their propaganda and identity. We are therefore obliged to depend mainly upon the text of Galatians for reconstructing them, while using other Pauline letters and Acts as supplementary witnesses. But some scholars are suspicious about the reliability of Galatians as a source in this respect. Schmithals believes that Paul was ill-informed about the agitation of his opponents.[1] Similarly, Marxsen assumes that Paul misunderstood his opponents.[2] Of course, it is not entirely impossible that Paul was mistaken about the Galatian crisis. But the assumption is presented without any good reason and primarily to justify the unconvincing theory that the opponents were Jewish Christian Gnostics.[3] Because of this fundamental weakness, the hypothesis attracts little support from NT scholarship. Thus it seems safe to assume that Paul correctly grasped the major points at issue and successfully dealt with them, in view of the fact that we do not hear elsewhere about any further trouble in Galatia (cf. 1 Cor. 16.1), unlike what is found in the case of Corinth.[4]

To reconstruct the argumentative context on the basis of Galatians

1.   Schmithals 1972: 18.
2.   Marxsen 1968: 53.
3.   We will see the groundlessness of this theory later on.
4.   Cf. Barclay 1987: 76; Barclay 1988: 38.

only is an extremely difficult task. Galatians is, as Barclay points out,[1] a fierce work of polemic in which Paul, instead of treating his opponents' argument fairly and fully, reacts one-sidedly to them with all the rhetorical and theological powers at his command in order to win the Galatians back from their influence. This highly polemical nature of the letter can easily mislead inattentive interpreters into assuming, naively, that every statement by Paul is a rebuttal of a charge made against him by his opponents.[2] However, 'not everything that Paul denies is necessarily an accusation by his opposition, and not everything that he accuses his opponents of doing or thinking represents their actual goals and intentions'.[3]

How, then, should we begin to move from the text of Galatians to its argumentative context? Recently Barclay has provided some helpful criteria for mirror-reading Galatians, that is, for reconstructing the context: (1) each type of statement (assertion, denial, command, prohibition) is to be open to a range of interpretations; (2) a statement with emphasis and urgency may indicate a real bone of contention; (3) repetition may suggest an important issue; (4) an ambiguous word or phrase is a shaky foundation to build on; (5) an unfamiliar motif may reflect a particular feature in the situation responded to; (6) consistency is to be maintained in drawing a picture of the opponents; (7) finally, the results are to be historically plausible.[4] I think, however, that these criteria cannot be properly brought into play unless the overall structure of Galatians and the rhetorical function of its parts are taken into consideration. As far as the criterion of consistency is concerned, how can we presuppose only one front of opposition in Galatia without a thorough analysis of the structure of the letter? Moreover, it seems to me that criteria 2 and 3 to which Barclay frequently appeals in reconstructing the crisis in Galatia[5] do not guide us in a clear direction. There are many themes or words which repeatedly appear throughout the letter (e.g. the law, the Spirit and the flesh, Abraham, the cross of Christ, circumcision, and so on), and each of them receives emphasis in a variety of ways. How, then,

1. Barclay 1987: 75; Barclay 1988: 37.
2. For example, see Barclay 1987: 79-80.
3. Betz 1979: 6.
4. Barclay 1987: 85; Barclay 1988: 40-41.
5. Barclay 1987: 86ff.

without examining the rhetorical function of the parts of the structure, can we determine which issue is more important than others and how these issues are interrelated?

I propose, therefore, to start our task of reconstructing the rhetorical situation by deducing relevant implications from the structure of Galatians which I have already analysed in Chapter 1. The structure is closely bound up with Paul's way of dealing with the false gospel of his opponents. This is not to say that the structure reveals the whole content of their propaganda. I believe, however, that it discloses at least some important clues for our task, including central issues and their relationship with other issues. Thus the implications of the structure will, I hope, help us to draw a plausible picture of the opposition in Galatia which can be confirmed by external evidences.

This proposal may not be completely new. Brinsmead has already attempted to utilize his analysis of the rhetorical structure of Galatians for reconstructing the theology of the opponents. He fails, however, to relate properly the rhetorical analysis to his reconstruction, other than to demonstrate in his own way that there is one intruding theology rather than two (or more). Brinsmead bases his theory of the opposing theology largely upon the unproven premise that certain words, phrases, and statements of Paul directly reflect the language and thought of his opponents. For instance, he regards the law-tradition, among many traditions, as being central to the theology of the opponents. Since Paul connects the law with angels in 3.19 (cf. 1.8) and with τὰ στοιχεῖα τοῦ κόσμου and cultic calendar in 4.3, 8-10, Brinsmead jumps to the conclusion that for the opponents the law is the basis of cosmic order and that angels are the rulers of the universe. The Jewish law is 'the key that opens up the secrets of the cosmos and brings fellowship with the angelic rulers of the universe'.[1] This kind of interpretation is not entirely implausible, but I seriously doubt whether any theory built upon such an indefinite foundation carries conviction.[2] Moreover, Brinsmead's classification of Galatians as an apologetic letter is questionable. I think that the letter yields best sense when it is read in terms of deliberative rhetoric which allows exhortation to play an important role.[3]

---

1. Brinsmead 1982: 161.
2. Cf. Barclay 1987: 81-82.
3. See above Ch. 1.1.b.

2. The Implications of the Structure of Galatians

Here I will draw from my analysis of the Galatian structure in Chapter 1 the implications which are relevant for our purpose. In doing so, I will be involved, when necessary, in interacting with modern theories concerning the opponents in Galatia.

1. The letter to the Galatians as a whole is Paul's reaction to *one* intruding theology. This is evident from the fact that there is an essential unity to the entire argument of the letter. At the beginning of the body of the letter Paul sets forward the proposition of his argument: there is no other gospel than the gospel of Christ (1.6-10). After asserting the divine origin of his gospel, namely the gospel of Christ, in the subsequent narration, Paul develops two lines of argument in support of the proposition: no one can be justified by the works of the law but only by faith in Christ (3.1-14; cf. 2.14b-17); and the justified believer is no longer a slave of the law but a son of God (3.23–4.7; 4.21-31; cf. 2.18-21). On the basis of this theological argument, Paul, on the one hand, urges the Galatians not to receive circumcision for justification (5.1-12), and, on the other hand, exhorts them to walk by the Spirit, not by the flesh (5.13–6.10). These two lines of argument and their corresponding exhortations are based on one foundation, that is, the eschatological redemption of Christ (3.13-14; 3.25; 4.4-5; 5.1a, 13a). This fundamental grounding is first introduced in 1.4 in the prescript and finally restated in 6.14 in the postscript.[1]

This compels us to question seriously the validity of any two-front theories. According to Lütgert, Paul in Galatians simultaneously battles on two fronts: on the one hand against legalistic Judaizers in 3.1ff., and on the other hand against antinomian pneumatics in 5.13ff.[2] In his study Jewett does not find any separate libertinistic group in Galatia. He thinks, however, that Paul first argues, in 3.6–4.31, against nomism imported from Jewish Christians under the Zealot pressure and then, in 5.13–6.10, against libertinism which existed among the Galatians from the very beginning due to their Hellenistic background.[3] Betz sees the Galatian crisis from a slightly

1. See above Ch. 2.
2. Lütgert 1919; cf. Ropes 1929.
3. Jewett 1971a: 198-212, especially 209-12.

3. *The Argument and Identity of the Opponents*   101

different angle. In his view, after a period of initial enthusiasm, as a result of their acceptance of Paul's gospel, the Galatians fell into a problem of 'the flesh' (5.13, 16-17, 19; 6.12-13). This prompted the opponents to introduce the Jewish Torah covenant as the solution to the problem.[1] Bruce also discounts the thesis that Paul wages war on two fronts at the same time. He believes, nevertheless, that the section on the flesh, as distinct from the preceding argumentative section, is a warning against misinterpreting Paul's message of freedom in an antinomian sense.[2] Here we see clearly that the real crux of these explicit and implicit two-front theories lies in their direct correlation of the flesh and libertinism. They assume that the 'works of the flesh' is clearly indicative of the existence of antinomian licence. However, this need not be so. If we follow Paul's argument carefully, we realize that Paul rather associates the flesh with the *law*. Gal. 5.16 and 5.18, which correspond to each other, show that subjection to the desire of the flesh is identical to slavery under the law. This link between the flesh and the law is also found in the argumentative section. In the allegory of Hagar and Sarah (4.21-31), which is addressed to those who want to be under the law, it is demonstrated that those who are of the Sinai covenant are children born according to the flesh, like Ishmael. And in the rhetorical question in 3.3, directed at those who are considering a return from the Spirit to the law ('Having begun by the Spirit, are you now being perfected by the flesh?' [NASB]), we again see the link between the law and the flesh. Moreover, there is another link in 6.12-13: here Paul connects the flesh with circumcision which is intimately related to the law. Thus it is quite apparent that all the two-front theories are unfounded. I conclude, therefore, that throughout Galatians Paul fights on only *one* front.[3]

2. The *entire* letter is Paul's reaction to the propaganda of his opponents. In the proposition of the letter (1.6-10) Paul puts forward an antithesis: the false gospel of the opponents versus the gospel of Christ. This propositional antithesis is specifically developed in the argumentative and paraenetic sections.[4] This can be represented as follows:

1.   Betz 1979: 8-9, 253ff., 271ff.
2.   Bruce 1982a: 25; cf. Fung 1988: 243.
3.   Cf. Gordon 1987: 33ff.
4.   See above Ch. 1.2.b.ii.

1.6-10	the gospel of the opponents	versus	the gospel of Christ
3.1-14;	justification by the	versus	justification by faith
cf. 2.15-17	works of the law		in Christ
3.23–4.7;	slavery under the law	versus	sonship in Christ
4.21-31;			
cf. 2.18-21			
5.1-12	circumcision	versus	faith
5.13–6.10	the flesh	versus	the Spirit
6.12-16	circumcision	versus	the cross of Christ

This diagram clearly indicates that Paul combats the false gospel throughout the letter except in the narrative section. It is widely recognized, however, that even in the narrative section Paul responds to his opponents' remarks about his gospel and apostleship. This means that the letter as a whole must be taken into account for our reconstruction.

Recently Barclay warned of the danger of undue selectivity in attempting a reconstruction.[1] But he advances no specific reason why the letter should be analysed in its entirety as a response to the agitation of the opponents. The above diagram does, however, offer a firm basis for criticism of some writers who have attempted the reconstruction using only selected parts instead of the entire letter. Tyson limits his research to Paul's defensive statements found mostly in the narrative section which, he believes, indicate responses to charges made by his opponents.[2] I think, however, that he is wrong in perceiving Galatians to be defensive only. Rather it is predominantly offensive. We see that in order to dissuade the Galatians from adhering to the false gospel of his opponents Paul launches a devastating attack on the law. This he does in the argumentative section which Tyson largely disregards in his study. Schmithals builds his theory about the opponents on gnostic terminology found in Galatians 1–2 and 5.13-16, and dismisses 3.1–5.12 as 'current *topoi* of Paul's discussion with the *Jews* over the question of the law'.[3] This is hardly legitimate, since Galatians 3–4 contains Paul's most vigorous attack on his opponents' theology and provides the basis for the exhortation in 5–6. We encounter the same problem of undue selectivity in Hawkins's dissertation on 'the opponents of Paul in Galatia' (1971), in which the

1.   Barclay 1987: 79.
2.   Tyson 1968: 241-54.
3.   Schmithals 1972: 41, italics his; see also Schmithals 1983: 49-50.

writer develops his hypothesis by analysing various verses in isolation without considering the overall structure of Galatians at all.

3. The reference to 'a different gospel' in the proposition of the letter (1.6-10) indicates that the opponents were *Christians*, although we are not sure at this point whether they were Jewish or Gentile Christians. What is almost certain is that they believed in Jesus as the messiah. They seemed to claim that their own preaching was the true representation of the gospel of Christ, regarding Paul's gospel as an abbreviated one.

4. It is evident that *circumcision* is presented as a major demand of the opponents. In the recapitulation (6.12-17) Paul clearly restates their position: 'Those who want to make a good showing in the flesh compel you to be circumcised, only that they may not be persecuted for the cross of Christ...they want you to be circumcised, that they may boast in your flesh' (6.12-13). Although his polemic here is not to be taken at face value,[1] one thing is clear: the opponents demanded circumcision among the Galatians. This demand is certainly the reason for Paul's warning to the Galatians: 'Look, I, Paul, tell you that if you receive circumcision, Christ will be of no benefit to you. I testify again to every man who receives circumcision, that he is obliged to keep the whole law' (5.2-3; cf. 2.3-5). Moreover, the demand lies behind his sarcastic joke in 5.12: 'As for these agitators, they had better go the whole way and make eunuchs of themselves!' (NEB).

In view of the fact that circumcision is a major issue, it is rather striking that its terminology is completely absent in the argumentative section. But when we take into account the basis–inference relationship between theological argument in 3–4 and exhortation in 5–6 where the warning against circumcision appears, we may safely assume that the question of circumcision relates intimately to the central issue of the agitators with which Paul deals in 3–4.

5. Although not directly, the argumentative section betrays an important hint of a further central issue of the opponents. If we carefully follow the line of Paul's argument in Galatians 3–4, we find a peculiar point emerging. In 3.1-14 Paul argues that no one can be justified by the works of the law but by faith alone. This is followed by a transitional excursus, dealing with the purpose of the law in the salvation history in 3.15-22. On this basis Paul argues in 3.23–4.7 that

1. Betz 1979: 6; Barclay 1987: 75-76.

the justified believers are no longer slaves of the law but sons of God. Thereafter in 4.8-20 he appeals to the Galatians to follow him in remaining free from the bondage of the law. So far, Paul's argument progresses smoothly and its arrangement makes sense. It can thus be said that 3.1–4.20 forms a unit of argument. Oddly enough, however, to this unit Paul appends the allegory of Hagar and Sarah, the thrust of which is that the believers are not children of the slave woman Hagar but of the free woman Sarah. The allegory does not *introduce* any further or new argument but rather *confirms* the argument of 3.23–4.7 that the believers are not slaves but sons. If this is the case, why then does Paul use the allegory at this particular juncture? What rhetorical function does it perform? Moreover, it has been repeatedly pointed out that the so-called allegorical handling of the OT story is by no means characteristic of Paul for whom the literal text is of much more importance than for Philo.[1] This fact makes the purpose and motivation of the allegory all the more puzzling.

Many interpreters think that the allegory is invoked in a polemical situation.[2] The opponents appear to have argued that the Sarah–Isaac–the Sinai covenant–the present Jerusalem line alone represented the true descendants of Abraham. Paul takes up this argument, and inverts it by identifying the slave woman Hagar with the mother of the Jews who are under the slavery of the law, and the free woman Sarah with the mother of the believers in Christ. From this we may infer that the crux of the debate is the question: who are the real descendants of Abraham?

This question is already present, though implicitly, when Paul first introduces the figure of Abraham into his discussion of justification by faith alone. In 3.6, after a series of rhetorical questions in 3.1-5, he suddenly quotes Gen. 15.6 ('Abraham believed God, and it was reckoned to him as righteousness') only by an introductory formula καθώς,[3] and then, by putting his major emphasis on the expression 'the descendants of Abraham' which is not found in the quotation, draws its consequence that it is the people of faith who are the

---

1. Schrenk 1964: 758; Hanson 1974: 103; Barrett 1976: 10, 13-14; Cole [1965] 1983: 129; Fung 1988: 219.
2. E.g. Longenecker 1975: 127-29; Barrett 1976: 9ff.; Bruce 1982a: 218; Fung 1988: 219-20; cf. Cosgrove 1987: 220ff.
3. Cf. Barrett 1976: 6.

descendants of Abraham. Behind this, as Martyn suggests, there seems to be the issue of the identity of Abraham's descendants.[1] In this connection 3.29 is noteworthy: 'If you belong to Christ, then you are Abraham's offspring...' This verse is the conclusion of the discussion in 3.26-28. Here again the expression 'Abraham's offspring', which is not found in the discussion (cf. 3.16), receives emphasis. Thus it becomes quite clear that the identity of Abraham's descendants is the central issue found in the argumentative section. Seen from this perspective, the allegory of Hagar and Sarah is not a merely supplementary argument or an after-thought.[2] Rather, it can be viewed as a *climax* of Paul's assault on his opponents' theology.[3]

Taking into consideration the fact that Galatians 3–4 is the central part to fight against the false gospel of the opponents, I think it would be wise to regard the identity of Abraham's descendants as the major issue of the opponents.

6. Paul's speech against Peter in 2.14b-21 serves as a summary of both the argumentative section in 3–4 and the paraenetic section in 5.1–6.10. The simple assertion of justification by faith alone in 2.14b-17 is brought into the full argument in 3.1-14 which provides the basis for the exhortation to reject circumcision for justification in 5.1-12. On the other hand, the brief discussion of the new existence of the justified believer in 2.18-21 is further elaborated on in 3.23–4.31 and 5.13–6.10.[4] This suggests that the issue involved in Paul's conflict with Peter is in essence the same as the issue in Galatia. The conflict arises out of Peter's sudden withdrawal from table-fellowship with the Gentile Christians when 'certain men from James' came to Antioch. In Paul's view, the behaviour of Peter is to compel the Gentiles to '*Judaize*', that is, to live like Jews.[5] This is a serious misunderstanding of the new status of the Christian believers in Christ. It is a serious threat to the truth of the gospel of Christ. This action of Peter in Antioch is of the same nature as the agitation of the false teachers in Galatia.

---

1. Martyn 1983: 230-31.
2. Burton 1921: 251.
3. Cf. Ridderbos 1953: 173; Barrett 1976: 15.
4. See above Ch. 1.2.a.vi, b.ii.
5. Barclay 1988: 36 n. 1.

7. The narrative section in 1.11–2.21 also divulges a further clue about the opponents. This section is located between the proposition of the letter in 1.6-10 and the argumentative section in 3–4. It does not develop the antithesis between the false gospel of the opponents and the gospel of Christ which is put forward in 1.6-10 and runs through 3–6. This means that in 1.11–2.21 Paul is not involved in a theological debate with his opponents. Instead, he attempts here to establish the divine authority for his gospel and apostolic ministry before launching a formidable attack on the theology of his opponents in the argumentative section. This indicates that the issue of the opponents found in the narrative section 1.11–2.21 is *not* a major one.[1]

In the narrative section Paul claims the divine origin of his gospel and the independence of his apostleship. When, on the Damascus road, he received the revelation of the Son of God and the commission to preach him, he did not seek any human advice or authorization but immediately launched an independent mission (1.11-24; cf. 1.1). Later on, in order to defend this revelation, Paul went up to Jerusalem where the validity of his gospel and commission was acknowledged (2.1-10). For the sake of the truth of the gospel of Christ, Paul confronted even Peter face to face in Antioch (2.11-21).[2]

This claim of Paul seems to imply that the validity of his gospel and apostleship was questioned by his opponents. This does not necessarily mean that they *charged* Paul with his dependence upon the Jerusalem apostles for his gospel and apostleship, as many scholars suppose.[3] But it may be possible that Paul does not respond to their specific accusations but rather to their almost incidental statements about his personal credentials.[4]

8. Lastly, we can draw an inference as to the broad theological framework of his opponents from the perspective of Paul derived from the structure of Galatians. I have maintained in Chapter 2 that the understanding of the Christ event in terms of eschatological deliverance constitutes the basic viewpoint of Paul's argument in the letter. On the cross Christ has conquered the evil powers of the old

1.   Cf. Tyson 1968: 241-54.
2.   Cf. Dunn 1982: 470-71.
3.   Ropes 1929: 12-15, 18-21; Tyson 1968: 245-50; Schmithals 1972: 19-32; Brinsmead 1982: 93-106.
4.   Barclay 1987: 78.

gurated the new age (1.4; 6.14-15). This general point
ed in the argumentative section. Here Paul sees salva-
redemption from the curse of the law (3.13-14, 25;
luntarily took on himself the curse which his people
ause of their violation of the covenant law, and died
y doing this he has established the new covenant
id men. In Christ all humankind are one; the old
en Jews and Gentiles that existed under the old coven-
n has been invalidated (3.26-29). Now the believers
ite the new 'Israel of God' (6.16). It is remarkable
ts heavy emphasis upon the *discontinuity* with the old
or him the new covenant of grace abolishes the old
aw; the new age of freedom abrogates the old age of
slavery. This eschatological motif of discontinuity dominates Paul's
whole argument against his opponents. This implies that the agitators
in Galatia failed to grasp the radical newness of the new covenant and
the new age brought about by Christ. Probably they argued for 'the
salvation-historical combination of Torah and Christ',[2] stressing the
continuity of the Mosaic covenant dispensation.

In this connection it is worth discussing the extent to which the agitators demanded obedience to the law of the Galatians. At first glance
it is not directly apparent in the text of Galatians whether they
required the Galatians to keep the whole law. Considering the theological perspective of the agitators discussed just above, however, we
may suppose that they sincerely advocated obedience to the entire law
for full membership of the covenant community. Also Paul's severe
polemic against the law—the sharp antithesis between the law and
faith in 2.14-17, 3.1-14 and 5.1-12, the emphasis upon the inferiority
of the law to the Abrahamic promises in 3.15-22, the argument of the
temporary validity of the law and its strange function to bring men
under its bondage in 3.15–4.11, and the contrast between the law and
the Spirit in 3.1-5 and 4.21-31—suggests the *seriousness* of the
agitators' promotion of the law. Furthermore, by addressing the
Galatians as 'you who want to be under law' in the introductory
statement of the Hagar–Sarah allegory in 4.21, Paul points in the same
direction.

1. Cf. Beker 1980: 99-104; Barclay 1988: 96-105.
2. Beker 1980: 99.

There are, however, some scholars who oppose this view mainly on the basis of Gal. 5.3 and 6.13. Schmithals argues that the agitators did not lay upon the Galatians the obligation to keep the law in its entirety, because they themselves, as Gnostic libertines, were not concerned with the law at all.[1] More moderately, Jewett says that, in order to avoid Zealot reprisals for associating with lawless Gentiles (6.12), the agitators tactfully did not introduce the whole law to the Galatians but were content to achieve quick and notable results—circumcision and calendar observance (4.10).[2] Sanders suggests that the opponents of Paul may have employed 'a policy of gradualism', which introduced the details of keeping the law gradually, and first required fulfilment of some of the more important commandments like circumcision, food and days.[3] Others think that the opponents were insincere, or selective, in demanding the observance of the law.[4]

We should, however, reconsider the verses on which the above theories are based. First, let us look closely at 6.13a: 'those who are circumcised do not themselves keep the law'. This accusation of Paul against his adversaries is sometimes taken, as just seen above, to reveal only factual information and is thus used to argue that the opponents were not interested in keeping the law or that they taught only part of it. We should bear in mind, however, that the accusation is not a flat statement but a highly polemical one. It is not easy to prove precisely on what grounds Paul pronounces the charge. It seems that Paul here adopts a traditional argument against Jewish law-observance on the basis of his firm conviction of human inability to fulfil the law (cf. Acts 7.53; Gal. 2.16; 3.10; Rom. 2.17ff.; 7.7ff.; 8.3).[5] At any rate one thing is clear: by the statement Paul intends to discredit his opponents and to shock the Galatians. This seems to presuppose that the opponents seriously taught obedience to the entire law and that the Galatians believed them to be sincere in keeping it. If not, the polemical statement would be entirely pointless.[6]

Next, we turn our consideration to 5.3: 'I testify again to every man

1.   Schmithals 1972: 33-34; Schmithals 1983: 43-57.
2.   Jewett 1971a: 205-208; cf. Gunther 1973: 83.
3.   Sanders 1983: 29, 56 n. 58.
4.   Lightfoot 1880: 222; Schlier 1971: 231-32, 281; Mussner 1974: 347-48; Brinsmead 1982: 64-65, 119.
5.   Eckert 1971: 34-35; Betz 1979: 316.
6.   Cf. Howard 1979: 15; Barclay 1988: 63-64.

3. *The Argument and Identity of the Opponents* 109

who receives circumcision, that he is obliged to keep the whole law.'
From this solemn warning by Paul it could be inferred that the opponents simply disclaimed or subtly played down the connection between
circumcision and obligation to keep the entire law. It is more likely,
however, that Paul reminds the Galatians of the serious implications
of receiving circumcision about which they were not, apparently,
uninformed but remained naive.[1] We should note that in the warning
of 5.3 the accent falls on 'the whole law', perfect obedience to which
is impossible and even one transgression of which may incur the curse
of the law (cf. 3.10).

It therefore appears highly unlikely that the agitators' demand of
keeping the law was unorthodox or partial. It is almost beyond a
doubt, though not mentioned explicitly, that they insisted on the
observance of the whole law as the logical consequence of receiving
circumcision.

Some hold that the agitators understood the law in a Jewish-
syncretistic way. Georgi, in an article, argues:

> For these Jewish Christians, the law was not only that of their people, but
> that of the world in general. In their view it originated from the angels
> (Paul's unique and very concise expressions in 3.19c can best be
> explained as polemically accepted statements, which the opponents had
> understood positively), the determining powers of creation and fate
> (elemental spirits and spirit-powers in 4.3, 9; cf. also the meaning of the
> calendar in 4.10; all this was also known to the Galatians from their
> heathen background). Thus, for them, law and creation order, law and
> fate, were one.[2]

There is no evidence in the text of Galatians, however, that statements
like 3.19 and 4.3, 8-10 suggest that the opponents understood the law
in a mystical manner. Rather, Paul's connection of the law with
angels, τὰ στοιχεῖα τοῦ κόσμου and the cultic calendar here seems
to be his radical and sarcastic way of registering criticism against the
Jewish law.[3]

To summarize the implications drawn from the Galatian structure:

1. Kümmel 1975: 300; Betz 1979: 259-61; Barclay 1987: 75; Barclay 1988: 64;
Fung 1988: 222.
2. Quoted by Hawkins 1971: 53; cf. Köster 1959: col. 18; Brinsmead 1982:
115-37.
3. Eckert 1971: 91-93, 127-28; Betz 1979: 218; Bultmann [1910] 1984: 103.

(1) throughout the letter Paul battles on only one front rather than two; (2) the entire letter, not merely some parts of it, is Paul's reaction to the theology of his opponents; (3) the opponents were Christians; (4) circumcision is their major demand upon the Galatians; (5) the central issue in the argumentative section is the identity of the true descendants of Abraham; (6) Peter's action in Antioch to compel the Gentile Christians to live like Jews is essentially of the the same nature as the agitation of the false teachers in Galatia; (7) the validity of Paul's gospel and his apostleship was somehow questioned by his opponents; (8) finally, the agitators probably held to the continuity of the Mosaic covenant dispensation, combining the law and Christ and requiring adherence to the whole law. These data will be used as a basis for my reconstruction of the argument and identity of Paul's opponents in Galatia.

3. *The Argument and Identity of the Opponents*

a. *The Argument of the Opponents*

It has become traditional to discuss first the identity of the opponents and thereafter their argument. In my view, this is not the appropriate order in view of the fact that most of the implications outlined above concern the argument of the opponents. Betz is correct in observing that Paul in Galatians never addresses his adversaries directly (cf. 1.6-7; 5.7, 10, 12; 6.12-13) but concerns himself with the issues of the argument introduced by them into the Galatian congregations.[1] Thus it should be contended that their argument, to a considerable degree, determines their identity.

Paul first made his missionary visit to Galatia because of his bodily illness (δι' ἀσθένειαν τῆς σαρκός), and preached to the Galatians that faith in Christ is the only requirement for entering the new community of God (4.13). They welcomed Paul and his message with enthusiasm (4.14-15). Consequently they were converted from polytheistic paganism to worshipping the one God (4.8-9), and experienced the active presence of the Spirit (3.2-5). Some time after Paul left Galatia, certain agitators who introduced themselves as representatives of the Jerusalem Church arrived and advocated a different

---

1. Betz 1979: 5.

gospel (1.6-9).[1] They regarded Paul's gospel as an abbreviated gospel, though not a completely false gospel. So they tried, in addition to faith in Christ, to impose upon the Galatian Christians circumcision (6.12-13; cf. 5.2-3, 12) and observance of the whole Jewish law for full salvation or for the full status as God's people (cf. 3.3).

What, then, was the departure point of the agitators' argument in order to persuade the Galatians to accept their demands? This is not self-evident in the text of Galatians. In this regard, I believe, Perelman's statement about a rhetorical principle for an effective argumentation is illuminating:

> To make his discourse effective, a speaker must adapt to his audience. What constitutes this adaptation, which is a specific requisite for argumentation? It amounts essentially to this: the speaker can choose as his points of departure only the theses accepted by those he addresses.[2]

In the light of this principle I presume that the agitators began their argument with Abraham because he was recognized as the father of God's people and the original recipient of the divine covenant and of the promise concerning salvation for his descendants and all the nations on earth (Gal. 3.8).

Abraham is seen in Judaism as the first one who recognized the only God, the creator of the world and all things in it. He was born and grew up in Ur of the Chaldees, a place full of idols. But when he was young, he began to understand the human errors of idolatry and uncleanness and to worship the one true God (*Jub.* 11.15-17). Abraham appealed to his father and brothers to refrain from futile idolatry and to turn to the God of heaven. One night he set fire to the house of idols (*Jub.* 12.1-14; cf. *Apoc. Abr.* 1-7). Afterwards Abraham left Ur of the Chaldees and moved to Haran and then to Canaan (Gen. 11.31–12.5; *Jub.* 12.15–13.1; *Apoc. Abr.* 8). This emigration by Abraham to Canaan was the complete desertion of idolatry (cf. Philo, *Abr.* 68ff., *Migr. Abr.* 176ff.). Here we may suppose that the agitators in Galatia linked this tradition of Abraham with the Galatians' conversion from pagan polytheism to monotheism (Gal. 4.8-9).

Abraham is highly esteemed as an example of perfect obedience to God. It is said in *Jub.* 23.10, 'Abraham was perfect in all his deeds

---

1. See below Ch. 3.3.b.
2. Perelman 1982: 21; cf. Perelman and Olbrechts-Tyteca 1969: 65-66.

with the Lord, and well-pleasing in righteousness all the days of his life'. On the basis of Gen. 26.5, in which God says to Isaac, 'Abraham obeyed my voice and kept my charge, my commandments, my statutes and my laws', various Jewish traditions assume that Abraham kept the law even before it was written.[1] It is understood that this obedience of Abraham was expressed as faithfulness to God in times of trial. According to *Jubilees*, when God tried Abraham through his country, famine, the wealth of kings, his wife, circumcision, and Ishmael and Hagar, he was found faithful (17.17-18). Even in the most difficult test—to sacrifice Isaac, his beloved son—Abraham remained faithful to God (*Jub.* 18.1-16). With this in view Mattathias, in his testament, asks his sons, 'Was not Abraham found faithful when tested, and it was reckoned to him as righteousness?' (1 Macc. 2.52). It is note-worthy that here Gen. 15.6 is interpreted in relation to Gen. 22.1-18. Abraham's faith is seen as *faithfulness* in the test of Isaac's sacrifice. According to Jewish theology, his faith is by no means opposed to his good works; rather, it is a meritorious achievement.[2] Perhaps this is one of the reasons why Paul makes a sharp distinction between faith and the works of the law in Gal. 3.1-14 and denies the existence of the law before its promulgation at Sinai in 3.17.

By virtue of his meritorious works Abraham received the promises from God (see Sir. 44.19-21). God said to Abraham that his descen-dants would be numerous (Gen. 12.2; 13.16; 15.5; 17.4-5; 18.18; 22.17). He further promised to him that in him and in his descendants all the nations would be blessed (Gen. 12.3; 18.18; 22.18; cf. 26.4; 28.14) and that to him and to his descendants a land would be given (Gen. 12.7; 13.15; 15.18; 17.8; cf. 24.7).[3] Furthermore, God gave to Abraham the promise of an everlasting covenant, saying that he would be God to him and to his descendants after him (Gen. 17.7). Here it should be noted that the three promises of the blessing of all the nations, the land and the everlasting covenant were addressed to Abraham and *to his descendants*. This is to say that in order to have a

1. See e.g. *Jub.* 16.28; Sir. 44.20; *2 Bar.* 57.2; Philo, *Abr.* 5-6, 60-61, 275; *b. Yom.* 286; *m. Kid.* 4.14.
2. Billerbeck 1926: 186ff., especially 200-201; Jeremias 1964: 8; Dibelius 1976: 170; Betz 1979: 139; Baird 1988: 368.
3. In postexilic Judaism the land came to mean the world in an eschatological sense; see *Jub.* 17.3; 22.14-15, 29-30; 32.18-19; *1 En.* 5.6-7; Sir. 44.21; *4 Ezra* 6.55-59; cf. Mt. 5.5; Rom. 4.13; Heb. 11.16.

share in the promises it is of decisive importance to belong to the
descendants of Abraham (cf. Gal. 3.16). This argument of the agitators seemed to cause Paul to interpret the 'seed' (σπέρμα) of
Abraham in a somewhat arbitrary manner in Gal. 3.16 (cf. Rom.
4.16; 9.8, 27).

At this point the agitators may have raised a question: who are the
true descendants of Abraham? They then appear to have argued that
not all the descendants of Abraham were his true seed. Before Isaac
was born, Abraham had fathered Ishmael by Hagar, Sarah's maid.
Later, by the enabling power of God, he begot Isaac by Sarah, his
wife. One day Sarah saw that the maid's son, Ishmael, mocked Isaac.
She then said to Abraham, 'Drive out this maid and her son, for the
son of this maid shall not be an heir with my son Isaac' (Gen. 21.10;
cf. Gal. 4.30). God took Sarah's part, saying to Abraham who was
distressed because of Ishmael, 'Whatever Sarah tells you, listen to her,
for *through Isaac* your descendants shall be named' (Gen. 21.12, italics mine). Thus only the offspring of Isaac are the true descendants of
Abraham, while the offspring of Ishmael are reckoned with the
Gentiles (cf. *Jub.* 16.17-18). In this connection it is unlikely that the
agitators also employed the story of the election of Jacob instead of
Esau in their argument (cf. Rom. 9.11-13), because there is no evidence for this in the allegory of Hagar and Sarah in Gal. 4.21-31, or
elsewhere in Galatians.

The agitators probably connected the Sarah–Isaac line with the Sinai
covenant (cf. Gal. 4.24-25), as argued above (Ch. 3.2). They understood the Sinai covenant as the fulfilment and completion of the
Abrahamic covenant.[1] As he had promised to Abraham: 'I will establish my covenant between me and you and your descendants after you
throughout their generations for an everlasting covenant, to be God to
you and your descendants after you' (Gen. 17.7), he made a covenant
with the descendants of Abraham and Isaac at Sinai and revealed their
covenant obligations in the law which he ordained through angels by
the hand of Moses (cf. Gal. 3.19). While the Abrahamic covenant contains one condition, namely circumcision (Gen. 17.10), the Sinai
covenant requires a great number of obligations. These obligations
must be fulfilled for living in the covenant relationship with God. God
says: 'You shall keep my statutes and my judgments, by which a man

1. Cf. Lang 1976: 309ff.

may live if he does them' (Lev. 18.5; cf. Gal. 3.12). The failure to
observe them incurs a divine curse, for it is written, 'Cursed is he
who does not confirm the words of this law by doing them' (Deut.
27.26; cf. Gal. 3.10). So it is absolutely necessary to keep all of the
law for preserving salvation. The messiah did not come to abrogate
but to affirm and interpret the law (cf. Gal. 6.2; Mt. 5.17). In fact he
is a new Moses.[1] The Spirit has also come to prompt obedience to the
law, for God promised: 'I will put my Spirit within you and cause you
to walk in my statues, and you will be careful to observe my
ordinances' (Ezek. 36.27).

Furthermore, the link between the Sinai covenant and the present
Jerusalem in Gal. 4.25 seems to suggest that the agitators also included
Jerusalem in the Sarah–Isaac line. In their opinion, the church in
Jerusalem which consisted of the circumcised Jewish Christians was
the center of the new messianic community in which the disciples of
Jesus, especially James, Cephas and John, exercised considerable
authority as the 'pillars', and from which Paul's gospel and apostleship
were derived.

For the agitators, therefore, the Sarah–Isaac–Sinai covenant–
Jerusalem line alone represents the true sons of Abraham. Only these
offspring of Abraham are counted as the real people of God who are
heirs according to the promises given to Abraham (cf. Gal. 3.29). But
there is a possibility for the Gentiles to enter the people of God,
because God promised to Abraham that in him and in his descendants
all the nations would be blessed (Gen. 12.3; 18.18; 22.18; cf. Gal. 3.8).
If they want to become the real descendants of Abraham and heirs of
the promises, the Gentiles must, like Jews, be circumcised and obey
the whole law. It seems to me, however, that the agitators compelled
the Galatians to receive circumcision more urgently. For circumcision
is 'the sign of the covenant' which God solemnly commanded every
male in Abraham's family to accept (Gen. 17.10-14), and it is also 'the
seal of the law' which means that he who is voluntarily subjected to
circumcision is bound to fulfil the law.[2] In this connection it is

---

1. Paul's repeated emphases upon the salvific significance of the cross throughout Galatians (1.4; 2.20-21; 3.1, 13; 6.14; cf. 4.4; 5.1, 13) suggest, it seems to me,
that the agitators played down the message of the cross due to their failure to comprehend adequately the implications of the death of Christ.

2. Lightfoot 1880: 203.

possible that in order to support their circumcision campaign the agitators claimed, on the basis of Paul's circumcising Timothy in Acts 16.3, that Paul, himself a circumcised Jew, also preached circumcision (cf. Gal. 5.11) though he failed to teach the Galatians to accept it (cf. Gal. 1.10).[1]

The argument of the agitators which I have reconstructed above is well founded upon the biblical and Jewish texts. It demands a rational adherence to their obvious and straightforward meaning. Herein lies the compelling power of the argument.

By this forceful argument the agitators succeeded in persuading many of the Galatians to consider seriously accepting their demands, namely circumcision and the law. It seems that this somehow provoked the dissension and conflict within the Galatian congregations, endangering their bond of love (cf. Gal. 5.13-14; 6.1-2). I think that Paul's metaphorical expression of 'biting and devouring one another' in Gal. 5.15 probably reflects the actual case,[2] though he speaks in general terms in Gal. 5.13–6.10. It is very conceivable that the case was the concrete occasion of the general paraenesis.[3]

Betz, however, understands this in a different way. According to him, the 'concrete *Sitz im Leben*' for the paraenesis was the Galatians' problems with the flesh (5.13, 16-17, 19; 6.12-13) due to Paul's law-free gospel without a code of ethics. These problems provided an opportunity for the agitators to offer their gospel of the Torah covenant.[4] But there are problems with this view. In Gal. 5.21 Paul says that he has *already* warned about 'the works of the flesh' during his missionary visit to them. This suggests that he did not leave the Galatians without any ethical instructions, including a number of practical regulations, though we cannot tell exactly how extensive these instructions were or in what form they were given.[5] Moreover, if it was a concern about the moral disorder among the Galatians which induced the agitators to preach 'another gospel', why did they choose as the main theme of their argument the identity of the true

1.   Schlier 1971: 238-39; cf. Borgen 1982: 37-46.
2.   Burton 1921: 297; Guthrie 1973: 134; Arichea and Nida 1976: 132; Bruce 1982a: 242.
3.   Cf. Cosgrove 1988b: 158.
4.   Betz 1979: 8-9, 273; cf. Lull 1980: 34-39; Lategan 1985a: 97; Barclay 1988: 68-72.
5.   Cf. Lull 1980: 36.

sons of Abraham instead of the high moral standard of the law and its
comprehensiveness to govern all the aspects of life? Furthermore, it
should be kept in mind, as Betz himself recognizes, that the paraenesis
in 5.13–6.10 is of a *general* character.[1]

It can now be concluded that the agitators' success in Galatia is
attributable to their compelling argument. But was this the only
reason for their success? Was there not any internal factor in the
Galatian churches which implicitly (or explicitly) contributed to the
success? In this connection Barclay makes an interesting suggestion.[2]
By accepting Paul's gospel the Galatians abandoned their previous
worship of pagan deities. This involved a social disruption in their
relationships with family, friends, fellow club members, business
associates and civic authorities. As long as Paul was with them, they
could depend upon him. When he left Galatia, however, they were
faced with a high degree of social insecurity. They could no longer
participate in their traditional religious practices. Nor did they belong
to the Jewish synagogues which were tolerated in the Roman world,[3]
though they had much in common with the Jews. In consequence, they
were socially ostracized (cf. 1 Pet. 2.12, 15, 18-20; 3.1, 13-16; 4.3-5,
12-16).[4] With such an uncertain social position it is understandable
how excited the Galatians must have been about the agitators' message
inviting them to become *Jewish* Christians by accepting circumcision
and the law rather than to remain mere Christians.

b. *The Identity of the Opponents*
It is now necessary to try to identify the opponents of Paul in Galatia
in the light of the reconstruction of their argument above. In the
course of drawing the implications concerning their message and
identity from the structure of Galatians I excluded the possibility that
the opponents were composed of two different groups, legalistic
Judaizers and antinomian pneumatics.[5] I also argued that they were
neither Christian Gnostics,[6] nor Jewish Christian syncretists.[7] My line

1. Betz 1979: 273.
2. Barclay 1988: 56ff.
3. See Stambaugh and Balch 1986: 51-52.
4. Cf. Stambaugh and Balch 1986: 60-62.
5. See above Ch. 3.2.
6. See above Ch. 3.2.
7. See above Ch. 3.2.

of argument thus far has been that the opponents were Christians, since they preached a gospel, though fundamentally different from Paul's gospel (cf. 1.6-7), and that they believed in Christ, though not in the same sense as Paul did.[1] Arguing that the Sarah–Isaac–Sinai covenant–Jerusalem line alone represented the true descendants of Abraham, they required the Galatians to be circumcised and to obey the law in order to become genuine sons of Abraham and heirs of the promises given to Abraham by God. All this seems to suggest that the agitators were Jewish Christians.

Munck contends, however, that the Judaizing opponents were not Jewish Christians but Gentile Christians, principally on the grounds of the present participle with the article οἱ περιτεμνόμενοι in Gal. 6.13 which, to his mind, never means 'those who belong to the circumcision' but 'those who receive circumcision'.[2] For Munck, they were Paul's own converts. They were taught by Paul 'to think lovingly of the Jewish Christians and the earliest disciples, and lovingly of God's chosen people'.[3] Then, after Paul left Galatia, they began to read the OT for themselves and discovered that God commanded his people to be circumcised and to observe his entire law. They also heard that the Christians in Jerusalem were circumcised and kept the law. So they seriously considered undergoing circumcision and observing the law in order to become Jewish Christians. The Judaizing movement thus arose and spread among the Gentile Christians.[4]

This hypothesis of Munck cannot be sustained for at least two reasons. First, throughout Galatians Paul consistently refers to his opponents in the third person while addressing the Galatian Christians in the second person (1.7; 3.1; 4.17; 5.7, 10, 12; 6.12-13). This clearly indicates that the opponents were *intruders*, not Paul's own converts. Secondly, if it is true that the opponents of Paul came from outside Galatia, it follows that the present particle οἱ περιτεμνόμενοι is open to more than one interpretation: for example, it can be taken as a timeless present, denoting 'the people of circumcision' or 'advocates of circumcision',[5] though, as Goodwin says, 'the present

1. See above Ch. 3.2.
2. Munck 1959: 89.
3. Munck 1959: 131.
4. Cf. Hirsch 1930: 192-97; Michaelis 1931: 83-89.
5. Lightfoot 1880: 222; Ridderbos 1953: 223 n. 5; Schlier 1971: 281; Howard

particle generally represents an action as going on at the time of its leading verb'.[1] Or the participle can be taken as a middle voice with a causative force, meaning 'those who cause to be circumcised', for the subject of οἱ περιτεμνόμενοι in 6.13a is the same as the subject of 6.13b: 'they desire to have you circumcised'.[2]

If the opponents were Jewish Christians coming from outside, what connections did they have with the Jerusalem Church and its leaders? Baur, the Tübingen scholar, argues that the opponents in Galatia were legitimate representatives of the Jerusalem apostles. According to him, the history of the primitive church was marked by the conflict between Jewish Christianity and Gentile Christianity. At the Jerusalem Conference, reported in Gal. 2.1-10, Paul did not merely contend with the false brethren but with the Jerusalem apostles, the leaders of the Jewish church. The apostles were compelled, by the force of Paul's argument, to acknowledge his independent mission among the Gentiles. But they neither fully supported this mission nor recognized the validity of his law-free gospel. Instead they still maintained close ties with other Jewish Christians in Jerusalem who firmly believed in the necessity to observe the law for salvation. These other Jewish Christians were the trouble-makers who, without the opposition of the apostles, infiltrated Paul's churches in Galatia in order to impose circumcision and the law upon the Galatians.[3]

Lightfoot opposes this theory of Baur, correctly maintaining in his commentary on Galatians that the letter 'shows the true relations existing between St Paul and the Twelve'.[4] In the two visits of Paul to Jerusalem (Gal. 1.18-20; 2.1-10) there was a general acknowledgment by the Jerusalem apostles of the validity of his gospel and of his apostolic authority. Peter's withdrawal from table-fellowship with the Gentile Christians in Antioch need not point in the contrary direction, because the action was not motivated by his theological principles but by his fear of the Jews—a hypocritical action therefore. Unlike the apostles, the opponents of Paul held 'a Judaism of the sharp Pharisaic

1979: 17; Fung 1988: 303.
1.   Quoted by Hawkins 1971: 93.
2.   Jewett 1971a: 202-203; cf. Howard 1979: 18; Bruce 1982a: 270.
3.   Baur 1876: 121ff.
4.   Lightfoot 1880: 68.

type'.[1] They belonged to the mother church in Jerusalem and may even have been disciples of Christ. But they did not have the backing of the apostles.

Schoeps also takes issue with Baur, arguing that the contrast between Paul and the apostles which Baur suggests does not reflect the real historical situation of primitive Christianity. For Schoeps there were three groups within the early church: Paul's group, James' and Peter's group, and the Pharisaic Judaizers'. The deep gulf did not exist between Paul and these 'pillars', but between Paul and the Judaizers. The 'pillars' took a moderate middle position at the Jerusalem Council, making concessions in regard to the Gentiles' obligations to keep the law and giving sincere recognition to Paul's mission to the Gentiles. But the conservative Judaizers 'regarded circumcision as a *sine qua non* and defended the complete validity of the Mosaic law for all Christians whether of Jewish or Gentile stock'.[2] They were the instigators of disturbance in Paul's missionary churches. It was with them that Paul engaged in bitter conflict.

Numerous other scholars also dismiss as unfounded the thesis of Baur that the Jerusalem apostles stood behind the opponents of Paul in Galatia, and regard the right-wing party in the Jerusalem Church as the most probable opponents.[3] I believe that this view harmonizes well with the testimony of the Galatian letter (cf. Acts 15). The statement in Gal. 6.12-13 (cf. 5.2-3, 12) and the bitter polemic against the law in 3–4 suggest, as argued above (Ch. 3.2), that the opponents strictly required the Galatians to be circumcised and to keep the law for salvation.[4] But the account of the Jerusalem conference in 2.1-10 clearly indicates that their theological position was not supported by the leading apostles. Nevertheless, Paul's repeated mention of Jerusalem in 1–2 and 4.25-26 seems to imply that the opponents had some connection with the Jerusalem Church. Thus it is quite reasonable to conjecture that it was the right wing of the Jerusalem community that infiltrated the Galatian churches, preaching circumcision and fulfilment of the law. It is very likely that they were linked to the

1.   Lightfoot 1880: 27.
2.   Schoeps 1961: 66, italics his.
3.   E.g. Ridderbos 1953: 16-18; Kümmel 1975: 298-301; Longenecker [1964] 1976: 212-18; Bruce 1982a: 25-27; Sanders 1983: 18.
4.   See above Ch. 3.3.a.

'false brethren' described in 2.4. But it would be injudicious to relate too easily the opponents to the 'certain men from James' or to 'those of circumcision' in 2.12; to identify exactly who they were is an extremely difficult task because of the scarcity of internal and external evidences.[1] What is striking in Paul's description of the Antioch incident is, however, that he does not pronounce any criticism against the men from James or against James himself or against the people of the circumcision, but draws an analogy between the Judaizing behaviour of Peter and the agitation of his antagonists in Galatia.[2]

To sum up, the opponents of Paul in Galatia are Jewish Christians connected with the right-wing party in the Jerusalem Church. For them it is of decisive importance to be the true sons of Abraham in order to share in the Abrahamic promises of salvation, because the promises were given not only to Abraham but also to his descendants. But only those who belong to the Sarah–Isaac–Sinai covenant–Jerusalem line are counted as the genuine offspring of Abraham. If the Gentiles want to enter the people of God, therefore, they must, like Jews, receive circumcision and obey the law as the Jews do. By this forceful argument the opponents succeeded in persuading the Galatians to consider seriously accepting circumcision and the law. The letter to the Galatians is Paul's response to this situation of crisis.

1. Cf. Dunn 1983b: 3-57; Houlden 1983: 58-67; Cohn-Sherbok 1983: 68-74.
2. See above Ch. 3.2.

Part II

PAUL'S VIEW OF THE LAW

Chapter 4

PAUL'S UNDERSTANDING OF νόμος

In the light of the three preliminary considerations above (Part I) I
now attempt an analysis of Paul's treatment of the law in Galatians.
The Greek term νόμος appears 32 times in Galatians (and 72 times in
Romans). It sometimes occurs with the definite article (11 times) and
at other times without it (21 times). Some scholars have tried to
establish a difference in meaning between ὁ νόμος and νόμος.
According to Lightfoot, Paul uses ὁ νόμος to refer to the Mosaic law,
while using νόμος to mean law in general.[1] Stamm views ὁ νόμος as
the Mosaic law but the anarthrous νόμος as all sorts of legalism.[2] But
such distinctions are not based on sufficient grounds. It has often been
pointed out that the two forms, ὁ νόμος and νόμος, are used interchangeably without any distinction in meaning (Gal. 3.11-12, 23-24;
see also Rom. 2.23-27).[3] According to Bläser, the presence or absence
of the definite article can be explained by the following linguistic
rules:[4] (1) when νόμος is used in the genitive case, anarthrous νόμος
follows anarthrous substantive;[5] (2) in a prepositional phrase νόμος is
not usually accompanied by the article.[6] Thus it can be concluded that
Paul does not intend to differentiate ὁ νόμος from anarthrous νόμος.

In Galatians, as in other Pauline letters, νόμος is predominantly
used for the law of Moses given to Israel on Mount Sinai (3.17; cf.
4.24). There are a few exceptions to this. In a hypothetical statement

---

1.   Lightfoot 1880: 118; cf. Sanday and Headlam 1907: 58.
2.   Stamm 1953: 482; cf. Burton 1921: 458
3.   Grafe 1884: 5ff.; Wang 1971: 68-69; Longenecker [1964] 1976: 118-19;
Martin 1983: 272 n. 10; Moo 1983: 77; Räisänen 1983: 17.
4.   Bläser 1941: 10ff.
5.   Gal. 2.16; 3.2, 5, 10; see also Rom. 2.25; 3.20, 28; 10.4; 13.10.
6.   Gal. 2.19, 21; 3.11, 18, 21, 23; 4.4, 5, 21; 5.4, 18; see also Rom. 2.12, 13,
23; 3.20, 21, 27; 4.13, 14; 5.13; 6.14, 15; 7.7, 8, 9; 9.31; 10.5.

in 3.21b Paul uses νόμος (twice) to mean any divine law, though he cannot think of it without an awareness of the Mosaic law as its supreme example.[1] Another exception is νόμος in 4.21b, which plainly refers to the story of Hagar in the Pentateuch, not to the Mosaic legislation (cf. Rom. 3.21b; 1 Cor. 14.34).

A number of interpreters include νόμος in 5.23b in this category of exceptions, regarding it as law in general.[2] But I disagree with this view. In my opinion, Gal. 5.18-23 speaks of the relationship between the Spirit and the Mosaic law. 5.18 states that if the Galatians are led by the Spirit, they are not ὑπὸ νόμον, that is, under the curse of the Mosaic law (Gal. 3.10, 23; 4.4, 5, 21; Rom. 6.14, 15). My structural analysis shows that this statement is motivated by the statement of 5.23b which follows the long list of the fruit of the Spirit in 5.22-23a in contrast to the deeds of the flesh in 5.19-21.[3] Verse 23b says: κατὰ τῶν τοιούτων οὐκ ἔστιν νόμος. The literal meaning is that the law is not against such things that are the various manifestations of the Spirit.[4] The reason for this statement is that the whole law of Moses is fulfilled in the fruit of the Spirit whose principal manifestation is love (5.14). This is in full agreement with the thought of Rom. 8.4: 'in order that the requirement of the law might be fulfilled in us, who do not walk according to the flesh, but according to the Spirit' (cf. Rom. 13.10). All this clearly demonstrates that the νόμος in 5.23b refers to the Mosaic law.

Moreover, many scholars argue that ὁ νόμος τοῦ Χριστοῦ in 6.2 is to be understood in a figurative sense.[5] It seems, however, that 'the law of Christ' is not to be radically distinguished from 'the whole law' in 5.14 which is generally perceived as the Mosaic law,[6] since 'Bear one another's burdens' in 6.2 is nothing other than a specific expression of the general commandment 'You shall love your neighbour as yourself' quoted in 5.14.[7]

We may thus conclude that apart from in Gal. 3.21b and 4.21b Paul

1. Cf. Guthrie 1973: 107.
2. Burton 1921: 318; Guthrie 1973: 140; Moo 1983: 76; Yates 1985: 110.
3. See above Ch. 1.2.a.xiv.
4. Cf. Ridderbos 1953: 208; Ebeling 1985: 257; Fung 1988: 273.
5. E.g. Bultmann 1951: 259; Gutbrod 1967: 1071; Bauer 1979: 543; Fitzmyer 1981: 187; Räisänen 1983: 77-82.
6. Cf. Eckert 1971: 160-61; Hübner 1986: 37; Stuhlmacher 1986: 126.
7. See above Ch. 1.2.b.ii; cf. Sanders 1983: 97-98; Barclay 1988: 141.

uses νόμος to refer to the Mosaic law which is the sum of Israel's obligations given on Mount Sinai. This Pauline usage of νόμος fully accords with Hebrew usage of תּוֹרָה which means 'the sum of the covenant responsibilities imposed upon the people of Israel by their Sovereign on Mount Sinai' in Deuteronomistic and later literature (e.g. Deut. 4.8; 30.10; 32.46; Josh. 1.7; 8.34; 1 Kgs 2.3; 2 Kgs 17.13; Dan. 9.11; Neh. 8.14; 9.13-14, 34).[1]

The Mosaic Torah is for Paul regarded as a complete unit, since he always uses νόμος in the singular. He makes no distinction between its cultic-ritual and ethical aspects.[2] This is quite clear from his assertion that anyone who receives circumcision is obligated to keep (ποιῆσαι) the whole law (ὅλον τὸν νόμον) (Gal. 5.3) and from the fact that ὅλος ὁ νόμος is the same as ὁ πᾶς νόμος in 5.14 which is actually 'fulfilled' (πεπλήρωται) in Christian love.[3]

With such introductory comments we may now embark upon a discussion of Paul and the Mosaic law in Galatians. As already suggested in Chapter 2,[4] Paul basically understands the law on three different levels: (1) the law as the obligation of the Sinai covenant; (2) the law as an enslaving power; and (3) the law as an expression of love. Each of these levels will be dealt with individually in the following chapters. In the course of the discussion the syntagmatic and paradigmatic relations of the word νόμος to other words will be taken into account, in line with the conviction of structuralists that a certain concept must be understood in terms of its relationship to other concepts within a particular structure.

1. Westerholm 1986: 334-36; Westerholm 1988: 138-40; cf. Schechter [1909] 1961: 116-27; Dodd 1935: 33-34; Schoeps 1961: 29; Sandmel 1979: 48; Lapide 1981: 44.
2. Bultmann 1951: 260-61; Longenecker [1964] 1976: 119-20; Fitzmyer 1981: 187; Moo 1983: 84-85; cf. Räisänen 1983: 23-28.
3. Sanders 1983: 96-97; Barclay 1988: 137-42; cf. Hübner 1986: 37; Räisänen 1983: 26-27.
4. See above Ch. 2.2.b, e.

Chapter 5

THE LAW AS THE OBLIGATION OF THE SINAI COVENANT

1. *The Law is not an Entrance Requirement*

It has been argued that the main issue of the opponents in Galatia is the identity of Abraham's true descendants.[1] Regarding the Galatians (i.e. the *Gentile* Christians) as outsiders to the Abrahamic covenant, the opponents demanded that the converts of Paul accept circumcision and the Mosaic law, in addition to faith in Christ, in order to be fully integrated into the authentic children of Abraham who would have the right to inherit the promises given to Abraham.[2] To be sure, they did not argue against faith in Christ. But they considered circumcision and the law as additional entrance-requirements for membership in the community of God in the case of the Gentiles. In Paul's view, however, this creates an extremely serious theological problem. For him, in the new dispensation faith alone is the necessary and sufficient condition for admission into the people of God for all mankind, the Gentiles as well as the Jews. To require circumcision and the law as supplements to faith renders faith on its own insufficient. So to accept those extra requirements is to invalidate the atoning death of Christ and thereby nullify the grace of God (cf. Gal. 2.21; 5.4; Rom. 4.14). This is the reason why Paul gives an account of his view of the law in Galatians.

The law has, for Paul, various dimensions in the history of salvation. As far as the condition for membership in God's people is concerned, the law was never intended to be a means of access to salvation in God's plan. After an appeal to the Galatians' own experience in Gal. 3.1-5 that they have received the Spirit not by the works of the

---

1. See above Ch. 3.3.a; cf. Gundry 1985: 8ff.
2. Cf. Kuhn 1968: 727-44; McEleney 1974: 319-41; Nolland 1981: 173-94.

law but by the hearing of faith,[1] Paul takes up the case of Abraham to demonstrate his point: justification[2] is *only* by faith; it has nothing to do with the law.[3] Paul agrees with his opponents that Abraham is the father of God's people and that being a descendant of Abraham is crucial. But Paul refutes their argument on their own ground by offering a completely different understanding of the faith of Abraham.

The appeal to Abraham is exceptionally authoritative, because he is recognized as the ancestor of the people of God. It follows, for Paul, that Abraham's experience of justification by God must be the *model* for all of his children. He quotes Gen. 15.6 (LXX) in Gal. 3.6: 'Abraham believed God, and it was reckoned to him as righteousness' (MT: 'he [Abram] believed in Yahweh; and he reckoned it to him as righteousness'). The opponents, assuming the pre-existence of the law, interpreted the faith of Abraham as the faithful obedience of the law. In times of trial this faith was expressed as faithfulness to God which was most amazingly demonstrated in the test to sacrifice Isaac in Gen. 22.1-18. Thus the opponents understood the faith of Abraham in the sense of a meritorious achievement. This faith is not an anti-thetical concept of works but rather a kind of work. For the opponents, thus, the faith of Abraham was counted by God as a *real act* of righteousness.[4]

Paul, however, reads Gen. 15.6 in a completely opposite way. He does not find any implications of merit in Abraham's faith in the original context. The sentence 'Abraham believed God' in the context of Genesis means that he placed his confident trust in God to keep his promise that his offspring would be as innumerable as the stars in the heaven (Gen. 15.5). This *believing* was the *total acceptance* of God's promise. It was the appropriate human response to the grace of God. It was the diametrical opposite to any kind of meritorious work. In fact, the faith had no connection with the law at all, because the law came 430 years later (Gal. 3.17);[5] here the pre-existence of the law is

1.   See below Ch. 5.1.
2.   I understand that the term justification entails gaining a new relationship with God. Cf. Räisänen 1985: 545-46.
3.   Cf. Sandmel 1955: 29; Dahl 1966: 140.
4.   See above Ch. 3.3a; cf. Heidland 1967: 290; Ziesler 1972: 182-83.
5.   Cf. Lührmann 1988: 420-23.

denied. The faith of Abraham is explained more fully in Romans 4. The faith was in antithesis to works (4.2-4). It was a trust in the God 'who justifies the ungodly' (4.5) and 'who gives life to the dead and calls into being that which does not exist' (4.17). And it was a trust in the promise of God which was against every human hope (4.18-21). This radical faith was accounted as the basis of God's acceptance of Abraham.[1]

From this example of Abraham Paul, as the particle ἄρα suggests, derives the thesis that the men of faith (οἱ ἐκ πίστεως) are sons of Abraham (3.7). This means that those who believe *in the same way* as Abraham believed are his true children.[2] Here it follows that the kind of faith which Abraham put in God in response to his gracious promise is the determining factor which makes one a son of Abraham. This faith is the only way of becoming part of the people of God. This is also applicable to the case of the Gentiles in the new era. For 'the Scripture, foreseeing that God would justify the Gentiles by faith, preached the gospel beforehand to Abraham, saying, "All the nations shall be blessed in you"' (Gal. 3.8); here we notice that the blessing of Abraham is interpreted as justification.[3] Thus all men of faith (οἱ ἐκ πίστεως) who share the faith of Abraham, the Gentiles as well as the Jews, are justified 'along with Abraham, the believer' (Gal. 3.9; cf. Rom. 4.10-12). Note that the 'in you' (ἐν σοί) in v. 8 is now interchanged with 'along with' (σύν) Abraham in v. 9. This suggests that to be blessed in Abraham means to be justified in the same way as the believing Abraham.[4] Thus it is obvious, for Paul, that from the very beginning of the history of redemption God intended faith, not the law, to be the only means of justification.

Howard understands the term 'faith' used in the phrase οἱ ἐκ πίστεως (3.7, 9) to refer to 'the faith-act of God which fulfilled the promise'.[5] But this understanding ignores the strong logical

1. Cf. Gaston 1987: 47ff.
2. Hansen (1989: 112) thinks that the statements in Gal. 3.6-7 form an argument by enthymeme. According to him, there is the implicit premise between v. 6 (the explicit premise) and v. 7 (the conclusion): 'as God dealt with Abraham, so he will deal with all men'.
3. Cf. Cosgrove 1988a: 547 n. 1.
4. Johnson 1987: 195; Williams 1987a: 95; cf. Van Seters 1975: 272-78; Hays 1983: 203; Hooker 1989: 327.
5. Howard 1979: 57; see also Howard 1967: 459-65; Howard 1969: 335;

relationship between 3.6 and 7, namely a basis–inference relationship (ἄρα!).[1] It is most natural to see the faith as a *human* act like Abraham's believing response to the gracious promise of God.

Hays contends that the phrase οἱ ἐκ πίστεως is 'a deliberate catchword allusion' to the quotation of Hab. 2.4 in Gal. 3.11. The Habakkuk quotation should, Hays asserts, be understood as a messianic text which proclaims that the messiah (ὁ δίκαιος) will live by his faith (faithfulness). So the faith in οἱ ἐκ πίστεως carries the connotation of Christ's faith. Even 'Abraham's faith is a foreshadowing of Christ's [faith]'.[2] Such an interpretation could make good theological sense, but a careful consideration of Paul's argument does not, in fact, commend it. In the first place, we should remember that Paul uses the phrase οἱ ἐκ πίστεως immediately after appealing to Abraham's believing response to the free promise of God and his justification by God in 3.6. This shows that the faith in the phrase refers back to the faith mentioned in v. 6. Secondly, if we apply this logic to the flow of the argument, it is difficult to accept Hays's claim that the faith in the phrase ἐκ πίστεως in the Habakkuk citation in 3.11, which appears later, determines the meaning of the faith in ἐκ πίστεως in 3.7. I think, rather, that it is more logical to see the former as depending upon the latter. Thirdly, in 3.11a Paul claims that 'no one is justified by the law' and then quotes Hab. 2.4 to prove his own claim. Here we observe that the preceding claim is a statement of universal validity. This requires that the Habakkuk citation have universal applicability; otherwise the citation fails to establish convincingly the preceding universal statement. Thus the OT text must not be interpreted to speak of the messiah whose uniqueness as an individual is problematic for universal demonstrations.[3] Fourthly, even if we grant that the Habakkuk quotation might be understood messianically, it is impossible to interpret Abraham's faith as a foreshadowing of Christ's faith.[4] The reason is that the faith of Abraham is qualitatively different from that of Christ. Christ's faith is, as interpreted by Hays,[5] his faithful

Howard 1974: 212-15; cf. Gaston 1987: 58ff.
1. See above Ch. 1.2.a.vii.
2. Hays 1983: 201-202; cf. Hays 1991: 726.
3. Johnson 1987: 190.
4. Cf. Johnson 1982: 77-90; Williams 1987b: 431-47; Hooker 1989: 321-42.
5. Hays 1983: 201 and *passim.*

obedience unto death which has warranted redemption in which the believers participate. This is evidently a meritorious achievement. But Abraham's faith is total dependence on the God of promise, being totally devoid of any overtones of merit and having nothing to boast about (cf. Rom. 4.4). Finally, in my view there is no clear reference to Christ's faith but only to the Christian faith in Galatians. As Dunn convincingly argues,[1] even the passages of πίστις Χριστοῦ (Gal. 2.16, 20; 3.22) speak of the faith of believers. Note first that all the πίστις Χριστοῦ phrases in the letter (πίστις 'Ιησοῦ Χριστοῦ, πίστις Χριστοῦ in 2.16; πίστις τοῦ υἱοῦ τοῦ θεοῦ in 2.20; πίστις 'Ιησοῦ Χριστοῦ in 3.22) lack the definite article. This seems to indicate that the genitive of all these expressions is objective, because within earliest Christian speech the definite article in front of πίστις accompanied by a genitive '"almost invariably" denotes the subjective genitive'.[2] In Gal. 2.16 πίστις 'Ιησοῦ Χριστοῦ (v. 16a) and πίστις Χριστοῦ (v. 16b) are noun counterparts of the act of believing (πιστεύω in v. 16b). This occurrence of the two noun phrases along with the verb phrase is not redundancy[3] but repetition 'for the sake of emphasis and clarity'.[4] The same is true of the double reference to πίστις 'Ιησοῦ Χριστοῦ/believing in 3.22 (cf. 3.6, 8). The πίστις τοῦ υἱοῦ τοῦ θεοῦ in 2.20 also refers to the Christian faith rather than Christ's faithfulness, since the relative clauses, 'who loved me and gave himself for me', which immediately follow and define the phrase, are versions of the standard *pistis*-formula, that is, confessional formula.[5]

By the same kind of faith as Abraham's the Galatians have received the Spirit (Gal. 3.1-5). Here the manner of receiving the Spirit is described as ἐξ ἀκοῆς πίστεως in 3.2 and 5. This peculiar phrase is quite bewildering to many interpreters. For both ἀκοή and πίστις can have two different meanings: ἀκοή can denote either the act of hearing or what is heard, namely message or report; πίστις can also be taken as either the act of believing or what is believed, namely the

1. Dunn 1991: 731-40.
2. Dunn 1991: 733; cf. Burton 1921: 482; Hultgren 1980: 253.
3. Cf. Williams 1987: 435-35; Hooker 1989: 329.
4. Dunn 1991: 739.
5. Kramer 1966: 118; cf. Berényi 1984: 490-537.

Christian message. The immediate context, however, determines the precise meaning of the phrase.

In the first place, we should note that ἀκοὴ πίστεως is set in contrast to ἔργα νόμου in 3.2 and 5. It is undeniable that ἔργα here refers to a human activity, namely observing (the law), in which the Galatians themselves actually took part (4.10). This compels us to take the corresponding word ἀκοή in an active sense, namely hearing.[1] Some scholars, however, appeal to the parallel passage in Rom. 10.16-17 in order to support the alternative understanding of ἀκοή, in Gal. 3.2 and 5, as message.[2] For them, both references to ἀκοή, in Rom. 10.16b and 10.17, refer to message or report, because the two verses are directly tied up with ἄρα. But ἀκοή in v. 16 must be distinguished from ἀκοή in v. 17. This is so because the inferential particle appearing at the very beginning of v. 17 does not connect v. 17 with v. 16 but with vv. 14-15, which mainly say that believing depends upon hearing which in turn depends upon preaching. This surely leads us to understand ἀκοή in v. 17 as hearing. I think, on the other hand, that v. 16 which contains ἀκοή used in the passive sense of what is heard (i.e. message) would more logically be placed after v. 17, because both v. 16 and vv. 18-21 speak of the same issue, namely Israel's unbelief.[3] Thus the appeal to Rom. 10.16-17 is irrelevant.

The next task is to determine the meaning of πίστις in the phrase ἀκοὴ πίστεως. For this we need to pay special attention to the adverb καθώς, which appears at the beginning of 3.6. This adverb is a marker of similarity in events and states.[4] It then follows that the Galatians' reception of the Spirit in 3.1-5 and Abraham's experience of justification in 3.6ff. are parallel. Abraham *believed* (ἐπίστευσεν) the God of promise and was justified; the Galatians received the Spirit ἐξ ἀκοῆς πίστεως. This parallel strongly suggests that πίστις in 3.2 and 5 refers to a human act like the believing of Abraham.

It therefore appears to be sensible to take both ἀκοή and πίστις in an active sense: ἀκοή means hearing; πίστις believing. These two

---

1. E.g. Lightfoot 1880: 135; Ridderbos 1953: 113 n. 3; Cole [1965] 1983: 89; Fung 1988: 132; Williams 1989: 86.

2. E.g. Hays 1983: 146-48; Johnson 1987: 186-88.

3. E.g. Barrett 1962: 204-205; Williams 1989: 86-87; cf. Murray 1965: 60-61; Cranfield 1979: 535-37.

4. Louw and Nida *et al.* 1988: 64.14; cf. Williams 1987a: 93-94.

human activities should not be regarded as distinct; rather, they are identical. For hearing is not a simple act of the ear; instead it is, like faith, 'a response of the self', that is, a response 'to a spoken word in a manner consonant with the intention of the speaker'.[1] By this hearing of faith the Galatians have experienced the Spirit, as Abraham was justified by believing the God of promise. This experience had nothing to do with the law, because the Galatians were *without* and *outside* the law at the time of their initial response to the gospel of Christ preached by Paul.

The Galatians' experience of the Spirit is the evidence that they have received the Spirit of sonship in their hearts and have been adopted as sons (Gal. 4.6; cf. 4.28-29). This means that God has accepted the Galatians, justified them, and given them a part in the blessing of Abraham.[2] Here we see that the universal promise, 'All the nations shall be blessed in you [Abraham]' (Gal. 3.8), finds fulfilment in the reception of the Spirit. In this connection it is to be noted that in Gal. 3.14b the Gentiles' sharing in the blessing of Abraham is set in parallel with receiving the promise of the Spirit, that is, the promised Spirit.[3] This parallelism also shows that the promise of the Gentiles' participation in Abraham's blessing is fulfilled in the bestowal of the promised Spirit. In my opinion, this fulfilment naturally leads to the fulfilment of the promise of the innumerable descendants of Abraham which is implied in 3.6. If the Gentiles (i.e. all the nations except the Jews) can, by faith, take a part in the blessing of Abraham and become his children, is not the promise of numerous descendants fulfilled?

We can thus say that the Spirit is the actual fulfilment of the two promises made to Abraham. If we put it in another way, the promises of Abraham are the promise of the Spirit, as many have observed.[4] In view of the fact that there is no mention of the Spirit in Abrahamic narrative in Genesis, this may appear a strange exegesis. But it is a way of reading the OT adopted by Paul who reinterprets the old saving acts of God in the light of the Christ event.

---

1. Williams 1989: 91.
2. Dahl 1977: 133; cf. Williams 1987a: 91-100.
3. The phrase ἡ ἐπαγγελία τοῦ πνεύματος should be understood as the promised Spirit, because the Spirit which was previously promised has now been bestowed upon the believers (Moule 1963: 176; Schlier 1971: 140-41; Betz 1979: 153; Bruce 1982a: 168; Fung 1988: 151-52).
4. E.g. Betz 1979: 152-53; Hill 1981–82: 199; Williams 1988: 714-16, 720.

It is noteworthy that the term ἐπαγγελία used in connection with the Spirit in 3.14 is introduced here for the first time in Galatians. It is picked up for further discussion in the following sections (3.16, 17, 18, 19, 21, 22, 29; cf. 4.23, 28). This implies that there is a close link between the promise of the Spirit and the promise(s) mentioned in 3.16-29. The promises in Gal. 3.16 are probably the promises of the land, since the exact words καὶ τῷ σπέρματί σου in 3.16 are found in connection with the promises of the land (Gen. [LXX] 13.15; 17.8; cf. 12.7; 15.7; 24.7). In the rest of Galatians 3 following 3.16 I think that this promise of the land is continually in view, since there is no indication of other promises. The land originally refers to the land of Canaan. For Paul, however, it means the world in an eschatological sense (Rom. 4.13). This promise of the land should not be sharply differentiated from the other two promises in Gal. 3.6 and 8, for the possession of the world is realized by the inclusion of the *numerous* (3.6) *Gentiles* (3.8) in the family of Abraham. If this is the case, it is to be said that the promise of the land made to Abraham is also fulfilled in the gift of the Spirit. Thus it is clear that the coming of the Spirit has fulfilled all the promises given to Abraham.

If the Gentile Galatians have, by faith, received the Spirit and thereby the actual fulfilment of all the Abrahamic promises, it is altogether clear that participation in the promises is based on faith alone, not on the law which was added 430 years later (Gal. 3.18). From this fundamental point of view Paul refutes the argument of the opponents that the Galatians must accept circumcision and the law so as to inherit the promises.[1] For Paul, faith is the *only* way of becoming the legitimate sons of Abraham and of sharing his promises. It has been God's intended means of salvation from the beginning. It is not God's second attempt to save all mankind after his first unsuccessful attempt through the law.[2] The law was *never* planned to be the condition for entering the people of God at all.

1. Cf. Cosgrove 1988a: 536-49.
2. Cf. Hübner 1986: 31.

2. *The Law is the Condition for Staying in the Sinai Covenant*

Gal. 3.10-13, I think, serves as a bridge between 3.8, which contains the promise of the Gentiles' sharing in the blessing of Abraham by faith, and 3.14, which speaks of its fulfilment in the gift of the Spirit. In other words, the passage explains how the blessing of Abraham, namely justification by faith, has come to the Gentiles.[1] In doing so, the passage 3.10-13, especially 3.10 and 13, reveals a dimension of Paul's theology of the law.

Gal. 3.10 introduces the problem of the curse of the law. Although we have already given consideration to this verse,[2] I would like to deal with it again here from a slightly different perspective. Verse 10a says: ὅσοι γὰρ ἐξ ἔργων νόμου εἰσίν, ὑπὸ κατάραν εἰσίν. The phrase ἔργα νόμου has been understood traditionally to mean works done in conformity with the demand of the law.[3] Against this traditional understanding some other opinions have been recently advanced. Many scholars think that the ἔργα νόμου express the Jewish *mis*understanding of the law. Observing that the phrase always appears in direct contrast with faith as the basis of acceptance of God, they interpret it to mean legalistic observances of the law to *earn* the favour of God.[4] Fuller goes as far as to say that 'it involves trying to bribe God to impart blessing on the basis of the good works that one does'.[5] And it thus expresses 'a revolt against God rather than mere compliance with all the commands of the law'.[6] But, as I have argued above (Ch. 2.2.b), Paul does not view the death of Christ in terms of redemption from such a legalistic misinterpretation of the law in Gal. 3.13. Moreover, the fact that the phrase 'the works of the law' is interchanged with the law in Gal. 2.16, 21; 3.11 and 5.4[7] shows that Paul does not differentiate 'the works of the law' from the law as the

1. Cf. Sanders 1983: 22.
2. See above Ch. 2.2.b.
3. E.g. Moo 1983: 92ff.; Räisänen 1983: 177; Fung 1988: 113; Westerholm 1988: 116.
4. E.g. Burton 1921: 120; Bring 1961: 120ff.; Bring 1966: 21ff.; Cosgrove 1978-79: 146-48.
5. Fuller 1975-76: 33.
6. Fuller 1980: 93.
7. Westerholm 1988: 117-18.

sum of Israel's obligations imposed by their God at Sinai.[1] Further-more, in Romans 3–4 the word ἔργον which stands in parallel with τὰ ἔργα τοῦ νόμου is used in a neutral sense, not in a negative sense.[2] Thus it is undoubtedly clear that Paul himself does not see 'the works of the law' in the legalistic sense, whereas his opponents imposed them upon the Gentile Galatians, in addition to faith in Christ, for estab-lishing a right relationship with God.

Taking note of the specific issues raised in Gal. 2.1ff., 11ff.; 4.10; 5.2ff. and 6.12-13, Dunn does not consider 'the works of the law' as good works in general, but as particular observances of the law such as circumcision, food laws, special feast days. These works function as 'Jewish identity markers' which demonstrate the distinctiveness of the Jewish community in separation from the Gentiles.[3] But we should remember that the opponents in Galatia did not advocate only some ritual practices of the law but compliance with the law in its entirety.[4] Paul's interchange of 'the works of the law' and the law which was mentioned just above also suggests that we should not confine 'the works of the law' to a few observances of the law. In addition, it is worthwhile to take account of Moo's assertion that 'works' in Rom. 4.2 and 6, which are functionally equivalent to 'the works of the law' in 3.20 and 28, are not limited to cultic observances but refer to works in general.[5]

Gaston, presupposing that faith used in antithesis to ἔργα νόμου (Gal. 2.16; 3.2, 5; Rom. 3.28) refers to the faithfulness of Christ instead of faith in Christ, proposes that the ἔργα νόμου are to be taken as a subjective genitive: what the law works. The law, as an active power, produces a curse (Gal. 3.10), sin (Rom. 5.20), death (Rom. 7.11) and so forth.[6] But this argument is also based on a wrong premise. I have already contended that in Gal. 3.1-14 faith in connec-tion with justification refers to a human activity like the believing of

1. See above Ch. 4.
2. Rhyne 1981: 75-84; Moo 1983: 92-96; Westerholm 1988: 120-21.
3. Dunn 1983a: 107-11; Dunn 1985: 527-32; cf. Tyson 1973: 423-31; Heiligenthal 1984: 38-53; Lambrecht 1986: 114-15; Hamerton-Kelly 1990a: 108; Hamerton-Kelly 1990b: 62.
4. See above Ch. 3.2.
5. Moo 1983: 94-96; cf. Westerholm 1988: 119.
6. Gaston 1984: 39-46; Gaston 1987: 100-106.

Abraham (3.6).[1] If I am correct, 'the works of the law' must not be understood to refer to the activity of the law but to a *human* activity, namely human obedience to the law. Further, we should remember that in Romans 3–4 the 'works' corresponding to 'the works of the law' do not have a negative meaning but a neutral denotation.

I therefore conclude that the traditional interpretation of 'the works of the law' as works performed in compliance with the law is still valid. Thus the meaning of v. 10a should be that those who rely upon obedience to the law are under a curse.

The reason for the statement of v. 10a is provided by the quotation of Deut. 27.26 in v. 10b: 'Cursed is everyone who does not abide by all things written in the book of the law, to perform them'. It is a general view that the quotation indicates the *un*fulfillability of the law.[2] If this view is right, we can reconstruct Paul's reasoning this way:

1.   All who do not obey the law fully are cursed (10b).
2.   But no-one can obey the law fully (implied premise).
3.   Therefore, all who depend upon the obedience of the law are under a curse (10a).

Sanders, however, takes issue with this popular understanding of the verse, claiming that Paul here does not deal with the impossibility of keeping the law perfectly. He advances three reasons in support of his claim. First, Sanders argues that Paul's argument in Galatians 3 is terminological. Paul selects the Abraham story in order to assert that Gentiles are 'righteoused'[3] by faith. The story contains three crucial terms, namely 'Gentiles', 'righteous', and 'faith'. Gen. 15.6 (LXX) quoted in Gal. 3.6 connects the δικ-root with πίστις, while Gen. 18.8 in 3.8 provides the term ἔθνη. According to Sanders, the same terminological argument applies to Paul's quotation of Deut. 27.26 (LXX) in Gal. 3.10. The reason why Paul quotes this passage is that it serves his purpose to show that the law, in contrast to faith, brings about a curse, in contrast to the blessing of Abraham, because 'Deut. 27:26 is the only passage in the LXX in which *nomos* is connected with "curse"'. Thus, for Sanders, 'the thrust of Gal. 3:10 is borne by the

1.   See above Ch. 5.1.
2.   E.g. Drane 1975: 28; Bruce 1982a: 159; Moo 1983: 97-98; Schreiner 1984: 151-60; Schreiner 1985: 253-60; Gundry 1985: 24-25; Lambrecht 1986: 113.
3.   Sanders employs the awkward verb 'righteous' for justify.

words *nomos* and "cursed", not by the word "all", which happens to appear'.[1]

Secondly, Sanders pays attention to the relationship between the statements and their proof-texts, namely the OT quotations, in Gal. 3.10-12. Against the common view that the meaning of Paul's own statements depends upon what the proof-texts say, he contends that Paul's own statements give the clue to the meaning of the proof-texts. Thus in Gal. 3.10 Paul simply says that those who accept the law are under a curse. This also shows that the word 'all' does not play any significant role.[2]

Thirdly and finally, Sanders's argument concerns the function of Gal. 3.10-13 in the argument of Gal. 3.8-14. He thinks that Paul's main thesis of 3.8-14 is found in 3.8: the Gentiles are justified by faith, which is proved by the quotation of Gen. 18.18. Gal. 3.10-13 does not in itself advance any substantial argument but merely supports the thesis: 3.10 speaks of the opposite of the blessing stated in 3.8, namely the curse of the law; 3.11-12 reiterates that no one is justified by the law which is not of faith; and 3.13 shows how God removed the curse of the law. Verse 14, then, sums up the preceding argument, restating the positive point of 3.8: the blessing of Abraham coming to the Gentiles. This dependence of 3.10-13 upon 3.8 indicates that we should not expect any new argument in 3.10 such as the impossibility of keeping the whole law.[3]

Sanders then concludes that these three considerations are decisive arguments against the general opinion that one should not accept the law because no one can fulfil it entirely. Moreover, he points to Phil. 3.6b for further support for his argument concerning the fulfillability of the law.[4]

These arguments of Sanders give rise to many difficulties. I am not convinced by his first contention that Paul's argument in Galatians 3 is merely terminological. I do not agree that Paul simply chooses the story of Abraham because it provides important terms which Paul looks for. In my opinion, Paul is, in a sense, forced to take the story

---

1. Sanders 1983: 21, italics his.
2. Sanders 1983: 21-22.
3. Sanders 1983: 22.
4. Sanders 1983: 23-24; cf. Stendahl 1976: 80-81; Betz 1979: 145 n. 71.

because his opponents used it for their argument.[1] More importantly, it seems to me, the reason why Paul chooses the Abraham story is that Abraham who stands at the beginning of the redemptive history is, in his view, the prototype of justification by faith. So it is wrong to argue that Paul quotes Deut. 27.26 in Gal. 3.10b because the OT text connects the words 'law' with 'curse'. As seen above (Ch. 2.2.b), the Deuteronomic text as a *whole*, including of course these two important terms, should be taken into account if we want to understand Paul's argument in 3.10-13. In the text the very term 'all' which Sanders ignores, together with 'everyone' as well as the phrase 'the book of the law' substituted for just 'this law', plays a highly significant role in suggesting the universal human plight as the presupposition of Christ's redemption from the curse of the law in 3.13.

I must confess that it is difficult to accept Sanders's second argument as well. He simply contends without providing any substantiation that Paul's own assertions in Gal. 3.10-12 determine the meaning of proof-texts and not vice versa. Is this convincing? Of course there is some merit in Sanders's contention. But, as Schreiner tellingly shows, all of the OT quotations in Gal. 3.10-13 actually *explain* and *strengthen* Paul's argument by giving a rationale for his introductory statements.[2] My analysis of 3.10 also shows that the quotation of Deut. 27.26 gives a reason why all who rely upon the works of the law are under a curse: cursed is everyone who does not keep all the precepts of the law.[3] Here the premise of the impossibility of keeping the law perfectly is obviously implied.

Sanders's third argument is that Gal. 3.10-13 is subordinate to the thesis of 3.8 which is reiterated in 3.14. But my reading of the text of 3.8-14 does not support this argument. Verse 14 which starts with ἵνα clearly speaks of the result of Christ's redemption from the curse of the law in v. 13. This problem of the curse is first introduced in v. 10. So 3.10-13 is not just subsidiary to 3.8 and 3.14, but shows how the promise in 3.8 finds its fulfilment in 3.14 through the redemption of Christ.[4] This leads me to question Sanders's contention that there is no

---

1. See above Ch. 3.3.a.
2. Schreiner 1985: 257-58.
3. See above Ch. 2.2.b.
4. See above Ch. 2.2.b.

indication of the idea of the unfulfillability of the law in 3.10 in view
of the subordination of 3.10-13 to 3.8.

Finally, I would like to deal with Phil. 3.6b from which Sanders
claims support for the idea of the fulfillability of the law. In this verse
Paul says that he was blameless 'as to the righteousness in the law'. At
first glance this statement seems to suggest that Paul's observances of
the law must have been without fault. It should be noted, however,
that in its immediate context Phil. 3.6b refers to Paul's *pre*-conversion
assessment of himself. As a scrupulous Pharisee Paul might have
thought that his obedience to the law was perfect (this probably
included offering sacrifices in the temple for his failures).[1] But in the
brilliant light of the Christophany on the road to Damascus, Paul not
only realized his terrible sin of persecuting the church[2] but also his
own religious-moral bankruptcy which he could not have perceived in
the dim light of Judaism.[3] This involved his revolutionary realization
that his unconscious conflict with the law, suppressed during his past
Pharisaic time, was in fact a universal experience (cf. Romans 7).[4]

I therefore feel confident to assert that Sanders's arguments are not
valid. It remains defensible to accept the traditional view that Gal. 3.10
implies the impossibility of obeying the law perfectly. This is supported by Rom. 1.18–3.20 and 7.1-25 (cf. Gal. 5.3). Sanders argues,
of course, that even in these passages Paul does not say that the law
cannot be kept perfectly.[5] But his argument is very unsatisfactory.[6]

A number of scholars hold that Paul rejects the law as a means of
justification because no-one can fulfil it perfectly.[7] Does this suggest
that if anyone keeps the law fully he can be justified, that is, enter the
community of God? Does this then mean that the law and faith are
rival means of justification? Such a view does not accord with Paul's
understanding of the law. For Paul, the law which was given 430
years later does not nullify the promise (Gal. 3.17), not being

    1.   Cranfield 1979: 847; Schreiner 1984: 158; Schreiner 1985: 261-62; Espy
1985: 181 n. 33.
    2.   Cf. Kim 1984: 280-81, 287, 345-46.
    3.   Cf. Espy 1985: 175.
    4.   Theissen 1983: 244; cf. Beker 1980: 241.
    5.   Sanders 1983: 27-29, 78, 123-32.
    6.   See Schreiner 1985: 263-78; cf. Espy 1985: 166-77.
    7.   E.g. Wilckens 1974: 81-104; Wilckens 1982a: 165-72; Moo 1983: 96-99;
Hübner 1986: 18-20.

contrary to it (Gal. 3.21). Inheritance does not come from the law
(Gal. 3.18).[1] So the law was never planned to be a means of having a
share in the promise. Indeed, it was never meant to set aside the divine
plan of justification by faith.[2] Gal. 3.11 says that justification cannot
come by the law because it comes only by faith. 3.12 goes on to say
that the law is not compatible with faith.[3] Thus the law *in principle*
does not represent an alternative way of justification. Even if anyone
obeys it flawlessly, he cannot thereby enter into a right relationship
with God. The law cannot serve as a basis for determining the
relationship.

If we really want to understand Paul's teaching of the law in
Gal. 3.10-13, we should pose the question: why does the law curse
those who fail to obey it perfectly? We have already briefly discussed
this question above (Ch. 2.2.b). But here I would like to elaborate
upon some points of the discussion. We have observed that Paul, in
quoting Deut. 27.26 which pronounces a curse upon the transgressor
of certain prescripts, replaces 'this law' in the original text with 'the
book of the law' in Gal. 3.10b, thus extending the application of the
Deuteronomic curse-text to the whole Mosaic law.

It must be emphasized that the Mosaic law was addressed to the concrete community of Israel who had a special relationship with
Yahweh, not to an assumed recipient. Noth writes:

> The Old Testament laws envisage throughout a particular community of
> people resident on Palestinian soil, whose distinguishing feature consisted
> in the fact that 'Yahweh the God of Israel' was its God, a God whose
> connection with this community was founded upon definite historical
> events of the past. That common link with Yahweh was constitutive for
> the community envisaged by the Old Testament law-codes is too evident
> and too generally attested to need detailed proof (sic).[4]

This special relationship of Israel with Yahweh actually began with
Abraham. When Abraham was ninety-nine years old, Yahweh appeared
to him, giving freely a promise: 'I will establish my covenant between
me and you and your descendants after you throughout their
generations for an everlasting covenant, to be God to you and to your

1. Cf. Kline 1968: 23.
2. Cf. Robertson 1980: 174-75.
3. Cf. Sanders 1978: 106.
4. Noth 1966: 20.

descendants after you' (Gen. 17.7). Being faithful to this promise, Yahweh later entered into a covenant with Isaac and then with Jacob. This covenant with the Patriarchs of Israel was the main motive of his deliverance of Israel from the bondage of Egypt. The Exodus narrative actually starts this way: 'God heard their [the sons of Israel] groaning, and God remembered his covenant with Abraham, Isaac, and Jacob' (Exod. 2.24). Through the great saving event Yahweh showed his faithfulness to the covenant and established himself to be the God of Israel. He then gave the law to his people at Sinai in order that they might lead a holy life before their God.

It is apparent, therefore, that the covenant was *first* established by God's gracious initiative and that *thereafter* the law was proclaimed. In other words, the covenant precedes the law. This is to say that the law is not the precondition of the covenant but its result. The law has nothing to do with the establishment of the covenant. It is not a means of entrance into the covenant. But obedience to the law is a proper response to the grace of God who has taken an initiative to establish the covenant. This means that the law is the *obligation* of the covenant. The observance of it enables Israel to remain in relationship with God. Lev. 18.5 quoted in Gal. 3.12 affirms: 'He who practises them [the statutes and ordinances of the law] shall live by them'. The 'life' here is not to be taken to refer to life in the world to come, but to life within the covenant, that is, staying in the covenant relationship with God.[1] This remaining in the covenant involves enjoying the blessing of life. For this blessing is included in the covenant. Noth notes: 'In fact the blessing contained in *Deut.* XXVIII (apparently intended in respect of future fulfilment of the law) was already present before the law, for it rests on a previously given divine promise'.[2] So obedience to the law does not *earn* the blessing, but *permits* the covenant and the blessing to continue. This obedience is no more than the *duty* of the people of the covenant who have experienced God's electing grace and thus cannot make any claim to a reward. However, the transgression of the law indicates repudiation of covenant-loyalty to God, and so means the breaking of the covenant. This incurs a curse. This curse is the curse of God, the law-giver. It involves separation from God and

---

1.   Cf. Ladd 1968: 142 n. 3; Kaiser 1971: 19-28; McComiskey 1985: 121; Dunn 1988b: 601.

2.   Noth 1966: 126.

his holy community and the forfeit of the blessing in the covenant. This eventually brings death.

Here we should bear in mind that 'fulfilment and non-fulfilment, blessing and curse, are not both on the same level—nor, from the point of view of the law, are they two open possibilities offered for man's selection', as Noth states.[1] The fulfilment of the law is human duty, not a matter of choice. It does not earn any reward but simply ensures that the blessing belonging to the covenant remains. On the contrary, transgression and its result, curse, are what people can choose by their free will. Thus Noth goes on to say, 'there is only one possibility for man of having his own independent activity: that is transgression, defection, followed by curse and judgment'.[2]

In Paul's view, all the people of Israel were under the curse of the law due to their failure to keep the law completely. This is definitely implied in Gal. 3.10, 13, 22, 23 and 4.4-5 (cf. Rom. 2.17-29). Sanders argues, however, that the Jewish people in the time of Paul believed that the means of atonement provided by the law itself, namely sacrifice and repentance, were sufficient to atone for transgression.[3] But Paul realized that these means of atonement were inadequate in the light of the new saving event of God in Christ. In this connection we may suppose that Paul further appreciated the prophets' message of imminent doom because of Israel's guilt, in spite of the available means of atonement.

Paul understands the redemption of Christ as removing the curse of the law upon Israel. Gal. 3.13 says, 'Christ redeemed us from the *curse of the law*, having become a *curse* for us' (italics mine). Here the first person plural ('us') refers to the Jewish people.[4] Because the Jews serve as the representative of all the nations,[5] this particular saving act of Christ to redeem the Jews from the curse of the law has brought about a universal consequence, namely the Gentiles' participation in the blessing of Abraham (3.14). Here we see the fulfilment of the universal promise made to Abraham, in Gen. 12.3 (cf. 18.18; 22.18; 26.4; 28.14) and quoted in Gal. 3.8, through the mediation of Christ.

1. Noth 1966: 128.
2. Noth 1966: 131.
3. Sanders 1977: 422.
4. See above Ch. 2.2.b.
5. See above Ch. 2.2.b.

Now it becomes quite evident that Paul understands the law in Gal. 3.10-13 from the standpoint of the covenant. For him, the law is the obligation of the covenant between God and his people, the covenant which was graciously initiated by God. It can never give access to salvation, even if it could be perfectly observed. Obedience to the law only allows the covenant and the blessing in it to continue. But the transgression of the law brings about the curse, expelling the transgressor from the covenant. This function of the law as the stipulation of the Sinai covenant is terminated on the cross (cf. Rom. 10.4), for Christ has established a new covenant by his unprecedented saving act.[1] Such a concept of the law does not allow any idea of legalism or of meritorious works.

The same idea of the law is also found in other Pauline letters. Rom. 10.1-10 speaks of two different forms of righteousness: Israel's own righteousness and 'God's righteousness' (v. 3). The former is equated with 'the righteousness which is from the law' (v. 5); the latter with 'the righteousness from faith' (v. 6). These two are set in antithesis. It has been held that Israel's righteousness, namely righteousness from the law, refers to self-righteousness from legalistic observances of the law.[2] There is no clue here, however, that Paul thinks the Jews' righteousness from the law is intrinsically mistaken. It must also be noted that Paul does not condemn Israel's zeal for God, which is actually zeal for the law, but rather commends it (v. 2). According to Dunn, Israel's own righteousness (ἡ ἴδιος δικαιοσύνη) refers to '*Israel's* righteousness, righteousness which is Israel's alone, theirs and nobody else's—or, alternatively expressed, covenant righteousness, the righteousness which is Israel's by virtue of their being the chosen people of God'.[3] To support this view Dunn offers an interpretation of the two words, ἴδιος and στῆσαι, which are used in direct connection with the righteousness of Israel in Rom. 10.3. For him, as suggested in Bauer,[4] the ἴδιος has the sense of 'mine (and not yours)' as 'peculiar to me';[5] the στῆσαι does not denote 'an act of creation'

1.   Cf. Fensham 1966: 219-26.
2.   E.g. Ridderbos 1975: 139-42; Beker 1980: 247; Wilckens 1980: 220.
3.   Dunn 1987: 221-22, italics his; cf. Howard 1969: 336; Wright 1978: 83; Gaston 1979: 66; Sanders 1983: 38.
4.   Bauer 1979: s.v.
5.   Dunn 1987: 221; Dunn 1988b: 587.

but 'a setting or establishing or confirming of something which is already in existence'.[1]

To explain Israel's righteousness from the law Paul quotes Lev. 18.5 in Rom. 10.5: 'the man who does them [the statutes and ordinances of the law] shall live by them'. This OT text is also cited in Gal. 3.12 to argue that the law as the covenant obligation does not rest upon faith. According to Dunn, the passage is 'a typical expression of Israel's sense of obligation under the covenant—"do and thus live"'.[2] It does not criticize 'doing' as an attempt to earn divine favour, but says that keeping the law is necessary for life within the covenant. If this is the case, the righteousness of Israel, namely the covenant righteousness, is a matter of doing the law and living in the covenant. Here we see that the law is understood as the condition for maintaining the covenant righteousness, not as leading to self-righteousness. This function of the law was brought to an end by Christ who has, by atoning for Israel's transgressions,[3] established God's righteousness for all humankind (10.4).[4]

The same salvation-historical contrast appears in Phil. 3.9: Paul's own righteousness (righteousness by the law) versus God's righteousness (righteousness by faith in Christ). Paul regards the former righteousness as 'loss' in the light of knowledge of Christ (3.8). Like Israel's own righteousness in Rom. 10.3, Paul's own righteousness by the law here has customarily been interpreted as self-righteousness based on man's achievements.[5] But we do not find any suggestion that the righteousness is inherently wrong. On the contrary, it is counted as 'gain' in 3.7. We should note further that Paul includes his righteousness by the law among other *covenant privileges*, namely circumcision, belonging to Israel and zeal for the law in 3.5 and 6. This shows that the righteousness is not legalistic self-righteousness

---

1. Dunn 1988b: 595; cf. Bauer 1979: s.v.
2. Dunn 1987: 223.
3. Cf. Westerholm 1988: 129, 162, 172.
4. In my opinion, the τέλος νόμου in Rom. 10.4 means the termination of the law as the obligation of the Sinai covenant. Cf. Bultmann 1955: 36-66; Cranfield 1964: 48-53; Schneider 1964: 410-22; Howard 1969: 331-37; Meyer 1980: 59-78; Rhyne 1981: 95-121; Rhyne 1985: 486-99; Badenas 1985; Linss 1988: 5-12.
5. E.g. Bultmann 1951: 266-67; Beare 1959: 106; Ernst 1974: 98.

but the covenant righteousness. If so, it follows that the law is the obligation of the covenant.[1]

Paul's opponents in Galatia also understood the law in the framework of the covenant, though they required the Gentile Galatians to observe the law as a means of admission to the true descendants of Abraham, regarding the Gentiles as proselytes. They believed that they were elected by God by virtue of Abraham's faithful obedience and put in the covenant with God and that they should keep the law to live in the covenant. For them, Christ was a new Moses who came to affirm the law and to strengthen the Sinai covenant.[2] But their error lies in the failure to grasp that Israel broke the covenant by their disobedience, and that Christ died on the cross in order to remove the resulting curse upon them and thereby enacted a new covenant, creating a new people of God.[3]

The rabbinic Judaism of Paul's day has traditionally been regarded as a religion of work-righteousness, especially in connection with the interpretation of the well-known Pauline antithesis between law and faith.[4] But this view has long been opposed by Jewish scholars like Schechter (1909), Montefiore (1914) and Schoeps (1961), and by Christian experts in early Judaism like Moore,[5] Limbeck (1971) and especially Sanders (1977). On the basis of his massive analysis of Tannaitic literature, the Dead Sea Scrolls and some apocryphal and pseudepigraphical writings, Sanders vigorously rejects the traditional understanding of rabbinic Judaism as a legalistic religion. He persuasively argues that the Jews of the first century perceived the law quite differently. They put great emphasis upon the grace of God in freely electing Israel and in making his covenant with them. For them the law was not given as a way to enter into the covenant but as the way to stay in the covenant. Sanders calls this pattern of the Jewish religion 'covenantal nomism'. He briefly defines it thus:

1. Cf. Sanders 1983: 44-45; Watson 1986: 78; Räisänen 1987: 408-10.
2. See above Ch. 3.3.a.
3. On the other hand, Paul confirms the continuing validity of the election of Israel on a different level in Romans 9–11. Cf. Beker 1990: 40-55.
4. See Sanders 1977: 33-59.
5. Moore 1921: 197ff.; Moore 1927–30.

covenantal nomism is the view that one's place in God's plan is established on the basis of the covenant and that the covenant requires as the
proper response of man his obedience to its commandments, while providing means of atonement for transgression.[1]

This thesis of Sanders has been enthusiastically embraced by Räisänen
and Dunn.[2] Even Neusner, who is very critical of Sanders, acknow-
ledges that his work is 'a complete success' as far as its attempt to
demonstrate the fundamental nature of the covenant idea in rabbinic
literature is concerned.[3]

In brief, Gal. 3.10-13 shows that Paul comprehends the law in the
context of the Mosaic covenant. The law is not a means of *entering*
into the covenant but the way of *living* in the covenant. The law, as
the stipulation of the covenant, brings about a curse upon its transgressor. This idea of the law is also found in Rom. 10.1-10 and
Phil. 3.9. As far as the relationship between the law and the covenant
is concerned, the opponents in Galatia and the first-century Palestinian
Judaism basically agree with Paul.

3. *The Law as a Symbol of Israel's Distinctiveness*

It has been a recent trend to maintain that the social function of the
law is the key to Paul's criticism of the law. Dunn is a leading figure
of this trend.[4] According to Dunn, 'the works of the law' in Galatians
refer to particular observances of circumcision, the food laws and
Sabbath which are 'widely regarded as characteristically and distinc-
tively Jewish'.[5] This shows that Paul does not disparage the law per se
or good works in general but 'the law as fixing a particular social
identity, as encouraging a sense of national superiority and presump-
tion of divine favour by virtue of membership of a particular
people'.[6] The curse of the law (Gal. 3.10) from which Christ
redeemed us (3.13) is, then, 'the curse which falls on all who restrict
the grace and promise of God in nationalistic terms, who treat the law

1. Sanders 1977: 75; for a fuller definition see p. 422.
2. Räisänen 1980a: 65-68; Dunn 1983a: 97-100.
3. Neusner 1978: 180.
4. Cf. Heiligenthal 1984: 49-50; Watson 1986: 49-72; Gordon 1987: 38ff.
5. Dunn 1983a: 107.
6. Dunn 1985: 531.

as a boundary to mark the people of God off from the Gentiles'.[1]

This novel idea of Dunn, though interesting, has many weaknesses. First of all, as I have already discussed,[2] the expression 'works of the law' is not to be interpreted as doing certain parts of the law but as the works demanded by the entire law. Secondly, Paul's attack on the law is much more radical, as Räisänen rightly observes.[3] It is not directed towards the particular social function of the law but towards the law as a whole. When Paul speaks of the law which curses (3.10, 13), produces transgressions (3.19), enslaves (3.23ff.), and is connected with the power of sin (3.22), the demonic spirits of the world (4.3, 9) and flesh opposing the power of the Spirit (5.16-18), he undoubtedly has in mind the whole law. Thirdly and lastly, it is far-fetched to think of the death of Christ in terms of liberation from such a nationalistic understanding of the law. We should know that it was not wrong at all for Israel to be separated from the ungodly nations in order to obey the law. The guilt of Israel did not lie in possessing the law which naturally served as their boundary marker but in failing to keep it perfectly. Paul, in fact, understands Christ's death as the means of eschatological redemption from the present evil world in which the law, sin, demonic spirits and flesh act as evil powers.

We can thus conclude that Dunn's thesis is unsatisfactory. Yet this is not to deny that there are some sociological implications of the law in Galatians. When Peter withdrew himself from table fellowship with the Gentile Christians in Antioch, fearing the Jews, and in so doing compelled the Gentiles to live like Jews, Paul, before presenting his argument of justification by faith, said to Peter, accepting provisionally the Jewish point of view, 'We are Jews by birth and not sinners from Gentiles' (2.15). This statement draws attention to the customary Jewish distinction between the Jews and the Gentiles. The Jews regarded the Gentiles as sinners. The reason is not only that the Gentiles did not keep the law but also that they did not even have it. They were completely outside the law. They were thus called οἱ ἄνομοι (cf. Rom. 2.12; 1 Cor. 9.21). In contrast, the Jews regarded themselves as the people of the law, for they had been given the law and were under solemn obligation to keep it due to their covenant relationship with God. This

1. Dunn 1985: 536.
2. See above Ch. 5.2.
3. Räisänen 1985: 544, 548.

law was originally planned to bind Israel to their God. Its aim was to establish the lordship of God in his people's life by regulating its every aspect whether it dealt with moral, civil or cultic matter. So obedience to the law inevitably involved *separation* from the heathen nations and from all their profane, idolatrous customs and habits. In this connection it should be noted that in Deut. 7.1-11 and Ezra 10.11 the command to obey the law (or the will of God) goes hand in hand with the command to be separated from ungodly nations (cf. Deut. 26.18-19; Neh. 13.3). In my opinion, God's repeated calling of Israel to holiness (e.g. Lev. 11.45; 19.2; 20.7), which is actually the call to observe the law, implies the demand that they should separate themselves from their neighbouring people worshipping other gods.[1] Thus the law which was originally given as the obligation of the covenant naturally assumed a social function in the actual life of Israel within the covenant, namely *identifying* Israel as the people of God and *distinguishing* them from the foreign nations.

I have rejected Dunn's idea that the works of the law refer to particular observances of the law such as circumcision, the food laws, and the Sabbath.[2] But I readily concede that Dunn is correct in saying that those cultic practices were especially characteristic of the distinctiveness of the Jews.[3] For the ritual laws were unique to Israel alone, whereas the moral aspects of the law could be applicable to all the people on earth.[4] It is well known that circumcision remained a powerful identity symbol of membership of the covenant people in the eyes of the Gentiles as well as of the Jews themselves (Gen. 17.9-14). No wonder, then, that the Galatian Christians were, like Titus (Gal. 2.3), compelled to receive circumcision and considered it as a serious matter. The observance of the food laws was also regarded as one of the core symbols of the Jewish identity. 1 Maccabees describes the martyrs as those who 'stood firm and found the courage to refuse unclean food' and who 'chose death rather than contamination by such fare' (1.62-63). Neusner writes: 'Of the 341 individual Houses' [of Shammai and Hillel] legal pericopae, no fewer than 229...approximately 67 per cent of the whole, directly or indirectly concern

1. Cf. Snaith 1944: 24ff.; Seebass 1976: 226; Kaiser 1983: 140-41.
2. See above Ch. 5.2.
3. Dunn 1983a: 107ff.; cf. Meeks 1983: 97; Sanders 1983: 102.
4. Cf. Douglas 1966: 62-65, 128; Mol 1976: 233; Dunn 1985: 524-25.

table-fellowship'.[1] Thus it is understandable that the issue in Antioch was the Jewish food laws (Gal. 2.11-14).[2] With regard to the Sabbath, Stambaugh and Balch say that keeping the Sabbath and meeting at the synagogue 'were the most well-known symbols of Judaism' in the time of the early synagogues.[3] It is well known that in order to keep the Sabbath holy the rabbis extended the few biblical verses on the Sabbath into a great number of rules so that these rules were compared to 'mountains hanging from a hair'. It is noteworthy that the Jewish calendar which the Galatians have adopted through the persuasion of the agitators includes the Sabbath (Gal. 4.10).

The law, especially its ritual items, therefore functioned as an identity symbol of Judaism in differentiating the Jews from the Gentiles. It constituted a dividing wall between the Jews and the Gentiles (Eph. 2.14-15). Christ has, however, broken down the wall by inaugurating a new era. On the cross he removed the curse of the law under which the Jews were placed, and has thereby established a new covenant. Now in Christ a new people of God has emerged, replacing his old people. By faith in Christ not only the Gentiles but also the Jews can enter the new people who are described as 'a new creation' (καινὴ κτίσις) (Gal. 6.15; 2 Cor. 5.17). In Christ, thus, the old distinctions between circumcision and uncircumcision and between the Jews and the Greeks mean nothing at all (3.28; 5.6; 6.15). The social function of the law to mark the Jews out from the other nations has come to an end. All who belong to Christ are one (3.28).

---

1.   Quoted from Stambaugh and Balch 1986: 100.
2.   Cf. Sanders 1990: 283ff.
3.   Stambaugh and Balch 1986: 86.

Chapter 6

THE LAW AS AN ENSLAVING POWER

1. *The Law and Sin*

Against his opponents' contention that the Gentile Galatians should
receive circumcision and the law in order to inherit the promise made
to Abraham, as seen in the preceding chapter, Paul argues that
Abraham by faith accepted the promise and that the Galatians by faith
received the Spirit which was the actual fulfilment of the promise of
Abraham. He then goes on to assert that the inheritance is not based on
the law (Gal. 3.18). For Paul the law, which came much later, had no
power to invalidate the promise (3.17). The law was not contrary to
the promise (3.21); rather, it prepared the way for its fulfilment. The
law was originally given as the obligation of the Sinai covenant. Yet it
was broken and thus pronounced a curse upon those who transgressed
it, particularly Israel. From this curse of the law Christ redeemed
them so that the Abrahamic promise was fulfilled (3.13-14). With this
fulfilment the law as the covenant obligation gave way. Thus it was
temporally limited to the period between the promise and its
fulfilment. This period of the law is something like a parenthesis.

At this point Paul raises a question about the purpose of the law in
the history of redemption. In Gal. 3.19a he formulates it this way: τί
οὖν ὁ νόμος; This question is elliptical.[1] The word τί here can be
understood as 'why'[2] or 'what'.[3] No matter how we take it,[4] the context clearly suggests that the question primarily concerns the function,
purpose and significance of the law in the divine plan of salvation, not
its nature.

1. Blass and Debrunner 1961: §480.5.
2. E.g. RSV; NASB; Bruce 1982a: 175.
3. E.g. Betz 1979: 161; Belleville 1986: 55.
4. Cf. Burton 1921: 187.

Paul answers the question: τῶν παραβάσεων χάριν προσετέθη (3.19b). The verb προσετέθη refers back to the giving of the law 430 years later than the promise of Abraham (3.17). The prepositional phrase τῶν παραβάσεων χάριν is not unambiguous, for the χάριν may denote either purpose (1 Tim. 5.14; Tit. 1.5, 11; Jude 16) or reason (1 Jn 3.12; cf. Lk. 7.47; Eph. 3.1, 14).[1] If the former is the case, the phrase may mean 'for the purpose of (or for the sake of) transgressions', namely to produce or provoke transgressions. In the second case, it can mean 'because of transgressions', namely to check, deal with or prevent transgressions. This latter view agrees with the traditional Jewish understanding of the Torah as a hedge against sin.[2] Keck and Lull think along this line.[3] To my mind, however, there is no evidence in Galatians or elsewhere in Paul which supports this position.

The majority of interpreters regard the first option as representing Paul's intention here. In doing so, however, they do not provide sufficient evidence drawn from Galatians itself but mainly appeal to Rom. 3.20; 4.15; 5.13, 20; 7.5, 7-24 and 1 Cor. 15.56.[4] But in my opinion Galatians alone, especially the immediate context of 3.19b, divulges sufficient indications to support the majority view. First of all, 3.8-14 states that the promise was made to Abraham long before the law was promulgated and was fulfilled through the cross of Christ which removed the curse of the law imposed upon Israel owing to their transgressions. This means when the promise was given, there was no law; when it was fulfilled, however, the law, especially its transgressions, was presupposed. It follows that the law came to help the promise to find fulfilment through Christ *by producing transgressions*, not by preventing them. If the law had enabled Israel to keep its demands, it could certainly have abolished the promise (cf. 3.15, 17).

Secondly, Paul's forceful denial that the law is against the promise (3.21) can be understood *only* when we presuppose a possible attack by his opponents on his disparaging definition of the law in 3.19-20,

1. Bauer 1979: s.v.
2. Cf. Schoeps 1961: 194ff.; Betz 1979: 165.
3. Keck 1979: 74; Lull 1986: 482ff.
4. E.g. Cranfield 1964: 46; Eckert 1971: 82; Betz 1979: 165; Ebeling 1985: 193; Fung 1988: 159-60.

especially the statement in 3.19b: 'it was added for the purpose of transgressions'.[1] Since the opponents firmly believe that the law and the promise are compatible, they would immediately ask in reaction to the provocative statement: do you mean, then, that the law contradicts the promise?

Thirdly, we should note the *enslaving* function of the law. Gal. 3.23 says, 'before faith came, we were confined under the law, being shut up to the faith which was later to be revealed'. This bondage under the law is described as being equivalent to bondage under the elemental spirits of the world in 4.3 and 8-9. This negative character of the law compels us to take the preposition χάριν to indicate purpose.

Lastly, we are to pay attention to the παράβασις employed in the prepositional phrase in question. The word is a *legal* term; it does not refer to sin in general but to a concrete act of breaking a promulgated law or an explicit command.[2] According to Rom. 4.15 and 5.14, there was ἁμαρτία but no παράβασις between Adam and Moses because the law had not yet been given.[3] So παράβασις is not something which is antecedent to but something which is subsequent to the coming of law. How, then, can we interpret the phrase τῶν παραβάσεων χάριν to mean 'because of transgressions' as if these transgressions had taken place without the law?

We can therefore safely take the χάριν in a telic sense. Gal. 3.19b means that the law was added *for the purpose of* producing transgressions. This function of the law is more than one of revealing sin (ἁμαρτία) as transgression (cf. Rom. 3.20), though it does include it.[4]

In this connection it is worthwhile to consider Rom. 5.20a: νόμος δὲ παρεισῆλθεν, ἵνα πλεονάσῃ τὸ παράπτωμα. It is not so easy to determine the precise meaning of the term παράπτωμα. In 5.15, 17 and 18 the term is used to describe Adam's sin (παράβασις) in 5.14. This leads many scholars to see παράπτωμα as equivalent to παράβασις.[5] Yet, in 5.20 παράπτωμα is parallel to ἁμαρτία which

---

1. Cf. Bandstra 1964: 128; Lambrecht 1977–78: 492; Betz 1979: 173-74.
2. Schneider 1967: 739-40.
3. Cf. Lull 1986: 484.
4. Cf. Burton 1921: 188; Mussner 1974: 245; Fung 1988: 160.
5. E.g. Barrett 1962: 113; Murray 1965: 207-208; Michel 1966: 140; Wilckens 1978: 322 n. 1070.

was in the world before the law (5.13). There is, however, no instance in which παράπτωμα shares in the personal use of ἁμαρτία.[1] All these observations seem to indicate this: παράπτωμα has a broader connotation than παράβασις, a violation of a commandment or a law which did not exist between Adam and Moses, but it is not the same as ἁμαρτία. According to Cranfield, παράπτωμα, being equivalent to ἁμάρτημα (Rom. 3.25), refers to 'a false step, a going astray (it is cognate with παραπίπτειν), and so a misdeed' which disrupted humanity's relationship with God.[2] If this is correct, we can understand Rom. 5.20a this way: the law came in to increase sinful deeds which had occurred. This thought is not an exact parallel to that of Gal. 3.19b. But there is no essential difference between the two references. They basically concern the same thing: the law was given to aggravate the existing situation (cf. 1 Cor. 15.56; 2 Cor. 3.6, 7, 9). Thus it is not necessary to assume a theological development from Galatians to Romans in this respect.[3]

Returning to Gal. 3.19b, a question may be raised: how does the law produce transgressions? Unfortunately, in this regard Galatians is silent. If, however, we accept Rom. 5.20a as a parallel (not exact but approximate) to Gal. 3.19b, we can find an answer to the question in Romans, since Rom. 7.5ff. offers a clarification of the abrupt statement of Rom. 5.20a.[4] Although the assertions of Rom. 5.20a and Gal. 3.19b are slightly different, they share one and the same explanation. In Rom. 7.5 Paul states that τὰ παθήματα τῶν ἁμαρτιῶν were aroused through the law in men who were in the flesh. This Greek phrase means passions of sins, that is, passions which express themselves in concrete acts of sin rather than in false striving for self-righteousness, as implied in the plural form of the Greek words παθήματα and ἁμαρτιῶν.[5] The thought is specifically elaborated in Rom. 7.8ff. In the absence of the law sin was inactive (at least relatively). When the commandment 'Thou shall not covet' appeared on the stage, however, sin, through this commandment, took occasion

1.   Michaelis 1968: 172 n. 11; cf. Räisänen 1983: 144 n. 81; Hübner 1986: 80.
2.   Cranfield 1975: 284; cf. Michaelis 1968: 172; Louw and Nida *et al.* 1988: 88.297.
3.   Cf. Hübner 1986: 80-81.
4.   Cf. Beker 1980: 239; Snodgrass 1988: 104.
5.   Dunn 1988a: 364; cf. Bandstra 1964: 127-28; Bornkamm 1975: 126; Hübner 1986: 72ff.; Morris 1987: 285-87.

to stir up in man coveting of every kind (πᾶσαν ἐπιθυμίαν). This account is an obvious allusion to the fall story in Genesis 3, in which the serpent (sin) tempted Adam to eat the forbidden fruit by means of the commandment not to eat it.[1] Notice that the expression 'sin deceived (ἐξηπάτησέν) me' in v. 11 is reminiscent of the woman's complaint 'the serpent deceived (ἠπάτησέν, LXX) me' in Gen. 3.13.[2] It can be said, therefore, that by providing an operational base for sin to kindle people's sinful passions, the law served, though not directly, to provoke transgressions.[3]

Hübner ascribes the negative function of the law expressed in Gal. 3.19b to its origin from the demonic angels. In order to avoid any cynical comment on God's dealing with people for salvation, he interprets the participial clause διαταγεὶς δι' ἀγγέλων in 3.19d to mean 'ordained *by* the angels', taking the διά causatively to express source.[4] For Hübner, the mediator in 3.19d-20a does not represent God but a plurality, that is, the angels. This implies God's lack of involvement in giving the law. Moreover the rhetorical question 'Is the law then contrary to the promises of God?' in v. 21a at once becomes comprehensible if the intention of the angelic (non-divine) law to drive people to transgressions is presupposed.[5]

However, I do not find this analysis of Hübner convincing. First, the participial clause in 3.19d should be regarded as being connected with the verb of the main clause in 3.19b προσετέθη, because the participle διαταγείς modifies the main verb. The passive form of προσετέθη seems to suggest God as the giver of the law. It should be observed that the verb is qualified by the subordinate clause ἄχρις οὗ ἔλθῃ τὸ σπέρμα ᾧ ἐπήγγελται in 3.19c. This temporal clause clearly refers to God's design with regard to the law (cf. 3.22). This indicates that the προσετέθη is a divine passive. Hübner is aware of

---

1. Barrett 1962: 143; Bruce 1975: 268-69; Hübner 1986: 74-75; Dunn 1988a: 400.

2. I think that Rom. 7.7-13 depicts the Christian Paul's look in hindsight at the plight of Israel under the law, including himself before his conversion (Beker 1980: 238-42; Moo 1986: 122-35; cf. Cranfield 1975: 342-44; Karlberg 1986: 65-74; Westerholm 1988: 181-82).

3. Cf. Hübner 1986: 70-78.

4. Cf. Bauer 1979: s.v., διά III.2.b.

5. Hübner 1986: 26-29; cf. Schweitzer 1931: 69ff.; Schoeps 1961: 183; Drane 1975: 32-34; Räisänen 1983: 128-33.

this objection. In order to get away from the difficulty he simply presupposes 'an accumulation of perspectives' in the text.[1] Yet he fails to provide any concrete example which can be a parallel to 3.19b-d.[2] It is also noteworthy that in Acts 2.41, 47; 5.14 and 11.24 the verb προσετέθη is used with God as the agent.[3] Thus it becomes obvious that it is *God* who added the law to provoke transgressions.

Secondly, in interpreting the baffling verse of 3.20 (ὁ δὲ μεσίτης ἑνὸς οὐκ ἔστιν, ὁ δὲ θεὸς εἷς ἐστιν), as briefly stated, Hübner holds that the plurality affirmed in the phrase ἑνὸς οὐκ refers to a plurality of persons, namely the angels.[4] A serious difficulty with this opinion is, however, that a mediator never one-sidedly represents a plurality of persons in one party but always stands between two parties. This is the reason why most commentators view the ἑνὸς οὐκ as referring to two parties.[5] Even if the view of Hübner that the mediator represents the angels is granted, it does not necessarily exclude the possibility that God is ultimately responsible for giving the law, since we can assume at least two intermediaries, namely the angels and Moses, between God and Israel.[6] Here we should bear in mind that the law is the obligation of the covenant which is a kind of *contract* between God and his people.

Thirdly, the statement of 3.21c clearly assumes that the law originated from God, since the hypothetical notion 'if a law had been given which was able to impart' in v. 21c cannot take place without supposing the divine origin of the law.[7] This shows that it is wrong to presuppose the angelic authorship of the law in order to grasp the thrust of the rhetorical question in 3.21a.

Fourthly, there are many other indications in Galatians that the law is divine: Paul's zeal for the law before his conversion (1.14); the curse of God invoked over the transgressors of the law (3.10); and the fulfilment of the whole law in Christian love (5.14; cf. 6.2).

Finally, although there is no direct reference to the presence of

1. Hübner 1986: 27-28.
2. Cf. Räisänen 1983: 153 n. 127.
3. Fallon 1979: 652.
4. Cf. Oepke 1937: 619.
5. E.g. Lightfoot 1880: 146-47; Burton 1921: 190-91; Ridderbos 1953: 140; Betz 1979: 171; Fung 1988: 161-62.
6. Cf. Bruce 1982a: 179.
7. Wang 1971: 98; Räisänen 1983: 132.

angels at the promulgation of the law in the OT, the idea that the angels participated as God's assistants at the revelation was quite popular in Paul's time (e.g. Deut. 33.2, LXX; Josephus, *Ant.* 15.136; *Test. XII Patr.*, *T. Dan* 6; *Jub.* 1.29-2.1; Acts 7.38, 53; Heb. 2.2).[1] I believe that in Gal. 3.19d Paul simply shares this tradition. In this connection Bandstra makes the interesting suggestion that the angelic mediation fits into the purpose of the law to stimulate transgressions, since the angels are thought to serve to uphold God's justice and to carry out his judgment (e.g. Exod. 23.21; 2 Sam. 24.16; 2 Kgs 19.35; Isa. 37.36; Heb. 2.2).[2]

All these considerations together make Hübner's interpretation implausible. It is *by God*, I am claiming, that the law was intended to serve to produce transgressions. This does not say that God is responsible for sin. Rather it seems to mean that the law still remained in God's hands, serving his redemptive plan, though it assumed the negative function in encountering the power of sin.

In any event, the consequence of the giving of the law is: [ἀλλὰ] συνέκλεισεν ἡ γραφὴ τὰ πάντα ὑπὸ ἁμαρτίαν (3.22a; cf. Rom. 11.32).[3] It is remarkable that the singular γραφή is not accompanied by any OT quotation, in view of the fact that in Paul (and also in the NT in general) the term usually refers to a specific passage in the OT (Gal. 3.8; 4.30; Rom. 4.3; 9.17; 10.11; 11.2). It is also notable that the γραφή is described in personal terms. These observations suggest that it refers to the entire Scripture which is invested with the authority of God.[4] The συγκλείω can be taken in various senses,[5] but is undoubtedly used here in the negative sense of 'to shut up', 'to confine', or 'imprison'. The neuter plural τὰ πάντα probably refers to all people (cf. Jn 6.37, 39), since the entire argument here is on the personal

1. For discussions of these texts, see Callan 1980: 550-54; Bandstra 1989: 223-40; cf. Gaston 1987: 36-37.
2. Bandstra 1964: 151-57.
3. Although the ἀλλά connects Gal. 3.22 with the preceding hypothetical assumption in v. 21 by showing a contrast between them, my structural analysis demonstrates that v. 22 actually stands in an result–reason relation to 3.19b. See above Ch. 1.2.a.viii.
4. Cf. Guthrie 1973: 107; Cosgrove 1978-79: 160; Ebeling 1985: 192-93; Belleville 1986: 56; Fung 1988: 164.
5. See Michel 1971: 744-47.

level.[1] The expression ὑπὸ ἁμαρτίαν means under the *bondage* of sin, a supreme power of the old age, as the συγκλείω suggests.[2] This understanding of sin fits into the broad framework of Paul's eschatological understanding of the Christ event in Galatians (1.4; 6.14-15).[3] The picture behind the statement in 3.22a seems to be that of the jail. The Scripture is represented as the magistrate, all people as the prisoners, and sin as the jailer.[4]

2. The Bondage of the Law

After dealing with the law and sin in the transitional section in 3.15-22, Paul goes on to describe the slavery of the law in antithesis to the sonship in Christ in 3.23–4.7. The slavery is expressed as being ὑπὸ νόμον in 3.23 and 4.4-5 (cf. 4.21; 5.18). Then it is compared with being ὑπὸ παιδαγωγόν (3.25), ὑπὸ ἐπιτρόπους καὶ οἰκονόμους (4.2) and ὑπὸ τὰ στοιχεῖα τοῦ κόσμου (4.3). Here it is important to note that these ὑπό phrases are parallel to ὑπὸ ἁμαρτίαν in 3.22. This indicates that, like bondage under sin, slavery under the law is also the effect of the function of the law to stimulate transgressions.

Before considering the import of the diverse analogies of the law we should first investigate the meaning of the phrase ὑπὸ νόμον in the context of Galatians. This is a legitimate order of interpretation. In my opinion, it is wrong to adopt the approach followed by a number of interpreters,[5] that is, to consider first the role of the metaphors παιδαγωγός (3.24-25) and ἐπίτροπος and οἰκονόμος (4.2) in the Graeco-Roman social context in order to understand the phrase ὑπὸ νόμον. I regard it as essential to determine the significance of the metaphors by first examining what Paul is trying to say by ὑπὸ νόμον, *not* vice versa.[6]

The peculiar phrase ὑπὸ νόμον first appears in 3.23. It is accompanied by the verb ἐφρουρούμεθα and the participle συγκλειόμενοι

1.   Guthrie 1973: 107; Betz 1979: 175 n. 116; Fung 1988: 164 n. 65; cf. Bruce 1982a: 180; Belleville 1986: 56-57.
2.   Cf. Burton 1921: 196; Belleville 1986: 56.
3.   See above Ch. 2.
4.   Guthrie 1973: 107; cf. Fung 1988: 164.
5.   Longenecker 1982: 53-61; Belleville 1986: 59ff.; Young 1987: 150-76; cf. Lull 1986: 481-98.
6.   Cf. Gordon 1989: 150.

6. *The Law as an Enslaving Power* 157

(ὑπὸ νόμον ἐφρουρούμεθα συγκλειόμενοι),[1] and thus refers to the condition of the Jews[2] before the coming of faith. A variety of opinions exists about the Jewish situation under the law. Gordon understands the situation in a positive light, regarding the function of the law as that of guarding or protecting Israel from the profane idolatry of the Gentiles. For him, the verb φρουρέω suggests protective custody. Even the συγκλείω has the connotation of confinement which serves a positive purpose.[3] It is true that the law functioned to protect Israel from the idolatrous influence of the ungodly nations in the OT. However, that is not the point here. Note the structural parallelism between ὑπὸ ἁμαρτίαν in 3.22 and ὑπὸ νόμον in 3.23. Does this not indicate that being under the law here is something which is strongly negative? Moreover, it is unlikely that the verb συγκλείω, used negatively in connection with the enslaving power of sin in v. 22, would immediately thereafter in v. 23 hint at a positive connotation.[4] Furthermore, the negative function of the law to produce transgressions as expressed in 3.19b[5] clearly speaks against any attempt to perceive the function of the law in 3.23 as a positive one.

Belleville thinks that being under the law is neutral. According to her, the Jews need strict supervision (including punishment for their wrongdoings) and custodial care of the law, because they are held in the custody of sin's prevailing influence.[6] But this interpretation also fails to take into consideration seriously the parallelism of ὑπὸ ἁμαρτίαν and ὑπὸ νόμον. In my opinion, if being ὑπὸ ἁμαρτίαν refers to the slavery of the evil power of sin, as interpreted above,[7] then we are not permitted to see any positive element in the confinement under the law. Also, the statement of 3.19b rules out this possibility.

1. Lull (1986: 487-88) takes the present participle συγκλειόμενοι as a substitute for an imperfect which indicates a continued action prior to that of the main verb, mainly in order to justify his mistaken interpretation of 3.19b that the law was added because of the transgressions that had occurred. But it is more natural to see the present participle as denoting the same action which is expressed by the principal verb (Burton 1894: §120; Burton 1921: 199; Young 1987: 170).
2. See above Ch. 2.2.b; cf. Gaston 1979: 62-63.
3. Gordon 1989: 153-54; cf. Michel 1971: 746; Cosgrove 1978–79: 163.
4. Cf. Belleville 1986: 57.
5. See above Ch. 6.1.
6. Belleville 1986: 60; cf. Longenecker 1982: 58-59 ; Lull 1986: 488.
7. See Ch. 6.1.

Young proposes a negative interpretation to existence under the law. For him, to be under the law is to be under the law's restriction rather than its protection or correction. Positing that Paul's attack in Galatians is directed against Jewish religious nationalism and exclusivism, Young claims that the restriction of the law involves preventing Israel from free association with the Gentiles.[1] By the same token Howard argues that being under the law means to experience 'the suppressing force of the law which separated Jew from Gentile and held back the universal unity which was destined to come'.[2] I have already repudiated this kind of sociological interpretation as indefensible.[3]

What, then, is the exact nature of existence under the law? It has been noted above that being ὑπὸ νόμον in 3.23 is parallel to being ὑπὸ ἁμαρτίαν in v. 22 and that the same verb συγκλείω is used in connection with both existences. Here we see that the law, like sin, is also depicted as a custodian. It holds its prisoners in custody with a view to *suppression*, not protection. For this reason the verb φρουρέω used besides συγκλείω[4] in association with the phrase ὑπὸ νόμον in v. 23 is to be taken in the sense of a restrictive confinement, though it is elsewhere employed in the sense of a protective guarding (2 Cor. 11.32; Phil. 4.7; 1 Pet. 1.5). The statement of v. 19b also lends support to this understanding.

We now turn to the passage in 4.4b-5a, where the expression ὑπὸ νόμον occurs twice, in order to give a further clarification of the character of the bondage of the law: ἐξαπέστειλεν ὁ θεὸς τὸν υἱὸν αὐτοῦ, γενόμενον ἐκ γυναικός, γενόμενον ὑπὸ νόμον, ἵνα τοὺς ὑπὸ νόμον ἐξαγοράσῃ. Here, too, being ὑπὸ νόμον is described as a bondage, as suggested by the term ἐξαγοράζω which has a connotation of deliverance or liberation. It is common to regard being under the law here as being under obligation to keep the law.[5] To my mind, however, it is absurd to think that being under such an obligation is a desperate (or non-exit) situation from which Christ redeemed his

1.   Young 1987: 170ff.
2.   Howard 1979: 61-62.
3.   See above Ch. 5.3.
4.   See just above.
5.   Stott 1968: 106; Arichea and Nida 1976: 90; Fung 1988: 182 n. 73; Louw and Nida *et al.* 1988: 37.7.

people. We should not forget what Paul says in 3.13a: 'Christ redeemed (ἐξηγόρασεν) us from the curse of the law, having become a curse for us.' Note that the same verb ἐξαγοράζω is employed here as in 4.5. In fact, 3.13a and 4.4b-5a form a parallelism. As argued already,[1] the first person plural pronouns in the quotation of 3.13a refer to the Jews only. According to 3.10, they were under a curse (ὑπὸ κατάραν) because of their failure to fulfil the law. We can now change the structure (not the meaning!) of 3.13a so as to make its correspondence to 4.4b-5a more striking: Christ became a curse in order to redeem his people who were under the curse of the law. Note the parallelism between the two statements. This parallelism makes it clear that those ὑπὸ νόμον in 4.5a are the Jews under the curse of the law. What naturally follows then is that existence under the law in 4.4b-5a means existence under the curse of the law.[2]

It is perplexing that Paul employs the metaphor παιδαγωγός in Gal. 3.24-25 (cf. 1 Cor. 4.15) to describe the bondage of the law, that is, existence under the curse of the law. The figure of pedagogue was widely known in Graeco-Roman society.[3] He was not a teacher (διδάσκαλος) but a household-slave who accompanied the free-born boy wherever he went, especially to school. His task consisted of protection of the boy from all kinds of dangers and supervision of his general conduct which involved reproach and punishment for his bad manners. The pedagogue kept the lad under his control and restricted his liberty until he reached the age of puberty.[4]

According to Lull and Young,[5] however, there was a big gap between the ideal and the actual. It was quite common to put old and decrepit slaves in charge of children while appointing fit and young slaves to manage more demanding works such as financial affairs. Plutarch lamented this practice of using the most useless slaves for the important early discipline of the children (*Mor.* 4A-B). The pedagogues were supposed to assist their charges to realize and achieve

1. See above Ch. 2.2.b.
2. Cf. Ridderbos 1953: 156; Betz 1979: 176; Bruce 1982a: 196; Lategan 1991: 82, 85.
3. See Longenecker 1982: 53-56; Belleville 1986: 59-60; Lull 1986: 489-94; Young 1987: 150-69; cf. Hanson 1988: 71-76.
4. Plato was of the opinion that a child should be treated as a slave during his minority (*Leg.* 7.810E).
5. Lull 1986: 493; Young 1987: 159.

virtue, but many, if not most of them, were not educated but rough and abusive men. They often failed to advise well or to provide a good example to be followed. What they taught best were 'petty and childish duties' (Plutarch, *Mor.* 439F). Yet this teaching was often accompanied by threats or whipping. It is not surprising, then, that the pedagogues gained a bad reputation for being rude and harsh. It is true, however, that there were some good pedagogues who attracted respect and affection.[1]

What, then, is Paul's point in using the pedagogue metaphor for the law? To be sure, the primary task of the pedagogue was to protect children from all sorts of harm and to teach them proper manners. But there is no indication in the context of 3.24-25 that the law played such a protective and educative role, as observed above. The context rather suggests that the unpleasant restraint of the pedagogue is the force of the analogy.[2] It should be noted that the comparison of the law with the pedagogue in v. 24 is motivated by the situation depicted in v. 23: 'before faith came we were confined under the law, kept under restraint... *so that* (ὥστε) the law has become our pedagogue...' This demonstrates that Paul employs the pedagogue metaphor in order to describe vividly the enslavement of the law. For Paul, subjection under the pedagogue amounts to imprisonment, that is, lack of freedom, and thus is comparable to slavery under the law, the plight of the Jews before (or outside) Christ.

In this connection some construe the dominion of the law in an existential way. Taking the preposition εἰς in the phrase εἰς Χριστόν in 3.24 to express the goal, they think of the enslaving function of the law as oppressing individuals and creating a growing passion for liberty in Christ.[3] However, the εἰς must be taken in a temporal sense in the light of many temporal references in 3.19-25: ἄχρις (v. 19), πρό (v. 23), εἰς τὴν μέλλουσαν πίστιν (v. 23), ἐλθούσης δὲ τῆς πίστεως (v. 25), οὐκέτι (v. 25). This understanding is further substantiated by the fact that in 4.1-7 also Paul uses different images to stress the temporal limits of the law's subjugation (see below). Thus it is clear that Paul here speaks of a non-exit situation of people under

1. See Lull 1986: 490; Young 1987: 165-68.
2. Young 1987: 170-71; cf. Westerholm 1988: 196.
3. Luther [1891] 1979: 340-41; Ridderbos 1953: 146; Cole [1965] 1983: 108; cf. Cousar 1982: 79.

the law before the coming of Christ *in terms of salvation history*, not in terms of subjective psychology.[1]

Paul in 4.2 sets forth another analogy of bondage under the law: being ὑπὸ ἐπιτρόπους καὶ οἰκονόμους.[2] There has been much discussion on the precise meaning of the two titles and the legal system behind them which Paul has in mind.[3] In general, however, ἐπίτροπος is a legal term for the guardian, appointed by the father or by the court, who managed the household and the property of a minor until he attained his majority. On the other hand, οἰκονόμος usually means a steward who administered the household and the estate of his master (cf. Lk. 12.42; 16.1, 8; Rom. 16.23; 1 Cor. 4.1-2; Tit. 1.7; 1 Pet. 4.10). We should note, however, that there is no clear instance of the use of οἰκονόμος for one who has charge of the person or estate of a minor heir.[4]

It is puzzling that here the administrative term οἰκονόμος occurs in association with the legal term ἐπίτροπος. It is unlikely that in combining the two terms Paul has in mind the Roman law which stipulates that a minor is to be under a *tutor* (ἐπίτροπος) until the age of 14, and thereafter under a *curator* (κουράτωρ) until the age of 25.[5] For if Paul had been thinking of this law, he could have used the phrase ἐπίτροπος καὶ κουράτωρ instead of ἐπίτροπος καὶ οἰκονόμος. Moreover, it does not seem that Paul has a historical succession of guardians in mind. The single preposition ὑπό and connective καί (ὑπὸ ἐπιτρόπους καὶ οἰκονόμους) implies that the minor is *at the same time* 'under guardians and stewards'.[6] It is possible, however, that the combination of the two terms takes place because of the references to slavery in 4.1 and 3, since οἰκονόμος can be the one

1. E.g. Burton 1921: 200; Bultmann 1951: 266; Beker 1980: 55; Fung 1988: 169; Westerholm 1988: 196.

2. The basic thought of Gal. 3.23-29, that is, the antithesis between slavery under the law and freedom in Christ, is repeated in 4.1-7, though with some elaboration. This is implied in the opening words λέγω δέ in 4.1 (cf. 3.17; 5.16; Rom. 15.8; 1 Cor. 1.12) which may be rendered as 'this is what I mean' (NEB) or 'let me put it this way' (Bruce 1982a: 192).

3. E.g. Ramsay 1900: 391-93; Burton 1921: 212-15; Hester 1967: 119-22; Belleville 1986: 60-63.

4. Burton 1921: 212.

5. Cf. Ramsay 1900: 392-93.

6. Belleville 1986: 62.

who superintends the slaves of his master.¹ It is also plausible that
Paul in his use of the two titles is merely referring to those who had
effective control of the person and estate of a child. In some cases the
ἐπίτροπος might delegate some of his responsibilities to the
οἰκονόμος.²

Whatever the case, the point of the analogy is clear: as Paul explicitly states in 4.1, the minor heir does not differ at all from a slave as
long as he is put under guardians and stewards. Although he is theo-
retically the owner and master, he is in reality without control over
his life and possessions. By the same token, the Jews under the curse
of the law have no capacity for self-determination and freedom,
though they have received the promise to inherit the eschatological
land.³

Further, Paul equates slavery under the law with bondage ὑπὸ τὰ
στοιχεῖα τοῦ κόσμου in 4.3ff. The phrase τὰ στοιχεῖα τοῦ κόσμου
here is simply τὰ στοιχεῖα in 4.9. This implies that the emphasis
within the phrase is placed on the ideas conveyed by τὰ στοιχεῖα
rather than τοῦ κόσμου.⁴ The word στοιχεῖον basically means a
member or component of a row or series, probably being derived
from στοῖχος, 'a row', 'a series', 'a line'. In Hellenistic and Classical
literature the plural, τὰ στοιχεῖα, is principally used in two senses:
(1) elements of knowledge or fundamental principles (e.g. Plato, *Leg.*
7.790C; Xenophon, *Mem.* 2.1.1; Plutarch, *Lib. Ed.* 16.2; Heb. 5.12),
and (2) the physical elements of the universe such as earth, water, air,
and fire (e.g. Plato, *Tim.* 48B; Diogenes Laertius 7.134-35; *4 Macc.*
12.13; Philo, *Dec.* 31; *Op. Mund.* 146; Hermas, *Vis.* 3.13; Justin
Martyr, *Dial.* 62.2; 2 Pet. 3.10, 12). As the references in brackets
show, however, this second sense is predominant in Jewish and
Christian literature of the NT period. In the second century CE
another meaning of στοιχεῖα appears. Justin Martyr in his *Second
Apol.* 5.2 employs the word to refer to heavenly bodies, especially the
sun, the moon, and other planets which influence seasonal events in
nature (see also *Dial.* 23.3; Theophilus of Antioch, *Autol.* 1.6, 2.35).

1.	Betz 1979: 204; cf. Longenecker 1982: 56.
2.	Belleville 1986: 63; cf. Burton 1921: 213-14; Michel 1967: 150; Longenecker
1982: 56.
3.	See above Ch. 5.1.
4.	Burton 1921: 516; cf. Bandstra 1964: 541ff.

We also find the word denoting spiritual beings such as demons and spirits in the *T. Sol.* (8.1-2; 18.1-2) which may not be earlier than the third or fourth century CE.[1]

How, then, does Paul understand τὰ στοιχεῖα τοῦ κόσμου in Galatians (cf. Col. 2.8, 20)? There has been a wide variety of interpretations of Paul's intended meaning of the phrase. (1) Assuming the inclusion of the law in the στοιχεῖα, some scholars interpret the phrase as elementary religious teachings by which people lived prior to Christ.[2] (2) Howard takes up the most frequent meaning of στοιχεῖα in the first century CE and proposes that τὰ στοιχεῖα τοῦ κόσμου refer to the elements of the universe which the Gentiles worshipped as gods.[3] (3) Schweizer makes a slightly different suggestion. While agreeing that στοιχεῖα mean the four elements of the universe, he denies that the Galatians elevated them to the status of gods. Rather, he thinks, they feared the elements as 'forces' (δυνάμεις) threatening continually the existence of the world by their 'mighty strife'.[4] (4) Bandstra also regards στοιχεῖα as primary, inherent components, but understands the κόσμος quite differently. He takes this term in a theological sense, and views τὰ στοιχεῖα τοῦ κόσμου as law and flesh which constitute the fundamental forces operative in the world in opposition to God.[5] (5) Schlier, appealing to 4.10, understands the στοιχεῖα to refer to stars which were revered as spiritual beings, in spite of the lack of any pre-Pauline attestation of the usage.[6] (6) Betz thinks that the στοιχεῖα include both the physical elements and the heavenly bodies which were thought of as exerting their control over men.[7] (7) Quite unexpectedly, Reicke identifies the στοιχεῖα with the angels mentioned in 3.19, noting that the former is represented in fairly personal fashion.[8] (8) Finally, other interpreters offer a somewhat loose understanding of the στοιχεῖα. Observing that

1. For the history of the use of στοιχεῖον, see Burton 1921: 510-14; Delling 1971: 670-83.
2. Lightfoot 1880: 167; Burton 1921: 510-18; Ridderbos 1953: 154; Carr 1981: 75; Belleville 1986: 67-69.
3. Howard 1979: 66-67; cf. Wink 1978: 225-48.
4. Schweizer 1988: 455-68; cf. 1970: 245-59.
5. Bandstra 1964: 57-68.
6. Schlier 1971: 192.
7. Betz 1979: 204-205; cf. Hübner 1986: 33.
8. Reicke 1951: 261ff.; cf. O'Brien 1984: 135-36.

both Judaism and paganism are forms of bondage to the στοιχεῖα, they consider the στοιχεῖα as covering all the things which people serve as their gods, including the Jewish law.[1]

In order to decide which one of these various solutions is most plausible, I would like here to consider the context in which the term στοιχεῖα is used. First of all, it is important to note that in 4.3-5 *bondage* under the law is parallel to *bondage* under τὰ στοιχεῖα τοῦ κόσμου. This does not necessarily mean that the law is identical to the στοιχεῖα or that the law is included in the στοιχεῖα. As observed above, in 3.22-23 Paul equates being under sin with being under the law. However, he never asserts that the law is sin (see e.g. Rom. 7.7). The same can be said for his comparison of the law to παιδαγωγός in 3.24-25 and to ἐπίτροπος and οἰκονόμος in 4.1-2. This observation makes the interpretations (1), (4) and (8) unlikely. Secondly, the description of the Galatians' past in 4.8 suggests that the στοιχεῖα were regarded by pagans as gods. Verse 8 reads: 'at that time, when you did not know God, you were enslaved to those who in nature (φύσει) are not gods'. The expression 'those who in nature are not gods' reminds us of a typical Jewish polemic against Gentile polytheism (Isa. 37.19; Jer. 2.11; 5.7; 16.20; Ep. Jer. 14, 22, 28, 49, 50, 64, 68, 71).[2] For Paul as a Christian Jew, pagan gods are not really 'gods' at all. The close conjunction in thought between vv. 8 and 9 shows that these counterfeit gods are identical with the στοιχεῖα in v. 9. In this connection it is noteworthy that the στοιχεῖα are described as being 'weak and beggarly'. This consideration permits only interpretations (2), (5) and (6) as possibilities. Lastly, we should notice the connection between the Galatians' attempt to return to the slavery of the στοιχεῖα in 4.9 and the calendar observances in 4.10 (cf. Gen. 1.14) which were usually associated with star worship.[3] This eliminates interpretation (2) from the remaining possibilities.

Our choice, then, is between interpretations (5) and (6). Interpretation (5), which understands the στοιχεῖα to refer to the heavenly bodies revered as spiritual beings, fits into the passage of 4.8-10 quite nicely. It was not uncommon to regard the stars as living beings in the ancient world. The main difficulty with this position is, however, that

1.   Delling 1971: 684-85; Esser 1976: 453; Bruce 1982a: 204; Fung 1988: 191.
2.   Howard 1979: 67, 98 n. 224; Bruce 1982a: 201; cf. Betz 1979: 214-15.
3.   Cf. Schlier 1971: 206.

there is no pre-Pauline attestation to the use of στοιχεῖα for the stars. Of course it is certainly not impossible to suppose that Paul is the first person to use the word στοιχεῖα to refer to the stars. It is precarious, however, to build a theory on such a thin foundation. But we cannot simply ignore the suggestion of 4.10. Thus it would be wise to assume, as the interpretation (6) does, that both the stars and the elements of the universe are included in the στοιχεῖα. It is well known that the use of the στοιχεῖα for the elements of the universe was predominant in the religious literature of antiquity, and that the elements as well as the stars were conceived as divine beings in the Gentile world of Paul's time (cf. Wis. 13.2; 7.17; Philo, *Vit. Cont.* 3-5).

I conclude, therefore, that στοιχεῖα refers to both the heavenly bodies and the elements which were worshipped as gods in paganism. For Paul, they represent *demonic forces* which dominate 'this present evil age' in view of his eschatological understanding of the redemptive work of Christ in Gal. 1.4 and 6.14,[1] and which enslave not only the Gentiles but also the Jews before and outside Christ.[2] Thus we can understand Paul's reason for equating slavery under the στοιχεῖα with slavery under the law. It is because both the στοιχεῖα and the law are enslaving powers which constitute and dominate this evil world. Being under these powers means absence of freedom and subjection to oppression.

Finally, we should observe that Paul relates existence under the law to subjection to the flesh in 5.16-18. Verse 18 reads: 'If you are led by the Spirit, you are not under the law (ὑπὸ νόμον)'. This statement is a reinforcement of that in v. 16: 'Walk by the Spirit, and you will not carry out the desire of the flesh'. The correspondence between these two statements implies that submission to the flesh is tantamount to being under the law.

This association of the law with the flesh is not new. It has already taken place in 3.2-3 and 4.21-31. In the former place the flesh seems to refer to the circumcised flesh (cf. Ch. 3.3.a); in the latter it denotes

1. Cf. Rom. 8.38, 16.20; 1 Cor. 2.6, 8; 5.5; 7.5; 8.5; 10.19-20; 15.24; 2 Cor. 2.11; 4.4; 11.14; Eph. 6.12; Col. 1.16; 1 Thess. 2.18; 3.5.
2. The 'we' who were held in bondage under the στοιχεῖα in Gal. 4.3 primarily refers to the Jews, since the first person plural certainly means the same as 'those who were under the law' in 4.5; on the other hand, the 'you' who are about to turn back again to the στοιχεῖα by accepting the Jewish law without doubt refers to the Galatian Gentiles.

the basis of natural procreation. The flesh in 5.16ff. including 5.13 is, however, viewed from quite a different perspective. It is presented as a *personified power* which stands in dualistic antithesis to the Spirit, the enabling power of the new era. It 'sets its desires against the Spirit' (5.17) and produces its works against the fruit of the Spirit (5.19-21). For Paul the flesh is also an enslaving power of the old age, just like the law. Subordination to the rule of this power leads helpless people to transgress the law and thereby brings them under the curse of the law. For this reason it can be said that subjection to the flesh is equivalent to slavery under the law.

In summary, for Paul the law was given in addition to the promise in order to produce transgressions. The consequence is that the law imprisoned all the transgressors under its curse. Paul compares this imprisonment to being under the restrictive supervision of a pedagogue (3.25) and under the control of guardians and stewards (4.2). Further, he connects this confinement with the enslavement to other powers in the old age (1.4; 6.14): sin (3.22), the demonic forces (4.3, 9), and flesh (5.13, 16ff.).

Bondage under the law is the main characterization of the existence of the Jews before the coming of Christ. This particular slavery represents the universal human plight under sin, demonic powers and flesh. It is, however, the prologue to the redemption of Christ.

3. *Freedom from the Bondage of the Law*

After comparing being ὑπὸ νόμον with being ὑπὸ παιδαγωγόν, Paul declares in Gal. 3.25 that with the coming of Christ, the dominion of the law was brought to an end: ἐλθούσης δὲ τῆς πίστεως οὐκέτι ὑπὸ παιδαγωγόν ἐσμεν. The coming of faith here corresponds to the coming of Christ in 3.19c, 24 and 4.4.

How Christ came is described in 4.4b: ἐξαπέστειλεν ὁ θεὸς τὸν υἱὸν αὐτοῦ. This statement probably refers to God's act of sending his Son out of his previous state into this world. Although the verb ἐξαπέστειλεν does not necessarily assume the pre-existence of the Son,[1] the idea may well have been in Paul's mind in writing the verse, since he believed in it (1 Cor. 8.6b; 10.4; Phil. 2.6; Col. 1.15-17). Some suppose that the statement in 4.4b is part of pre-Pauline

1. Rengstorf 1964: 406.

material.[1] Even if this is so, it is highly probable that the notion of the Son's pre-existence was still present when Paul wrote the verse, in view of the fact that the idea is not unique to Paul but popular in the early Christian community (cf. Jn 1.1ff.; Heb. 1.2; Rev. 3.14).

Verse 4b further describes the manner of the appearance of the Son: γενόμενον ἐκ γυναικός, γενόμενον ὑπὸ νόμον. The former phrase clearly refers to his birth out of a woman, since the γίνομαι in it is used as 'a quasi-passive of γεννάω' (cf. 1 Esd. 4.16; Tob. 8.6; Wis. 7.3; Sir. 44.9; Jn 8.58).[2] The aorist participle γενόμενον indicates that the events of God's sending his Son and of the Son's birth from a woman were coincident (cf. Phil. 2.7).[3] Here it is emphasized that at his birth Christ assumed human nature and became a *real* human being (cf. Jn 1.14). This indicates 'the descent to the level of those whom he came to redeem'.[4]

The latter phrase is a bit perplexing. Burton views it as 'made subject to law' rather than 'born under the law'.[5] However, the participle γενόμενον here, as in the former phrase, probably denotes an action coinciding with that of the main verb ἐξαπέστειλεν. So it is more sensible to understand the phrase to mean 'born under the law'. Many interpreters see it as referring to Christ's birth in the Jewish people who were subject to all the requirements of the law.[6] However, we should remember my previous argument that 'under the law' in the given context means 'under the curse of the law'.[7] If this assumption is correct, what Paul means here is that at his birth Christ took upon himself the curse which the Jews had incurred because of their non-fulfilment of the law.[8] To my mind this points to the *deep condescension* of his incarnation.

This humiliating incarnation is the first significant step of Christ's redemptive work. It led him to be subject to all human weaknesses, to be misunderstood, despised, rejected, to suffer and eventually to die

1. Schweizer 1972: 374.
2. Bruce 1982a: 195.
3. Bruce 1982a: 196; Fung 1988: 182.
4. Burton 1921: 217; cf. Ridderbos 1953: 155.
5. Burton 1921: 218; cf. Schlier 1971: 196; Betz 1979: 207.
6. Burton 1921: 218; Arichea and Nida 1976: 90; Cole [1965] 1983: 115-16; cf. Fung 1988: 182.
7. See above Ch. 6.2.
8. Cf. Bruce 1982a: 196.

on the cross. On the cross he was completely forsaken by God.[1] In this way Christ carried the curse of the law and exhausted it on behalf of his people. He thereby redeemed his people from the curse (3.13).[2] This particular redemption of the Jews brought about a universal consequence, namely the redemption of all people from sin, demonic forces and flesh, for the Jews served as the representative of all humankind. In fact, in his incarnation, suffering and death Christ fully indentified himself with the Gentiles as well as with the Jews.

In the second part of his speech to Cephas (2.18-21), which corresponds to 3.23–4.7,[3] Paul speaks from the standpoint of the beneficiary of the redemptive work of Christ: ἐγὼ γὰρ διὰ νόμου νόμῳ ἀπέθανον, ἵνα θεῷ ζήσω (2.19a; cf. Rom. 7.4). This statement is made against Cephas's falling back into the bondage of the law by his withdrawal from table fellowship with the Gentile Christians in Antioch.[4] The first person singular ἐγώ is not used to refer to Paul himself alone, but primarily to represent the Jewish Christians in general. This means that what Paul is talking about here is not so much his own personal experience as something that is true of any Jewish believer.[5] The law in 2.19a as in 3.23–4.7 refers to a power of the old age, as the antithesis between νόμῳ and θεῷ indicates. It is to this law that the Christians died. This means their complete *separation* from the power of the law.[6] The consequence is that the law no longer has any claim on or control over them.

The death took place διὰ νόμου. How should we understand this? We should notice that the main clause of 2.19a is rephrased in 2.19b: Χριστῷ συνεσταύρωμαι. Here we see the close link between the death to the law 'through the law' and the crucifixion of Christ. As seen above, the law played a role in the death of Christ. The curse of the law caused Christ to descend to this world in a human form and to die on the cross for his people. In this sense, it can be said, Christ died 'through the law'.[7] By virtue of their participation in the death of

1. I have argued above that the crucifixion is actually a strong evidence that Christ had already become a curse. See above Ch. 2.2.b.
2. Cf. Cousar 1982: 94-95.
3. See above Ch. 1.2.b.ii.
4. See above Ch. 1.2.a.vi.
5. Cf. Burton 1921: 132.
6. The dative νόμῳ as θεῷ is a dative of relation. Cf. Rom. 6.10-11.
7. Cf. Burton 1921: 134.

Christ by faith, the believers also died 'through the law' (cf. Rom. 6.6; 7.4).[1] Thereby they have been freed from the condemnation of the law and its dominion. For Paul this release from the power of the law is an eschatological transfer from the old aeon to the new aeon (cf. 1.4; 6.14). It follows that the release is at the same time the release from other old powers such as sin, demonic forces and flesh.

This release opened up a new possibility for all the believers to 'live to God', as the ἵνα clause expresses. This new life to God has been customarily understood as life in the service of God, taking the dative θεῷ as a dative of advantage.[2] This sense may not be entirely excluded here. But I do not believe that it is what Paul really has in mind. It is to be noted that in 2.19a living to God is in direct contrast with dying to the law, an old power. This implies that the new life means life which is intimately related to the power of God and surrendered to his sovereign control.[3] To put it simply, it is life under the rule of God, the new Master. 2.20a describes this life as life lived and controlled by Christ dwelling in the believers, the Lord of the new era. In 5.25 the life is further characterized as living by the Spirit, the enabling power of God (cf. Rom. 8.10).

1. Cf. Lightfoot 1880: 118; Zahn 1907: 113; Burton 1921: 132-34.
2. E.g. Burton 1921: 134; Ridderbos 1953: 103; Fung 1988: 123.
3. Ebeling 1985: 138; cf. Guthrie 1973: 89-90.

Chapter 7

THE LAW AS AN EXPRESSION OF LOVE

1. *The Law and Love*

I have argued above that the two distinctive functions of the law, the obligation of the Sinai covenant and an enslaving power, were terminated by the redemptive work of Christ. Does this mean that the law does not have any place in the Christian life whatsoever? Is Paul's attitude towards the law in Galatians completely negative, as some scholars suggest?[1]

As seen above (Ch. 3.3.a), the agitators' preaching of a different gospel caused confusion, controversy and strife among the Galatian Christians, and thereby seriously threatened their unity. Paul has this concrete situation in mind, I believe, when he warns in 5.15: 'But if you bite (δάκνετε) and devour (κατεσθίετε) one another, take heed that you are not consumed by one another'. Note the present tense of the verbs 'bite' and 'devour'. In response to this crisis Paul urges the Galatians at the outset of his second exhortation (5.13) not to use their freedom as an opportunity for the flesh but to serve one another through love. And he goes on to give the reason why loving one another is so imperative in 5.14: 'For the whole law (ὁ πᾶς νόμος) is fulfilled (πεπλήρωται) in one word, "You shall love your neighbour as yourself"'. This general injunction in 5.13-14 is given more specific expression in 6.1-2 (cf. Ch. 1.2.b.ii).[2] In v. 1 Paul exhorts the Galatians to restore in a spirit of gentleness one who is caught in any trespass. He then says in v. 2: 'Bear one another's burdens, and in this

---

1. Drane 1975: 3-59; Hübner 1986: 15-50.
2. I am not saying that Paul in 6.1-2 deals with an actual case of wrongdoing.

way you will fulfil (ἀναπληρώσετε[1]) the law of Christ (τὸν νόμον
τοῦ Χριστοῦ)'.

What needs to be observed here is that the law in 5.14 and 6.2 is
understood in a positive sense. Paul does not say that love supersedes
the law, making it useless, but that love is the fulfilment of the law (of
Christ). This is quite surprising in view of Paul's previous harsh
polemic against the law which he delivers up to 5.12—justification not
by the works of the law, the curse of the law, its transgression-
provoking function, and bondage under the law. At this point several
questions should be raised: how ought we to understand the positive
statements about the law in relation to the entirely negative view of
the law in previous sections? Does Paul, as Räisänen suggests,[2] contradict himself? Does he introduce a different kind of law? Or does he
put forward another dimension of the law?

A proper understanding of the positive statements about the law in
5.14 and 6.2 requires us first to discuss the identity of ὁ πᾶς νόμος
and ὁ νόμος τοῦ Χριστοῦ respectively. It is widely held that ὁ πᾶς
νόμος in 5.14 refers to the law of Moses. Hübner thinks, however,
that the popular view creates an internal discrepancy. In 5.3 Paul
urges the Galatians not to accept circumcision, for otherwise they
would have to keep the whole law (ὅλος ὁ νόμος). The implication of
this admonition is that the Galatians are not to obey the whole law.
But in 5.14 Paul goes on to claim that it is obligatory for Christians to
fulfil the whole law (ὁ πᾶς νόμος) through the commandment to love.
For Hübner this claim contradicts the injunction in 5.3 if Paul is
understood, as is usual, to speak of the same law in both passages. In
order to eliminate this problem, Hübner proposes that ὁ πᾶς νόμος in
5.14 should not be taken as identical with ὅλος ὁ νόμος in 5.3 but
rather as antithetical to it. According to him, the former, as the attributive position πᾶς suggests, refers to the totality of the law, while
the latter refers to the sum-total of the individual precepts of the law.
Thus, for Hübner, ὁ πᾶς νόμος does not refer to the Mosaic law but

---

1.   According to Metzger (1971: 598), this future indicative ἀναπληρώσετε is
slightly preferable to the aorist imperative ἀναπληρώσατε 'on the basis of early
and diversified external attestation (𝔓[46] B G and most ancient versions), as well as
transcriptional probability (scribes would be likely to conform the future to the
preceding imperatives, καταρτίζετε (v. 1) and βαστάζετε)'.

2.   Räisänen 1983: 62ff.

represents a radical reduction of its commands to a single command, that is, the love command which holds good for Christians. As such the expression is ironic, exploiting the Jewish understanding of the whole law. Therefore it is not a positive reference to the Mosaic law at all.[1]

It is certainly possible to suppose that Paul does not use ὁ πᾶς νόμος in 5.14 in exactly the same sense as he uses ὅλος ὁ νόμος in 5.3. Hübner may be right in arguing that ὁ πᾶς νόμος, with its unusual attributive position of πᾶς, emphasizes the totality of the law as distinct from the individual precepts of the law.[2] But I disagree with Hübner's contention that ὁ πᾶς νόμος does not refer to the Mosaic law at all but only to the love command. As seen just above, the main motivation for formulating this contention is the assumption that the statements in 5.3 and 5.14 stand in tension with each other if we suppose that Paul has the same law in mind in both statements. In my opinion this assumption is mistaken. To be sure, the statement in 5.3 does appear to imply that Christians are not bound to keep the whole law. However, we should bear in mind that Paul is talking here about the law in terms of the *Mosaic covenant*. This law is the obligation of the old covenant. For the essential meaning of Paul's warning in 5.3 is this: every one who receives circumcision to participate in the Sinai covenant is obliged to conform to all the demands of the law in order not to be brought under its curse (cf. 3.10). But the believers who depend upon the grace of Christ by faith are, as argued above, free from such an obligation (cf. 5.4). This is not to say, however, that the law which is an expression of God's holy will does not have any role at all in Christian ethics. Thus, I suggest that to interpret ὁ πᾶς νόμος in 5.14 to be a reference to the Mosaic law (as the majority of interpreters do) does not necessarily put 5.14 in conflict with 5.3.

Moreover, it is most unlikely that by the expression ὁ πᾶς νόμος Paul means, as Hübner suggests, the love command rather than the Mosaic law. If this were the case, I think, Paul would have given a clear indication of it. For, when Paul wrote 5.14, he must have been aware that the Gentile Galatians were so preoccupied with circumcision and the law that they would naturally understand his expression ὁ

1. Hübner 1986: 36ff.; cf. Hübner 1975: 243-48.
2. Cf. Robertson 1919: 419; Ridderbos 1953: 201 n. 3; Betz 1979: 274-75; Bruce 1982a: 241; Fung 1988: 245; Kertelge 1989: 335.

πᾶς νόμος to mean the Mosaic law. As far as I can see, however, there is no definite hint that Paul suddenly changed the meaning of νόμος in 5.14. In fact, the Greek word had never at any previous time meant anything radically different from Torah.[1]

Furthermore, we should notice that in 5.14 Paul, speaking of the fulfilment of ὁ πᾶς νόμος, quotes Lev. 19.18 ('You shall love your neighbour as yourself') which serves as a basis for a standard Jewish summary of the law.[2] Does this not indicate that Paul makes no sharp distinction between the whole law and the Mosaic law, though he does not fully agree with the Jewish notion of the summary of the law (see below)? Similarly, in Rom. 13.8 he says: 'he who loves his neighbour has fulfilled the law'. He then goes on to quote the same Levitical passage as summing up four of the Ten Commandments and 'any other commandment' (Rom. 13.8). Here it is even clearer that the law which is fulfilled in love is the Jewish law. In this connection Hübner advances the thesis that a significant development in Paul's thought about the law takes place from Galatians to Romans. Is it not natural, however, to expect Paul to refer to the same law when he cites the same OT passage in the two letters which are chronologically close to each other?[3] Thus we come to the conclusion that the common view of ὁ πᾶς νόμος as the Mosaic law is correct.

The question then remains: what about ὁ νόμος τοῦ Χριστοῦ in 6.2? This has been an extremely baffling phrase to many interpreters. It is not therefore surprising that a variety of opinions about the meaning of the phrase have been proposed. Davies claims that ὁ νόμος τοῦ Χριστοῦ is to be viewed as 'the law of the messiah', a new messianic Torah. In his opinion, Paul found in the words of Jesus the basis of a new kind of Christian halakah.[4] This claim is based on the alleged Jewish expectation of a new Torah which the messiah would bring. Davies adduces several rabbinic passages such as *Targ. Isa.* 12.3, *Qoh. R.* 2.1 and 12.1, *Targ. Song* 5.10, *Yal. Isa.* 26, and

---

1.   In the hypothetical statement in Gal. 3.21b Paul may well mean any divine law by νόμος, but even then he cannot conceive of such a law outside the framework of the Mosaic law. There is another instance where νόμος does not refer to the Mosaic legislation in particular: the law in 4.21b refers to the Pentateuch. See above Ch. 4; cf. Barclay 1988: 137.
2.   See Sanders 1977: 112-14.
3.   Cf. Sanders 1983: 96-97; Räisänen 1983: 27 n. 72; Barclay 1988: 137.
4.   Davies 1952: 92-93; cf. Davies 1948: 142ff.

Cant. R. 2.13, to show that in the messianic era a new Torah would be promulgated.[1] Here Davies is fully aware of the objection that the rabbinic passages which envisage the introduction of a new Torah are all of late date and the result of Christian influence.[2] But he argues that the absence of any specific early references to a new Torah may be due to deliberate surgery in view of the rabbis' counter-claims of the eternal validity of the Mosaic law against Christian propaganda of a new Torah, counter-claims which can be detected in *Deut. Rab.* 8 and *b. Šab.* 104a (cf. Justin Martyr, *Dial.*).[3] It is doubtful, however, whether the early Christian writers viewed the sayings of Jesus as a new Torah as against the Mosaic Torah.[4] Further, it is not likely, as Banks argues,[5] that the rabbinic passages to which Davies appeals concern the promulgation of a new Torah, but rather that these passages refer to a new interpretation of the Mosaic Torah. Billerbeck also asserts in his comment on Gal. 6.2:

> Even in rabbinic circles a 'Torah of the messiah' was spoken of; it was not, however, understood as a Torah which would supersede and replace the Torah of Moses, but rather as a new interpretation of the old Torah, which, by the power of God, the Messiah might bring and teach, so that his Torah would appear in a way as a new Torah.[6]

Thus we must conclude that Davies's thesis is highly implausible.[7]

Equally improbable is Stuhlmacher's thesis that the law of Christ is the Zion Torah, a prophetically envisaged new revelation (Isa. 2.2-4; 25.7-9; Jer. 31.31ff.; Ezek. 20; 36.22-28; 40-48; Mic. 4.1-4). According to Stuhlmacher, this Torah corresponds eschatologically to the Sinai Torah, but is not simply identical with it. The eschatological Torah goes forth from Zion, not from Sinai. Due to the gift of the Spirit and the destruction of death, this Zion Torah is to be of itself clear and livable. It is not directed to Israel alone but to all nations. In this way the new Torah brings to eschatological fulfilment the

1. Davies 1952: 69-76; cf. Schweitzer 1931: 187-93; Schoeps 1961: 171-75.
2. Cf. Klausner 1956: 446-49; Banks 1974a: 183-85.
3. Davies 1952: 86-89; cf. Longenecker [1964] 1976: 184-85.
4. Cf. Banks 1974a: 185.
5. Banks 1974a: 183-85.
6. Billerbeck 1926: 577.
7. Davies (1952: 90) himself admits that 'the evidence that we have been able to adduce in favor of a new Messianic Torah cannot be regarded as very impressive'.

spiritual intention of the Sinai Torah.[1] However, in the prophetic passages on which Stuhlmacher builds his thesis there is no indication of the anticipation of a *different* Torah from the Sinai Torah. Jer. 31.31-33 and Ezek. 36.22-28, which Stuhlmacher regards as 'the most distinctive evidence' for his daring idea, speak only of the supernatural change in people's *attitude* to the Mosaic Torah, not in the content of the Torah.[2]

Dodd understands the law of Christ to be a code of sayings of the Lord. He thinks that in a series of moral exhortations in Gal. 6.1-5 where the expression ὁ νόμος τοῦ Χριστοῦ occurs, Paul is alluding to Jesus' teaching in Mt. 23.4 and 18.15-16. Thus 'fulfilling the law of Christ' connotes the intention to carry out the precepts of Jesus Christ given to his disciples and handed down in the church.[3] It is true that Paul is acquainted with the sayings of Jesus (cf. Rom. 12.14; 13.7; 14.13, 14; 1 Cor. 7.10; 9.14; 11.23ff.; 1 Thess. 5.2, 13). It is far-fetched, however, to suggest that the terms βάρη (Gal. 6.2) and φορτίον (6.5) are echoes of φορτία βαρέα in Mt. 23.4, and that the admonition about restoring the falling brother in Gal. 6.2 is an allusion to the church order in Mt. 18.15-16, because the contexts of both Mt. 23.4 and 18.15-16 are very different from the context of Gal. 6.2 and 5.[4] Further, even if we willingly accept the suggestion of Dodd, I cannot agree with him that Paul regards the teaching of Jesus as a new law replacing the Mosaic law. Notice that in the entire letter to the Galatians Paul never appeals to Jesus' words to substantiate his exhortation. Instead, in Gal. 5.14 he quotes a passage from the Mosaic law, Lev. 19.18, in support of his injunction regarding mutual love. Dodd, on the basis of the statement of Gal. 5.18, believes that the Mosaic law is no longer valid for Christians.[5] As argued earlier,[6] however, ὑπὸ νόμον in this verse means no more than under the curse of the law. Moreover it is to be noted that in the immediate context (5.16-18) being under the law is compatible with subjection to the flesh which causes one to produce the works of the flesh (5.19-

1. Stuhlmacher 1986: 114ff., 125ff.; cf. Gese 1981: 80-92.
2. Cf. Räisänen 1983: 239-45; Kalusche 1986: 200-201.
3. Dodd 1953: 100-101, 108-109.
4. Cf. Barclay 1988: 129 n. 73.
5. Dodd 1953: 100.
6. See above Ch. 6.2.

21a) and thereby leads him to condemnation (5.21b). If I am correct, it then follows that Gal. 5.18 does not necessarily imply the complete abolition of the law in the new era.

Many scholars suggest that the law of Christ refers back to the commandment of love in 5.14.[1] But this view is not based on a correct observation of the syntactic structures of 5.14 and 6.2. In 5.14 the love commandment is presented as the *means* of the fulfilment of the whole law; however, the law of Christ in 6.2 is *something to be fulfilled* (i.e. the *object* of the fulfilment) by bearing one another's burdens, a concrete act of love. This clearly shows that the law of Christ is different from the love commandment.

Some interpreters take the νόμος in the expression ὁ νόμος τοῦ Χριστοῦ in a metaphorical sense.[2] In their opinion, the law of Christ does not refer to any specific legislation but to a governing principle of the Christian life which is paradigmatically manifested in Jesus Christ. However, this theory, including all the other preceding theories, ignores the close connection between 5.14 and 6.2. Both of these statements concern the same theme, the fulfilment of the law by love. Note that the main verbs of the two statements (πεπλήρωται in 5.14; ἀναπληρώσετε in 6.2) are synonymous, having the same verb-stem.[3] The essential difference is that 5.14 speaks in general terms while 6.2 speaks in specific terms.[4] Actually, the injunction 'Bear one another's burdens' in 6.2 is nothing more than a specific expression of the general commandment 'You shall love your neighbour as yourself' in 5.14. These observations compel us to understand the law of Christ in 6.2 to point to the same thing as the whole law in 5.14 does. Since the whole law refers to the Mosaic law, the law of Christ must be taken as *another reference to the Mosaic law.*[5]

In this connection there is an opposing view that the law of Christ cannot be regarded as the same as the Mosaic law in view of the flat

1. Gutbrod 1967: 1076; Furnish 1968: 64; Beker 1980: 105; Fung 1988: 288-89; cf. Bruce 1982a: 261; Hamerton–Kelly 1990b: 66-70.
2. Guthrie 1973: 143; Räisänen 1983: 80; Hays 1987: 175-76; Longenecker 1990: 275-76; cf. Burton 1921: 329.
3. I understand the implicit relationship of 6.2a and 6.2b to be condition–result. See above Ch. 1.2.a.xv.
4. My structural analysis shows that the pericopae 5.13-24 and 5.25-6.10 stand in general–specific relationship. See above Ch. 1.2.b.ii. Cf. Furnish 1972: 99.
5. Cf. Sanders 1983: 97-98; Barclay 1988: 131-32; Kertelge 1989: 333.

contrast between the law and Christ in Galatians.[1] In my opinion,
however, this view is not valid, because some of the dominant
oppositions in the letter include those between the works of the law
and faith in Christ and between slavery under the law and sonship in
Christ, but *not* between the law itself and Christ himself.

Here a question is posed: if the law of Christ, like the whole law in
5.14, is a reference to the Mosaic law, why does Paul call it, not just
'the law', as he usually does when speaking of the Mosaic law, but 'the
law *of Christ*'? It is noteworthy that in the entire Pauline letters this
phrase appears only in Gal. 6.2 (cf. 1 Cor. 9.21). In my view, as in
others',[2] it is used *polemically*. As my reconstruction of the argument
of the opponents shows,[3] the opponents combine the law and Christ in
order to reinforce their demand that the Galatians should accept the
Mosaic law to enter the covenant community of God. Paul vigorously
opposes this false theology that for the Gentiles the law is an entrance
requirement. But he agrees with the opponents that the law and Christ
are not irreconcilable entities. The opponents preached that Christ did
not come to abolish the Mosaic law but to affirm and reinterpret the
law (cf. Mt. 5.17).[4] Of course, Paul does not entirely concur with this
statement of the opponents, but he at least admits that Christ did not
completely abrogate the law and that it is therefore still valid for the
Christian in some sense (see below). If this is correct, we can then say
that Paul probably adopts the expression 'the law of Christ' from the
preaching of the opponents. But he uses it in a different context (i.e.
Christian paraenesis), so that on the one hand he blunts the force of
the opponents' argument and on the other hand demonstrates that his
gospel is not antinomian.[5]

If both ὁ πᾶς νόμος and ὁ νόμος τοῦ Χριστοῦ are references to
the law of Moses, how should we understand the statement in 5.14 and
6.2 that the law (of Christ) is fulfilled through love?[6] The key word
here is 'fulfil'. For this English word two Greek words are, as seen
above, employed in Galatians: πληρόω in 5.14; ἀναπληρόω in 6.2.

1. Eckert 1971: 160-61; Hays 1987: 276; cf. Hamerton-Kelly 1990b: 68.
2. Stoike 1971: 238ff.; Betz 1979: 300-301; Brinsmead 1982: 163ff.
3. See above Ch. 3.3.a.
4. See above Ch. 3.3.a.
5. Cf. Betz 1979: 300-301; Barclay 1988: 132-35.
6. The sentence of Gal. 6.2 can be changed this way: the law of Christ is
fulfilled through bearing one another's burdens (a concrete act of love).

But in Romans, where the two other mentions of fulfilling the law in Paul occur, only πληρόω is used (8.4; 13.8; cf. 13.10).

Some interpreters view πληρόω as synonymous with ποιέω.[1] As Betz correctly observes,[2] however, Paul makes a careful distinction between 'doing' and 'fulfilling' the law. For Paul, the Jews under the administration of the Sinai covenant are obliged to 'do' every precept of the law (Gal. 3.10, 12; 5.3; Rom. 10.5). In contrast, Christians under the administration of the new covenant are not under such an obligation, but 'fulfil' the law through love. 'Doing' the law is the main task of the Jews, the circumcised, but it is not required of Christians. In fact, Christians are *never* commanded to 'do' the law. 'Fulfilling' the law, however, describes the Christians'—and only the Christians'—relationship with the law (Gal. 5.14; 6.2; Rom. 8.4; 13.8; cf. Rom. 13.10; Mt. 5.17). As Van de Sandt observes, the combination of νόμος and πληρόω or its equivalent never appears in the Septuagint, apocryphal, pseudepigraphical or other Jewish literature.[3] Räisänen appeals to Rom. 2.14-15 against the distinction between 'doing' and 'fulfilling' the law, arguing that 'the Gentiles Paul had in mind could not "do" the law (or its ἔργον) in any other sense than the Christians "fulfilled" it, i.e. by living according to its central principle(s)'.[4] That the Gentiles sometimes 'do' by nature 'the things of the law' (τὰ τοῦ νόμου) cannot, however, be regarded as the same thing as that Christians 'fulfil' the law through love.[5]

Furnish[6] and several recent translations such as NEB, JB, TEV and NIV take the verb πληρόω to be equivalent to the verb ἀνακεφαλαιόω (sum up) in Rom. 13.9. But this position cannot be maintained for two decisive reasons. First, it must be noted that in Rom. 13.8-9 Paul uses both πληρόω and ἀνακεφαλαιόω but clearly distinguishes the

1. Schlier 1971: 245; Räisänen 1983: 63-64 n. 104; Hübner 1986: 49 n. 81; Thielman 1989: 82; cf. Burton 1921: 294-95; Ridderbos 1953: 201 n. 4; Cole [1965] 1983: 156.
2. Betz 1979: 275; cf. Westerholm 1986-87: 233; Barclay 1988: 139.
3. Van de Sandt 1976: 364-70; cf. Barclay 1988: 138-39.
4. Räisänen 1983: 63-64 n. 104.
5. See below; cf. Westerholm 1986–87: 233-34 n. 16; Barclay 1988: 141 n. 114.
6. Furnish 1968: 200; Furnish 1972: 97; cf. Van de Sandt 1976: 371-77; Cole [1965] 1983: 156.

former in the sense of 'fulfil' from the latter in the sense of 'sum up'.[1] Secondly, there is no parallel to the use of πληρόω in the sense of 'sum up' in the NT, the Septuagint, or in the ancient Greek literature.[2]

In my opinion, the best interpretation is to take πληρόω to mean 'satisfy the true intention of',[3] since Christians are free from the old obligation to keep all the individual precepts of the law but are not without the law (cf. 1 Cor. 9.20-21). The statement that the law is fulfilled through love means, then, that the real purpose or meaning of the law's demands is fully satisfied through love. This realization can be understood in line with the fulfilment of a divine prophecy or promise (cf. Mt. 5.17), since the claim to its eschatological fulfilment also often involves satisfying its purport without bringing about all the particular details of its original formulation.[4] In fact, the word πληρόω is frequently used to express the full realization of the divine will and plan in the NT (cf. Gal. 4.4), as Moule notes.[5]

Does this in turn mean that love annuls or replaces or absorbs the entire law? Not at all! Love without any specific guidance becomes 'a vague benevolence or impulsive improvisation based on romanticism'.[6] We should note that Paul unambiguously states: 'Love does no wrong to a neighbour' (Rom. 13.10) in the context where the fulfilment of the law is spoken of. This statement immediately follows the quotation of four commandments from the Decalogue. This indicates that love does not violate those commandments. Further, Paul declares in 1 Cor. 13.6 '[Love] does not rejoice in unrighteousness but rejoices in the truth'. All this demonstrates that although love is not limited to formal adherence to the individual commandments of the law it does not disregard them. Rather, 'love puts the law in proper perspective', so that the law is liberated from being abused by people.[7] It seems to follow that for Paul the law is ultimately *an expression of love*.

In rabbinic Judaism also we find that love is regarded as a kernel of

1. Burton 1921: 295; cf. Fung 1988: 246.
2. See Delling 1968: 283-310.
3. Westerholm 1986–87: 234-35; Barclay 1988: 140-41; cf. Dunn 1988a: 423; Louw and Nida *et al.* 1988: 33.144; Longenecker 1990: 242-43.
4. Cf. Burton 1921: 295; Barclay 1988: 139-40; Dunn 1988a: 423.
5. Moule 1967–68: 293-320.
6. Schrage 1988: 217.
7. Cousar 1982: 131.

all the commandments of the Torah.[1] Hillel said to a would-be proselyte: 'What is hateful to you, do not do to your neighbour: that is the
whole Torah, while the rest is commentary thereof; go and learn it'
(*b. Šab.* 31a).[2] In the same vein Rabbi Akiba later said: 'Thou shalt
love thy neighbour as thyself, that is a great principle in the Torah'
(*Gen. Rab.* 24.7). In this regard we may quote one further saying:
'Charity and deeds of loving-kindness are equal to all the *mitsvot* in
the Torah' (*t. Peah* 4.19; *p. Peah* 15b).

It is important to realize, however, that this position adopted by the
rabbis is not exactly the same as Paul's. For the rabbis, keeping the
essential commandment of love does not lead to ignorance of any
other commandments given by God. In fact, they never advocated the
abandonment of actual obedience to the many commandments in
favour of freedom to live according to the single principle.[3] For Paul,
however, loving the neighbour does not necessarily require Christians
actually to perform all the individual regulations. In Galatians Paul
explicitly excludes circumcision and some other items of the law for
Christians, especially for Gentile converts. In Christ circumcision
means nothing (5.6; 6.15; cf. 2.3ff.; 6.12-13; Rom. 2.25-29; 1 Cor.
7.19; Phil. 3.3). Moreover, it is against the truth of the gospel for a
Jewish Christian to withdraw himself from eating with Gentile
Christians in order to keep the Jewish food regulations (2.11ff.; cf.
Romans 14; 1 Corinthians 8, 10). This implies that the kosher laws are
totally irrelevant for Christians. Furthermore, for Gentile believers
the observance of festival days required by the Torah amounts to
returning to the previous worship of the elemental spirits of the world
(4.10; cf. Rom. 14.5-6; Col. 2.16-17).[4]

As noted above (Ch. 5.3), these three items of the law have in
common a nationalistic character: they are all typically Jewish. In
Judaism they function as powerful Jewish symbols to distinguish Jews
from Gentiles. In Paul's view, however, they are no longer valid for
Christians. Why is this so? Sanders thinks that Paul does not offer any

1. Cf. Sanders 1977: 112-14; Sanders 1978: 112-17.
2. The authenticity of this saying of Hillel is debatable. See Neusner 1971: 338-
39; Hübner 1975: 249.
3. Cf. Sanders 1977: 114.
4. Cf. Sanders 1983: 100-101.

theoretical explanation for this question.[1] In my opinion, however, the answer is to be found in Paul's understanding of the Christ event. For Paul, Christ bore on the cross the curse of the law on behalf of his people and thereby inaugurated a new era (Gal. 3.13). In this age of grace the blessing of Abraham has reached all the nations (3.8-9, 14). God has accepted the Gentiles as well as the Jews only on the basis of faith in Christ.[2] This understanding has brought about a revolutionary change in Paul's concept of 'neighbour'. When he was in the practice of the Jewish religion he interpreted 'neighbour' to mean fellow Jew, including the full proselyte, just as other Jews usually did. But now that he is a Christian, Paul takes the term 'neighbour' to refer to fellow Christians, whatever their race or nationality.[3] As a result Paul, unlike the Jews, understands Lev. 19.18 to be a commandment to love not only the Jewish Christian but also the Gentile Christian who does not have the Jewish badges (Gal. 5.14; cf. Rom. 13.8-10; 15.2; Eph. 4.25; Jas 4.12). For this reason Paul comes to the conclusion that loving the neighbour entails the abandonment of those distinctive Jewish observances (circumcision, food regulations and festival days) which sharply mark the Jews off from the Gentiles. The insistence on these practices on the part of the Jewish Christians *in* the Christian community, in spite of their acceptance of the Gentile Christians as brothers, means creating a division in the community and thereby poses a serious threat to its unity of love. In fact, it contradicts the truth of the gospel of Christ (cf. Gal. 2.14ff.). No wonder then that those observances are an object (although not the object) of Paul's attack in Galatians and in other letters, as seen above.

Does this suggest that 'the whole law' which finds its fulfilment in the love of the neighbour (Gal. 5.14) is a reduced law excluding those three items of the law, as some argue?[4] Here it is to be borne in mind, as seen above, that the word 'fulfilment' does not carry any idea of complying with the literal requirements of the law but conveys a notion of realizing the true intention of the requirements. So it is not wrong to suppose that 'the whole law' refers to the law in its entirety.

1. Sanders 1983: 100ff.
2. See above Chs. 2.2.b, 5.1.
3. Montefiore 1962: 161-63; cf. Greeven 1968: 316-18.
4. Räisänen 1983: 26-27; Sanders 1983: 103; Schreiner 1989: 59-65; cf. Hübner 1986: 36ff., 84ff.

In my view, Paul's logic behind the statement of Gal. 5.14 runs like this:

1. In the old covenant the observance of the law was Israel's response to the saving grace of God revealed in the Exodus.
2. In the new covenant loving the neighbour is the Christian's response to God's saving grace revealed in the Christ event.[1]
3. Therefore, loving the neighbour is the *eschatological fulfilment* of the law as a whole.[2]

We can now say that although some of the stipulations of the law are no longer pertinent for Christians, the true spirit of the *whole* law is in some way realized through love. Of course, this is not to say that only the inner meaning of the law is relevant to the new people of God (cf. Rom. 2.29; Phil. 3.3). As Brooten shows,[3] Paul continues in many places to use the law as a concrete ethical guide. In Gal. 5.14 he quotes Lev. 19.18. In Romans, where the same idea of love as the fulfilment of the law (13.10) also appears, Paul cites the Decalogue in 13.9 (cf. 2.21-22), and has in mind Lev. 18.22 and 2.13 in condemning same-sex love in 1.24-27. Further, in 1 Corinthians he explicitly appeals to the law when commanding women to be subordinate in 14.34 and is doubtless thinking of Lev. 18.8 and 20.11 in rebuking the sexual immorality in 5.1-5.

All this makes it clear, it seems to me, that in Paul's view the law, for Christians, continues to be an expression of God's will, particularly an expression of love (cf. Rom. 7.12), in spite of the above-mentioned nationalistic limitation.[4] It serves as a norm and standard of Christian conduct if it is rightly interpreted. It is very important to note, however, that Paul never commands the believer to do or obey the law.[5] Rather, he just states that the law is fulfilled through love. This means that the fulfilment of the law is the *result* of love.[6] The same thing is observed in Gal. 6.2, where the fulfilment follows

1.   For Paul loving the neighbour, which is not separated from loving God, 'is not just an aspect of the Christian's new life but its whole content and mode' (Furnish 1968: 199).
2.   Cf. Hooker 1982: 48-49.
3.   Brooten 1990: 71-89; cf. Deidun 1981: 157-60.
4.   Cf. Kaiser 1983: 34-37.
5.   Cf. Furnish 1968: 187, 191, 199.
6.   Westerholm 1986-87: 235-37; cf. Betz 1979: 275; Harnisch 1987: 291.

bearing one another's burdens, a specific act of love. This is also the case in Rom. 13.8: 'he who loves his neighbour has fulfilled the law'. Now it is quite understandable why statements about the fulfilment of the law in Paul never appear in the imperative mood.

2. The Law and the Spirit

Paul's view of the law in Gal. 5.14 is further developed in the following section (5.16-24), as the introductory λέγω δέ[1] in 5.16 (cf. 4.1) indicates. Here Paul asserts that the fulfilment of the law is *ultimately* the outcome of living according to the Spirit (cf. Rom. 8.4). For love is the fruit of the Spirit (5.22).[2] As the metaphor 'fruit' suggests, the Spirit is not an aid to love (noun, not verb) but the inner source and force of love.[3] Love in the believer is rooted in the inward action of the Spirit (cf. Gal. 5.6; Rom. 5.5). Thus the law eventually finds its fulfilment in the Christian life under the power of the Spirit.

This understanding motivates the statement which comes at the end of the list of virtues: κατὰ τῶν τοιούτων οὐκ ἔστιν νόμος (5.23b). There are some problems involved in this succinct statement. The first question is whether the phrase τῶν τοιούτων is to be taken as masculine or neuter. Some interpreters prefer the first option, since the plural of τῶν τοιούτων does not agree with the singular of καρπός. They think that the phrase corresponds with οἱ τὰ τοιαῦτα πράσσοντες in 5.21b.[4] For them, the statement means: 'there is no law against such people'.[5] It is to be noted, however, that the fruit is made up of nine virtues and that the τῶν τοιούτων appears straight after the virtues. Further, it is more likely, as is often pointed out,[6] that the phrase corresponds with τὰ τοιαῦτα in 5.21b, which refer to the works of the flesh, rather than οἱ τὰ τοιαῦτα πράσσοντες. Thus it seems

1. NEB: 'I mean this'; JB: 'Let me put it like this'.
2. Love, which heads the list of virtues in Gal. 5.22-23, is the summation of all the other virtues. Cf. 1 Cor. 13.4-7.
3. Cf. Deidun 1981: 81; Barclay 1988: 119-22.
4. Cole [1965] 1983: 169; cf. Ridderbos 1953: 208.
5. Cf. Aristotle, *Pol.* 3.13.1284a 14:...κατὰ δὲ τῶν τοιούτων οὐκ ἔστι νόμος, αὐτοὶ γάρ εἰσι νόμος ('but there is no law against such men, for they are themselves a law').
6. Burton 1921: 319; Lenski [1937] 1961: 293; Schlier 1971: 262-63; Betz 1979: 288.

more natural to understand the τῶν τοιούτων to refer to those virtues which are multiple manifestations of the fruit of the Spirit.

Another problem is how to understand the preposition κατά in front of τῶν τοιούτων. Most scholars take the κατά in the sense of 'against'. But the NEB translates it as 'dealing with'. This translation receives strong support from Styler.[1] The rationale behind this seems to be the argument that the manifold manifestations of the Spirit belong to a sphere with which the law has no relation.[2] But there is no evidence in Galatians to support this argument. As observed above, Christian life in the Spirit eventually results in the fulfilment of the law, not in the invalidation of the law. One might point to Gal. 5.18 for the argument: 'But if you are led by the Spirit, you are not under the law.' As I have repeatedly maintained, 'under the law' means under the curse of the law. So it is a mistake to infer from the verse that the law has no role to play in the realm of the Spirit or that the Spirit provides the believers with ad hoc guidance in the concrete circumstances, rendering all the external precepts of the law superfluous.[3] It is implied in 5.21b ('as I have forewarned' [καθὼς προεῖπον), as argued above (Ch.3.3.a), that Paul already gave some form of practical regulations to the Galatian believers through whom the power of the Spirit had been manifested (3.1-5). There is another point which decidedly opposes the NEB translation: κατά with the genitive is never used in the sense of 'dealing with' or 'concerning' in the NT, though κατά with the accusative sometimes denotes 'with respect to' or 'in relation to'.[4] It is not surprising, then, that the unusual translation is not taken up by the REB (which adopts the popular rendering).

There is one more problem. Many scholars take the νόμος in 5.23b in a general sense, translating οὐκ ἔστιν νόμος into 'there is no law'.[5] As argued above (Ch. 4), however, in the context there is no hint which points in this direction. Rather, v. 23b fits in well with the

1.   Styler 1973: 179 n. 11.
2.   Cf. Arichea and Nida 1976: 141; Bruce 1982a: 255; Barclay 1988: 123.
3.   Cf. Lull 1980: 117; Westerholm 1984: 239; Westerholm 1988: 214; Barclay 1988: 116.
4.   Bauer 1979: s.v.
5.   E.g. Burton 1921: 318; Guthrie 1973: 140; Yates 1985: 110; Longenecker 1990: 263; cf. Ridderbos 1953: 199, 208; Stott 1968: 149; Betz 1979: 288; Barrett 1985: 77; Fung 1988: 273.

thoughts in 5.14 and 18 where the Mosaic law is spoken of (see below).

In the light of the above discussion, therefore, 5.23b should be translated this way: 'The law is not against such things.'[1] As the 'against' expresses opposition and antagonism,[2] this statement means that the law does not take a stand against the virtues enumerated in 5.22-23a (while the works of the flesh lead to condemnation, as 5.21 [cf. 5.18] says).[3] In fact, the virtues are in full harmony with what the law intends. Thus the understatement of 5.23b has the effect of an emphatic assertion that the fruit of the Spirit fully satisfies the true intention of the law.[4]

It is to be kept in mind, however, that the Spirit does not automatically ensure that the believers produce the virtues against which the law cannot pronounce any condemnation. It is noteworthy that in 5.13 the flesh is described as a serious threat to the moral life of the Galatians, namely the Gentile Christians, who have already experienced the influence of the Spirit. The flesh is an evil power of the old era, which was defeated by Christ on the cross (cf. 5.24) but not completely eliminated. It is *still* active, having its own 'passions and desires' (5.24) and producing its 'works' listed in 5.19-21 which are diametrically opposed to the fruit of the Spirit in 5.22-23. And thereby the flesh brings people outside Christ under the curse of the law (5.18; cf. 5.21b). In fact, the flesh functions as the antagonistic force of the Spirit, the divine power of the new messianic era (cf. Rom. 8.5ff.). The coming of the Spirit has brought the believers into the irreconcilable conflict between the flesh and the Spirit. Thus 5.17 says: ἡ γὰρ σὰρξ ἐπιθυμεῖ κατὰ τοῦ πνεύματος, τὸ δὲ πνεῦμα κατὰ τῆς σαρκός, ταῦτα γὰρ ἀλλήλοις ἀντίκειται, ἵνα μὴ ἃ ἐὰν θέλητε ταῦτα ποιῆτε.

This verse has been a vexing problem to many interpreters. Here scholarly opinions differ considerably. Some, relating Gal. 5.17 to Rom. 7.14-25, think that v. 17 presents a picture of the battle of the flesh and the Spirit, the result of which is for the flesh to keep the

1. Cf. Jewish New Testament: 'Nothing in the *Torah* stands against such things'.
2. Louw and Nida *et al.* 1988: 90.31.
3. Cf. Ridderbos 1953: 208.
4. Cf. Burton 1921: 318; Barclay 1988: 122; Fung 1988: 273.

believers from following the leadings of the Spirit.[1] Others, in the light of the explicit promise in the preceding v. 16, presume that v. 17 speaks of the conflict between the flesh and the Spirit, the result (or the purpose) of which is for the Spirit to prevent the believers from satisfying the desires of the flesh.[2]

It must be noted, however, that v. 17, especially the main clause of v. 17b (ταῦτα γὰρ ἀλλήλοις ἀντίκειται), clearly expresses *mutual* opposition between the flesh and the Spirit rather than the one-sided victory of either the flesh or the Spirit. This is further supported by the fact that there is no explicit indication which requires us to take the phrase 'the things which you want to do' in the subordinate clause in v. 17b to mean specifically the desires incited by the flesh or the desires prompted by the Spirit. Does it follow that the believers are a helpless battlefield of the two antagonistic powers, as Burton thinks?[3]

In my opinion, 5.17 expresses the idea that 'in the Spirit–flesh conflict it is impossible for the believer to remain neutral: he either serves the flesh or follows the Spirit'.[4] Here two presuppositions are implied. One is that the ἵνα in v. 17b denotes result.[5] The other is that 'you want' in the ἵνα clause refers to the human free will, not to the will of the flesh or of the Spirit.[6] It follows then that the believer does not have the free assertion of his or her own will. For a moral action he or she should *choose* which influence to yield to, that of the flesh or that of the Spirit.

This is not to say, of course, that there is a deadlock between the flesh and the Spirit and thus that victory is entirely dependent upon the choice of the believer.[7] It is extremely important to remember, however, that Christ delivered his people from the present evil age and its rulers including the flesh (Gal. 1.4). The believers have crucified the flesh by participating in the cross of Christ (5.24). As a result,

1. Lightfoot 1880: 210; Althaus 1951: 15-18; Ridderbos 1953: 203-204; Dunn 1975: 267-68; Cole [1965] 1983: 158; Räisänen 1983: 115 n. 107.

2. Jewett 1971b: 106-107; Guthrie 1973: 135-36; Arichea and Nida 1976: 135.

3. Burton 1921: 302: 'Does the man choose evil, the Spirit opposes him; does he choose good, the flesh hinders him'.

4. Fung 1988: 251; cf. Kümmel 1974: 106.

5. E.g. Lightfoot 1880: 210; Betz 1979: 279-80; Bruce 1982a: 244; Fung 1988: 250; cf. Burton 1921: 301.

6. Cf. Ellicott 1867: 115; Lull 1980: 114; Fung 1988: 251.

7. Cf. Mussner 1974: 377-78.

they now live in the Spirit (3.1-5; 5.25).[1]

On this theological basis Paul commands the Galatian Christians in 5.16a to 'walk by the Spirit' (πνεύματι περιπατεῖτε) in order to resist the disposition of the flesh. This is a typical Pauline indicative–imperative relationship (cf. Ch. 1.2.a.xiv). 'Walking by the Spirit' involves a serious *decision* to follow the direction of the Spirit. The Spirit is the divine power of the new messianic era which is able to defeat the power of the flesh, an evil power of the old age. If the believers submit themselves to the directing and controlling power of the Spirit, therefore, they will not satisfy the desire of the flesh (5.16b).[2]

There is the other side of this truth: the Spirit not only supplies the power to resist the flesh but also the power to produce the fruit of the Spirit which is chiefly characterized by love (5.22-23). In 4.6 the Spirit is represented as causing the believers to recognize God as Father (cf. Rom. 8.15).[3] To my mind, this recognition inevitably accompanies the realization of God's love revealed in the cross of his Son. In fact, Paul claims in Rom. 5.5 that 'the love of God has been poured out in our hearts through the Holy Spirit given to us'. 'The love of God' here is God's love to us (subjective genitive), not our love to God, as the following three verses (vv. 6-8) clearly indicate. If so, we may say that the Spirit further leads—or rather compels (cf. 2 Cor. 5.14)—the believers to respond to the love of God. How to respond? For Paul, it should be done by loving their neighbours who are primarily fellow members of the community of God (cf. Gal. 5.13-14). As God demonstrated his love to his people by sacrificing his Son for them, the believers should show their love to God by serving their neighbours.[4] In Paul's view, this love of the believers which is enabled by the Spirit (cf. 5.6) is the fulfilment of the law. Thus Paul declares in 5.18 that if the believers are led by the Spirit, they are not under the curse of the law. But yielding to the influence

1. Cf. Cosgrove 1988b: 169ff.
2. Gal. 5.16b (καὶ ἐπιθυμίαν σαρκὸς οὐ μὴ τελέσητε) is a statement of a definite promise, as οὐ μή; with the aorist subjunctive expresses 'the most definite form of negation regarding the future' (Blass and Debrunner 1961: §365).
3. To be sure, in Gal. 4.6 it is the Spirit who cries, but he cries out of the hearts of the believers. It is noteworthy that in 2.20 there is no distinction between Christ's living in the believer and the believer's living by faith in the Son of God.
4. Cf. Hays 1987: 268-90.

of the flesh means renouncing the benefits of the Christ event and returning to the old bondage of the flesh. Its result is to produce the works of the flesh (5.19-21a), leading to condemnation. 5.21b says, 'those who practise such things [the works of the flesh] shall not inherit the kingdom of God' (cf. 6.8).

In conclusion, we can say that, while the law, as a result of the redemption of Christ, lost its two distinctive functions as the obligation of the Sinai covenant and as an enslaving power, for Paul the law still serves as an expression of God's will in spite of its nationalistic limitation, that is, distinguishing Jews from Gentiles.[1] It is significant, however, that Paul never commands the believer to obey the law. In the old covenant dispensation compliance with all the external demands of the law was the essential obligation of Israel. But this is no longer the case in the new covenant dispensation. What is required of the Christian redeemed by Christ is a much deeper commitment, the *total submission of his whole life* to the sovereign control of the Spirit (cf. Rom. 2.29; 7.6; 2 Cor. 3.6). The consequence is that the Christian is impelled and enabled to love his neighbour in response to God's grace unfolded in the cross. In this Christian love the whole intention of the law is fully realized. This implies, I believe, that for Paul all the commandments of the law explicitly or implicitly express the all-encompassing demand of love.[2]

1. Cf. Mohrlang 1984: 34-35.
2. Cf. Westerholm 1988: 199-201.

Chapter 8

CONCLUSIONS

In this study I have discussed Paul's view of the law in Galatians in the light of my preliminary consideration of the structure of the letter, the perspective of Paul, and the argument and identity of the opponents. Now it is time to draw from this discussion some implications for Pauline theology of the law, especially in relation to some of the most important current opinions. In doing so, it seems sensible first to gather together the main results of the discussion in summary form.[1]

νόμος occurs 32 times in Galatians. Whether with or without the definite article, the Greek word is used predominantly to refer to the Mosaic law imposed upon Israel on Mount Sinai (3.17; cf. 4.24), the two exceptions being in 3.21b and 4.21b where any divine law (whose supreme example is of course the Mosaic law) and the story of Hagar in the Pentateuch are in view respectively. For Paul the law is a complete unit without any distinction between its ceremonial and ethical aspects (cf. 5.3, 14).

The law functions on three different levels in Galatians. First, it serves as the *obligation of the Sinai covenant*. Abraham's experience of justification by believing the God of the free promise (3.6-9) demonstrates that the law which was added 430 years later than the promise (3.17) was never designed to be a means of justification which entails entering a relationship with God. This is further substantiated by the Galatians' receiving the Spirit by the hearing of faith (3.1-5) and not by the works of the law—the Spirit which is the actual fulfilment of the promise given to Abraham (3.14). For Paul, the law was rather the condition for staying in the covenant relationship with God. The law was originally addressed to the community of Israel who had already entered a special relationship with God. This means

---

1.   Summaries of the preliminary investigations are found at the end of their respective chapters.

that the covenant was first established by God's gracious initiative and then the law was proclaimed. It follows that the law had nothing to do with the establishment of the covenant but was given as a means for a proper response to the grace of God. It required Israel to live a holy life before God which inevitably entailed separation from the ungodly nations. Obedience to the law enabled Israel to remain in the covenant relationship with God (3.12). But its transgression incurred a curse, because it meant repudiating covenant-loyalty to God and so breaking the covenant. For this reason Paul states in Gal. 3.10 that all who fail to keep the law perfectly are cursed. Christ has removed this curse of the law on the cross and has established a new covenant (3.13). As a result, the old function of the law as the covenant obligation and its accompanying social role to mark the Jews out from the Gentiles were invalidated (cf. Rom. 10.4).

Secondly, the law functions as *an enslaving power*, seen from the perspective of the history of salvation. For Paul the law, in addition to the promise, was given by God in order to produce or provoke transgressions (Gal. 3.19; cf. Rom. 5.20) by providing an operational base for sin to kindle man's sinful passions (Rom. 7.5ff.). In consequence, all people were imprisoned under the power of sin (Gal. 3.22). More particularly, all the transgressors were kept in custody under the law (3.23). 'Under the law' here means 'under the curse of the law' in view of the statements in 3.10, 13 and 4.4-5. Paul compares this bondage of the law with being under a pedagogue (3.25), being under guardians and stewards (4.2), and being under the elemental spirits of the world (4.3, 9). The point of comparison here is lack of freedom, absence of self-determination, and subordination to foreign control. Further, Paul relates the existence under the law to subjection to the flesh in 5.16-18 which stands in opposition to the Spirit. However, with the coming of Christ the slavery of the law was brought to an end (3.25). At his birth Christ took upon himself the curse of the law, and carried it during his whole life on earth and eventually exhausted it on the cross on behalf of his people (3.13; 4.4). By virtue of their participation in the death of Christ by faith, the believers died in relation to the enslaving power of the law (2.19). Thereby they were liberated from it (5.1, 13) and now live under the sovereign rule of God, the new Master (2.19; cf. 2.20; 5.25).

Thirdly and lastly, in spite of the termination of the two aforementioned functions by the redemptive work of Christ, the law still plays a role as *an expression of God's will*, especially *an expression of love*, in Christian ethics. In Gal. 5.14 Paul claims that the whole law is fulfilled through loving the neighbour. In particular, in 6.2 he states that the law of Christ, which is a reference to the Mosaic law, is fulfilled through bearing one another's burdens, a concrete act of love. As the verb 'fulfil' ($\pi\lambda\eta\rho\acute{o}\omega$ in 5.14; $\dot{\alpha}\nu\alpha\pi\lambda\eta\rho\acute{o}\omega$ in 6.2) denotes 'satisfy the true intention of', these statements mean that the real purpose of the law is fully satisfied through love of the neighbour. However, loving the neighbour does not necessarily require Christians to keep all the precepts of the law. In Galatians Paul explicitly rules out circumcision, food regulations and festival days for Christians, especially Gentile converts. The reason is that the observance of these typically Jewish regulations on the part of the Jewish Christians in the Christian community creates a division in the community and so poses a serious threat to its unity of love. In spite of this nationalistic limitation the law continues to be an expression of God's will. It is noteworthy that in many places Paul explicitly and implicitly appeals to the law for his ethical teachings (Gal. 5.14; Rom. 1.24-27; 13.9; 1 Cor. 5.1-5; 14.34). It is striking, however, that he never commands his converts to do or obey the law. Instead, he simply declares that the fulfilment of the law is the result of love (5.14; 6.2; Rom. 13.8). In 5.22 Paul goes on to state that love is the fruit of the Spirit. It follows that the fulfilment is ultimately the outcome of walking by the Spirit. If the believer submits himself to the directing and controlling power of the Spirit, he is compelled and empowered to love his neighbours in response to God's love revealed in the cross. In this love of the believer the law finds the realization of its true intention. Thus for Paul the law is in essence an expression of love.

It is now appropriate to discuss the implications of this study for the current debate on Paul's theology of the law. It is, of course, not possible for me to engage in a detailed discussion of all the issues of the debate, because my research has been limited to Galatians only. Nonetheless, the discussion here will offer some significant help to settle the scholarly dispute over several broader issues of the theology.

1. *Paul does not misrepresent the law in Judaism.* Räisänen charges Paul with giving his readers a totally distorted picture of the Jewish law. The sharp antithesis between the works of the law and faith in Christ (or grace or the Spirit) in Gal. 2.16, 21; 3.2-5, 9-12; 5.4 and

Rom. 3.27-28; 4.2-5, 14; 6.14; 10.5-6 suggests, in Räisänen's view, that Paul understands the law as a rival soteriological principle. For Paul, the law serves as the Jewish gateway to salvation. It occupies a place analogous to that taken by Christ in the new dispensation.[1] This presentation of the law by Paul, Räisänen thinks, contradicts the Jews' own understanding of the law. For the Jews in Paul's day, according to Räisänen following Sanders,[2] the law is not the means of salvation. God's grace, revealed in the establishment of the covenant, precedes man's obedience. The keeping of the law on man's part is an expression of his willingness to remain within the covenant, not a legalistic achievement.[3] Räisänen thus concludes that Paul misrepresents the law in Judaism.[4] This charge is not new. About twenty years before, Schoeps contended that Paul completely misapprehended the law as a saving principle by wresting the law from the context of God's covenant with Israel.[5]

We have to keep in mind, however, that the well-known contrast between the works of the law and faith in Christ was set forth not against the alleged legalistic function of the law in Judaism, but against the demand of the opponents that the Gentile Galatians should, besides faith in Christ, accept circumcision and the law in order to become full members of the covenant community of God.[6] For this demand makes the law (and circumcision) an extra entrance requirement for the Gentile Christians. But for Paul, as seen above, the law was never intended to be a way of salvation in God's plan (Gal. 3.6-9, 17). Rather, it is the obligation of the Sinai covenant established by God.

---

1.   Räisänen does not understand that Bultmannian anthropocentric 'hard legalism' as a perverted attitude, arising from human pride, is envisaged in Paul's polemics against the law. In his view, what Paul attacks is the Jewish Torah-centric 'soft legalism' (1980a: 68-72; 1983: 168-76).

2.   Sanders 1977: 33-428, especially 75, 422-23.

3.   Cf. Westerholm 1988: 105-40.

4.   Räisänen 1980a: 63-83; Räisänen 1983: 162-91.

5.   Schoeps 1961: 213-18.

6.   Sanders likewise maintains: 'The argument of Galatians 3 is against Christian missionaries, not against Judaism, and it is against the view that Gentiles must accept the law *as a condition* of or as a basic requirement for membership. Paul's argument is not in favor of faith per se, nor is it against works per se. It is much more particular: it is against requiring the Gentiles to keep the law of Moses in order to be true "sons of Abraham"' (1983: 19, italics his).

Obedience to the law is an expression of gratitude for the grace of God and of willingness to remain in the covenant (3.10, 12, 13). In fact, the law has the role of the *imperative* based on the *indicative* of God's gracious act. Thus it is quite obvious that Paul understands the law within the framework of the covenant and that he does not misrepresent the law.

This leads us to ask: why does Paul then reject law-observant Judaism? Is it because Paul is now convinced that salvation is available only in Christ although there is no inherent deficiency in the covenantal nomism of Judaism, as Sanders argues?[1] Or is it because Judaism 'is nationalistic—bound by its own history and culture to the extent that God's saving activity is envisaged in racial and cultural terms'?[2] There are of course some elements of truth in both of these theories. But neither is entirely satisfactory. In my opinion, the reason for Paul's rejection of Judaism is that he realizes, in the light of the Christ event, that by carrying away the curse of the law fallen on the Jews because of their transgression (Gal. 3.10, 13) Christ has fulfilled the promise of universal salvation which had been given to Abraham (Gen. 12.3; cf. Gal. 3.8) and has thus established a new covenant with all mankind in him. For Paul, the old covenant is no longer valid because it was broken by Israel who failed to keep the law.[3]

2. *Paul's view of the law in Galatians is not entirely negative.*
According to Hübner, Paul in Galatians takes an unreservedly hostile attitude towards the law. The law was given by demonic angels with the evil intention of stimulating transgressions.[4] Christians are totally free from the law; they are bound to obey only the command to love (5.14). ὁ πᾶς νόμος (5.14), which is distinguished from ὅλος ὁ νόμος (5.3), is not a reference to the Mosaic law but to the love command.[5] Earlier, Drane similarly denied the divine origin of the law[6] and the existence of any positive statements about the law in Galatians.[7]

---

1. Sanders 1977: 551-52; Sanders 1983: 47.
2. Barclay 1988: 240; cf. Barclay 1986: 11; Wright 1978: 61-88; Dunn 1983a: 95-122; Dunn 1985: 523-42.
3. See above Chs. 2.2.b, 5.2.
4. Hübner 1986: 26ff.
5. Hübner 1986: 36ff.
6. Drane 1975: 32-34.
7. Drane 1975: 5: 'we... hear his [Paul's] repeatedly devastating denunciations

To be sure, in Galatians there is no explicit mention that the law is holy, righteous or good (cf. Rom. 7.12). In Paul's view, the law serves to provoke transgressions (3.19). It brings all the transgressors under its enslaving power (3.23ff.). Christians are neither under its slavery (5.1, 13) nor under obligation to keep all its precepts (5.3). However, this is not to say, as argued in Chapter 7, that the law has no continuing role to play in the Christian life. 'The whole law' in 5.14 does not refer to the love command but to the law of Moses. Its real intention is realized in love of the neighbour (5.14; 6.2; cf. Rom. 8.4; 13.8, 10) which is made possible by the power of the Spirit (5.22). It follows that for Paul the law still serves as an expression of God's holy will for Christians. It seems to me that this idea is also presupposed in Paul's understanding of the law as the obligation of the Mosaic covenant. If it is not holy and righteous, how can the law offer the covenant life (i.e. life within the covenant) to those who obey it (3.12) or pronounce a curse against those who breach it (3.10)? As argued above (Ch. 6.1), Hübner's contention of the angelic origin of the law is unfounded.

If this is the case, there is no good reason for assuming a substantial development in Paul's thought about the law between the time he wrote Galatians and Romans. It has usually been contended that whereas Galatians presents the law in an exclusively negative light, Romans presents it in a somewhat positive light.[1] As seen just above, however, Paul in Galatians does not deny the divine origin of the law, its holy character or its continuing (though limited) role in Christian ethics, though he does not assert these points as explicitly as he does in Romans. To my mind, there is no evidence for the evolutionary growth of Paul's understanding of the law between the two letters. Of course, Hübner points to this fact: the notion of the transgression-provoking function of the law expressed in Gal. 3.19b is not found in Romans, where only the idea of the sin-revealing function of the law is set forth (3.20; 7.7).[2] But it should be kept in mind, as argued above,[3] that the statement of Rom. 5.20a ('the law came in that the

of the Old Testament Law and all that it stood for'.

1.   Drane 1975: 3, 109-36; Wilckens 1982a: 154-90; Wilckens 1982b: 17-26; Hübner 1986: 15-100; for my brief summary of their arguments, see Introduction.
2.   Hübner 1986: 69-83, especially 78-79.
3.   See Ch. 6.1; cf. Bruce 1982a: 176.

sinful deeds [παράπτωμα] might increase') is not markedly different from that of Gal. 3.19b.[1] They basically express the same idea: the law was added to aggravate the existing situation. In my view, it is still reasonable to suppose that Paul, reflecting upon the implications of his Damascus road experience,[2] worked out the basic framework of his theology of the law during his long (approximately eighteen-year) Christian experience before writing Galatians, even before his second visit to Jerusalem described in Gal. 2.1-10. In this theological framework he handles particular issues in specific situations with different emphases and in different tones.[3]

3. *Paul is not inconsistent in his treatment of the law in Galatians.* Räisänen, from the viewpoint of common sense logic, contends that 'contradictions and tensions have to be *accepted* as *constant* features of Paul's theology of the law'.[4] There are many areas in which Räisänen perceives inconsistency. (1) The concept of the law oscillates between the Jewish Torah (Rom. 2.12ff.; 1 Cor. 9.20-21; cf. Gal. 2.14-15) and a universal force enslaving Gentiles as well as Jews (Gal. 3.13-14, 23-26; 4.5-6; Rom. 7.4-6). (2) Paul does not make an explicit distinction between the moral and the ritual aspects of the law (Gal. 5.3); but he tacitly reduces the whole Torah to a moral law (Gal. 5.14; Rom. 13.8-10). (3) Paul sometimes speaks of the abolition of the law (Gal. 2.19; 3.15-20, 24-25; 4.5, 21-31; Rom. 6.14; 7.1-6; 10.4; 2 Cor. 3) but at other times asserts its continuing validity (Gal. 5.14; Rom. 3.31; 8.4; 13.8-10; 1 Cor. 7.19). (4) Paul implies that nobody is able to fulfil the law (Gal. 3.10; 5.3; Rom. 7.14-25). Yet he states that some non-Christian Gentiles actually do the law (Rom. 2.14-16, 26-27) and that Christians can fulfil it (Gal. 5.14ff.; Rom. 8.4; 13.8-10). (5) While generally referring to the law as given by God (Rom. 7.22; 8.7; 9.4; 1 Cor. 9.8-9), Paul once in the course of a heated debate also suggests that the law originated from angels and is thus inferior (Gal. 3.19-20). (6) Finally, there is one more contradiction found in Paul's discussion of the purpose of the law. On the one hand, the law was intended to

1. The παράπτωμα in Rom. 5.20a has a broader connotation than the παράβασις in Gal. 3.19b which did not exist between Adam and Moses.
2. See above Ch. 2.2.e.
3. Cf. Davies 1982: 4-16; Martin 1989: 53-55.
4. Räisänen 1983: 11, italics his.

increase and engender sinning (Gal. 3.19; Rom. 5.20; 7.5, 7-11;
1 Cor. 15.56; cf. Gal. 3.21); on the other hand, it was designed to
lead to life (Gal. 3.12; Rom. 7.10, 12, 14).[1]

Space does not permit a detailed examination of all the arguments of
Räisänen which concern the statements about the law in Galatians. But
I would like here to offer a brief criticism against each of the
arguments enumerated above. First, the apparent contrast between the
'we' in Gal. 3.13 and the Gentiles in 3.14 suggests that the first person
plural pronoun does not include the Gentiles. This means that those
who are subject to the curse of the law (3.13) are the Jews in
particular. 'Those who are under the law' in 4.5 also refers solely to
the people of the law. For Paul says to the Gentile Galatians in 4.9 that
to succumb to Judaizing pressure is not to return to the law but to the
elemental spirits. This compels us to take the 'we' who were confined
under the law in 3.23 in an exclusive sense.[2] Thus it is clear that in
Galatians Paul consistently uses the term law to refer to the Mosaic
law given to Israel. Secondly, if the πληρόω in 5.14 is not used in the
same sense as ποιέω but denotes 'satisfy the true intention of', as
argued above (Ch. 7.1), it is not necessary to understand 'the whole
law' in v. 14 to mean a reduced moral law, but rather the Torah in its
entirety whose real purpose is realized in love.[3] Thirdly, when Paul
talks about the abolition of the law, he has in mind the two functions
of the law which are the obligation of the Sinai covenant and an
enslaving power. Yet this is not to say that the law as an expression of
God's will is also invalidated forever.[4] Fourthly, Paul never maintains
that the Christians automatically fulfil the law, but rather that they can
do it only if they submit themselves to the directing and controlling
power of the Spirit.[5] Fifthly, in Gal. 3.15-22 Paul argues, to be sure,
that the law is inferior to the promise. This does not mean that the law
was given by angels, not by God. Rather, what Paul is trying to
convey in 3.19b is that angels served as an intermediary between God
and Israel in giving the law.[6] Lastly, it is true that Paul simultaneously

1. Räisänen 1983: 16-161, 199-202; cf. Räisänen 1980b: 304-305.
2. See above Ch. 2.2.b.
3. See above Ch. 7.1.
4. See above Ch. 7.
5. See above Ch. 7.2; cf. Cranfield 1990: 77-85.
6. See above Ch. 6.1.

speaks of both a negative purpose of the law and its positive purpose. It should be borne in mind, however, that in doing so he adopts more than just one perspective. From the standpoint of the covenant, Paul views the observance of the law as the condition for remaining within the covenant (Gal. 3.12);[1] from the standpoint of the history of salvation, however, he understands the role of the law as producing transgressions in order to worsen the existing situation (3.19b).[2]

All this demonstrates that Räisänen's approach to the law in Paul is too simplistic and fails to grasp the complexity of Paul's thought, though his argument is often impressive. We must conclude that at least in Galatians Paul's remarks on the law do not contradict each other. I believe that if in interpreting his statements of the same subject in his other letters we take into account the entire rhetorical structure, the rhetorical situation, the historical and social context and various theological perspectives of each of the letters, most (if not all) of the charges of Paul's inconsistency will be found to lack any real foundation.[3]

1.   See above Ch. 5.2.
2.   See above Ch. 6.1; cf. Weima 1990: 219-35.
3.   Cf. Beker 1988: 364-77; Beker 1989: 352-65.

BIBLIOGRAPHY

Alt, A.
1953   'Die Ursprünge des israelitischen Rechts', in *Kleine Schriften zur
            Geschichte des Volkes Israel* (Munich: Beck'sche
            Verlagsbuchhandlung): 278-332.
Althaus, P.
1951   ' "Dass ihr nicht tut, was ihr wollt": Zur Auslegung von Gal. 5,17',
            TLZ 76: 15-18.
Arichea, D.C., Jr, and E.A. Nida
1976   *A Translators Handbook on Paul's Letter to the Galatians* (New York:
            United Bible Societies).
Aune, D.E.
1981   Review of Hans Dieter Betz, *Galatians: A Commentary on Paul's
            Letter to the Churches of Galatia*, *RelSRev* 7: 323-28.
1987   *The New Testament in its Literary Environment* (Philadelphia:
            Westminster Press).
Badenas, R.
1985   *Christ the End of the Law: Romans 10.4 in Pauline Perspective*
            (JSNTSup, 10; Sheffield: JSOT Press).
Bahr, G.J.
1968   'The Subscriptions in the Pauline Letters', *JBL* 87: 27-41.
Baird, W.
1957   'What is the Kerygma? A Study of 1 Cor. 15:3-8 and Gal. 1:11-17',
            JBL 76: 181-91.
1988   'Abraham in the New Testament: Tradition and the New Identity', *Int*
            42: 367-79.
Bandstra, A.J.
1964   *The Law and the Elements of the World: An Exegetical Study in
            Aspects of Paul's Teaching* (Kampen: Kok).
1989   'The Law and Angels: *Antiquities* 15.136 and Galatians 3:19', *CTJ* 24:
            223-40.
Banks, R.
1974a   'The Eschatological Role of Law in pre- and post-Christian Jewish
            Thought', in Banks 1974b: 173-85.
Banks, R. (ed.)
1974b   *Reconciliation and Hope: New Testament Essays on Atonement and
            Eschatology Presented to L.L. Morris on his 60th Birthday* (Grand
            Rapids: Eerdmans).
Barclay, J.M.G.
1986   'Paul and the Law: Observations on Some Recent Debates', *Themelios*
            12: 5-15.

| 1987 | 'Mirror-reading a Polemical Letter: Galatians as a Test Case', *JSNT* 31: 73-93. |

1988   *Obeying the Truth: A Study of Paul's Ethics in Galatians* (SNTW; Edinburgh: T. & T. Clark).

Barrett, C.K.

1962   *A Commentary on the Epistle to the Romans* (BNTC; London: A. & C. Black).

1976   'The Allegory of Abraham, Sarah and Hagar in the Argument of Galatians', in Friedrich, Pöhlmann and Stuhlmacher 1976: 1-16.

1985   *Freedom and Obligation: A Study of the Epistle to the Galatians* (Philadelphia: Westminster Press).

Bauer, W.

1979   *A Greek-English Lexicon of the New Testament and Other Early Christian Literature* (trans. and adapted by W.F. Arndt and F.W. Gingrich; 2nd edn, rev. and adapted by F.W. Danker and F.W. Gingrich; Chicago: University of Chicago Press).

Baur, F.C.

1876   *Paul, the Apostle of Jesus Christ*, I (trans. E. Zeller; London: Williams & Norgate, 2nd edn).

Beare, F.W.

1959   *The Epistle to the Philippians* (BNTC; London: A. & C. Black).

Beker, J.C.

1980   *Paul the Apostle: The Triumph of God in Life and Thought* (Philadelphia: Fortress Press).

1988   'Paul's Theology: Consistent or Inconsistent?', *NTS* 34: 364-77.

1989   'Paul the Theologian: Major Motifs in Pauline Theology', *Int* 43: 352-65.

1990   'Romans 9–11 in the Context of the Early Church', in Migliore 1990: 40-55 (40-55).

Belleville, L.L.

1986   ' "Under Law": Structural Analysis and the Pauline Concept of Law in Galatians 3.21–4.11', *JSNT* 26: 53-78.

Berkouwer, G.C.

1965   *The Work of Christ* (trans. C. Lambregtse; Grand Rapids: Eerdmans).

Berevnyi, G .

1984   'Gal 2.20: A pre-Pauline or a Pauline Text?', *Bib* 65: 490-537.

Betz, H.D.

1975   'The Literary Composition and Function of Paul's Letter to the Galatians', *NTS* 21: 353-79.

1976   'In Defense of the Spirit: Paul's Letter to the Galatians as a Document of Early Christian Apologetics', in E. Schüssler Fiorenza (ed.), *Aspects of Religious Propaganda in Judaism and Early Christianity* (Notre Dame, IN: University of Notre Dame Press): 99-114.

1979   *Galatians: A Commentary on Paul's Letter to the Churches in Galatia* (Hermeneia; Philadelphia: Fortress Press).

1985   *2 Corinthians 8 and 9* (Hermeneia; Philadelphia: Fortress Press).

Billerbeck, P.
1926   *Kommentar zum Neuen Testament aus Talmud und Midrasch*, III
                (Munich: Beck'sche Verlagsbuchhandlung).
Bläser, P.
1941   *Das Gesetz bei Paulus* (NTA; Münster: Aschendorff).
Blair, E.P.
1965   'Paul's Call to the Gentile Mission', *BR* 10: 19-33.
Blank, J.
1968   *Paulus und Jesus: Eine theologische Grundlegung* (StANT; Munich:
                Koesel-Verlag).
Blass, F., and A. Debrunner
1961   *A Greek Grammar of the New Testament and Other Early Christian
                Literature* (trans. and ed. R.W. Funk; Chicago: University of Chicago
                Press).
Borgen, P.
1982   'Paul Preaches Circumcision and Pleases Men', in Hooker and Wilson
                1982: 37-46.
Bornkamm, G.
1974   'The Revelation of Christ to Paul on the Damascus Road and Paul's
                Doctrine of Justification and Reconciliation', in Banks 1974b: 90-103.
1975   *Paul* (trans. D.M.G. Stalker; London: Hodder & Stoughton).
Bring, R.
1961   *Commentary on Galatians* (trans. E. Wahlstrom; Philadelphia:
                Muhlenberg).
1966   'Das Gesetz und die Gerechtigkeit Gottes: Eine Studie zur Frage nach
                der Bedeutung des Ausdruckes τέλος νόμου in Röm. 10:4', *StTh* 20:
                1-36.
Brinsmead, B.H.
1982   *Galatians—Dialogical Response to Opponents* (SBLDS; Chico:
                Scholars Press).
Brooten, B.J.
1990   'Paul and the Law: How Complete was the Departure?', in Migliore
                1990: 71-89.
Bruce, F.F.
1969   *New Testament History* (London: Nelson).
1975   'Paul and the Law of Moses', *BJRL* 57: 259-79.
1982a   *The Epistle of Paul to the Galatians: A Commentary on the Greek Text*
                (NIGTC; Exeter: Paternoster Press).
1982b   'The Curse of the Law', in Hooker and Wilson 1982: 27-36.
Büchsel, F.
1964   'ἀρά κτλ', *TDNT*, I, 448-51.
Bultmann, R.
1951   *Theology of the New Testament*, I (trans. K. Grobel; New York: Charles
                Scribner's Sons).
1955   'Christ the End of the Law', in *Essays Philosophical and Theological*
                (trans. J.C.G. Greig; London: SCM Press): 36-66.
1968   'πείθω κτλ' *TDNT*, VI, 1-11.

[1910] 1984 *Der Stil der paulinischen Predigt und die kynisch-stoische Diatribe* (Göttingen: Vandenhoeck & Ruprecht).

Burton, E.D.
1894   *Syntax of the Moods and Tenses in New Testament Greek* (Edinburgh: T. & T. Clark, 2nd edn).
1921   *A Critical and Exegetical Commentary on the Epistle to the Galatians* (ICC; Edinburgh: T. & T. Clark).

Byrne, B.
1979   *'Sons of God'—'Seed of Abraham': A Study of the Idea of Sonship of God of all Christians in Paul against the Jewish Background* (AnBib; Rome: Biblical Institute Press).

Callan, T.
1980   'Pauline Midrash: The Exegetical Background of Gal. 3:19b', *JBL* 99: 549-67.

Caneday, A.
1989   ' "Redeemed from the Curse of the Law": The Use of Deut. 21:22-23 in Gal. 3:13', *TrinJ* 10: 185-209.

Carr, W.
1981   *Angels and Principalities: The Background, Meaning and Development of the Pauline Phrase 'hai archai kai hai exousiai'* (SNTSMS; Cambridge: Cambridge University Press).

Chamblin, J.K.
1977   *Gospel according to Paul: An Inductive Study* (ThD dissertation, Union Theological Seminary in Virginia; Ann Arbor: University Microfilms International).
1986   'Revelation and Tradition in the Pauline *euangelion*', *WTJ* 48: 1-16.

Clements, R.E.
1965   *Prophecy and Covenant* (SBT; London: SCM Press).

Coetzee, J.C.
1985   'The Pauline Eschatology', in A.B. Du Toit (ed.), *Guide to the New Testament. V. The Pauline Letters: Introduction and Theology* (trans. D.R. Briggs; Pretoria: N.G. Kerkboekhandel): 311-42.

Cohn-Sherbok, D.
1983   'Some Reflections on James Dunn's "The Incident at Antioch (Gal. 2:11-18)" ', *JSNT* 18: 68-74.

Cole, R.A.
[1965] 1983 *The Epistle of Paul to the Galatians: An Introduction and Commentary* (TNTC; Leicester: Inter-Varsity Press).

Combrink, H.J.B.
1979   *Structural Analysis of Acts 6:8-8:3* (STS; Cape Town: Dutch Reformed Church Publishers).
1982   'The Macrostructure of the Gospel of Matthew', *Neotestamentica* 16: 1-20.

Cooper, K.T.
1982   'Paul and Rabbinic Soteriology', *WTJ* 44: 123-39.

Cosgrove, C.H.
  1978-79   'The Mosaic Law Preaches Faith: A Study in Galatians 3', *WTJ* 41:
             146-64.
  1987   'The Law has given Sarah no Children (Gal. 4:21-30)', *NovT* 29: 219-
             35.
  1988a   'Arguing Like a Mere Human Being: Galatians 3.15-18 in Rhetorical
             Perspective', *NTS* 34: 536-49.
  1988b   *The Cross and the Spirit: A Study in the Argument and Theology of
             Galatians* (Macon, GA: Mercer University Press).
Cousar, C.B.
  1982   *Galatians* (Interpretation; Atlanta: John Knox).
Craigie, P.C.
  1976   *The Book of Deuteronomy* (NICOT; Grand Rapids: Eerdmans).
Cranfield, C.E.B.
  1964   'St. Paul and the Law', *SJT* 17: 43-68.
  1975   *A Critical and Exegetical Commentary on the Epistle to the Romans*, I
             (ICC; Edinburgh: T. & T. Clark).
  1979   *A Critical and Exegetical Commentary on the Epistle to the Romans*, II
             (ICC; Edinburgh: T. & T. Clark).
  1990   'Giving a Dog a Bad Name: A Note on H. Räisänen's *Paul and the
             Law*', *JSNT* 38: 77-85.
Cronje, J.v.W.
  1986   'Defamiliarization in the Letter to the Galatians', in J.H. Petzer and
             P.J. Hartin (eds.), *A South African Perspective on the New Testament:
             Essays by South African New Testament Scholars Presented to
             B.M. Metzger during his Visit to South Africa in 1985* (Leiden: Brill):
             214-27.
Cullmann, O.
  1957   *Christ and Time: The Primitive Christian Conception of Time and
             History* (trans. F.V. Filson; London: SCM Press).
Dahl, N.
  1966   'The Story of Abraham in Luke–Acts', in L.E. Keck and J.L. Martyn,
             (eds.), *Studies in Luke–Acts* (Nashville: Abingdon Press): 139-58.
  1977   *Studies in Paul: Theology for the Early Christian Mission*
             (Minneapolis, MN: Augsburg).
Davies, W.D.
  1948   *Paul and Rabbinic Judaism: Some Rabbinic Elements in Pauline
             Theology* (London: SPCK).
  1952   *Torah in the Messianic Age and/or the Age to Come* (JBLMS;
             Philadelphia: Society of Biblical Literature).
  1982   'Paul and the Law: Reflections on Pitfalls in Interpretation', in Hooker
             and Wilson 1982: 4-16.
Deidun, T.J.
  1981   *New Covenant Morality in Paul* (AnBib; Rome: Biblical Institute
             Press).
Deissmann, G.A.
  1909   *Bible Studies: Contributions Chiefly from Papyri and Inscriptions to*

| | the History of the Language, the Literature, and the Religion of Hellenistic Judaism and Primitive Christianity (trans. A. Grieve; Edinburgh: T. & T. Clark). |
| 1911 | Light from the Ancient East: The New Testament Illustrated by Recently Discovered Texts of the Greco-Roman World (trans. L.R.M. Strachan; London: Hodder & Stoughton). |

Delling, G.
1968   'πλήρης κτλ', *TDNT*, VI, 283-310.
1971   'στοιχέω, συστοιχέω', *TDNT*, VII, 666-87.

Denney, J.
1905   *The Death of Christ* (London: Hodder & Stoughton).

Dibelius, M.
1976   *A Commentary on the Epistle of James* (rev. H. Greeven; trans. M.A. Williams; Hermeneia; Philadelphia: Fortress Press).

Dodd, C.H.
1935   *The Bible and the Greeks* (London: Hodder & Stoughton).
1953   'ἔννομος Χριστοῦ', in J.N. Sevenster and W.C. van Unnik (eds.), *Studia Paulina: In Honorem Johannis de Zwaan* (Haarlem: Bohn): 96-110.

Donaldson, T.L.
1986   'The "Curse of the Law" and the Inclusion of the Gentiles: Galatians 3.13-14', *NTS* 32: 94-112.

Doty, W.G.
1973   *Letters in Primitive Christianity* (Philadelphia: Fortress Press).

Douglas, M.
1966   *Purity and Danger* (London: Routledge & Kegan Paul).

Drane, J.W.
1974   'Tradition, Law and Ethics in Pauline Theology', *NovT* 16: 167-78.
1975   *Paul: Libertine or Legalist?* (London: SPCK).

Dunn, J.D.G.
1975   'Rom. 7.14-25 in the Theology of Paul', *TZ* 31: 257-73.
1982   'The Relationship between Paul and Jerusalem according to Galatians 1 and 2', *NTS* 28: 461-78.
1983a   'The New Perspective on Paul', *BJRL* 65: 95-122.
1983b   'The Incident at Antioch (Gal. 2:11-18)', *JSNT* 18: 3-57.
1985   'Works of the Law and the Curse of the Law (Galatians 3:10-14)', *NTS* 31: 523-42.
1987   ' "Righteousness from the Law" and "Righteousness from Faith": Paul's Interpretation of Scripture in Romans 10:1-10', in G.F. Hawthorne and O. Betz (eds.), *Tradition and Interpretation in the New Testament: Essays in Honor of E. Earle Ellis for his 60th Birthday* (Grand Rapids: Eerdmans): 216-28.
1988a   *Romans 1–8* (WBC; Dallas: Word Books).
1988b   *Romans 9–16* (WBC; Dallas: Word Books).
1991   'Once more, ΠΙΣΤΙΣ ΧΡΙΣΤΟΥ', in *Society for Biblical Literature Seminar Papers*: 730-44.

Dupont, J.
1970   'The Conversion of Paul, and its Influence on his Understanding of
            Salvation by Faith', in W.W. Gasque and R.P. Martin (eds.), *Apostolic
            History and the Gospel: Biblical and Historical Essays Presented to
            F.F. Bruce on his 60th Birthday* (Exeter: Paternoster Press): 176-94.
Du Toit, A.B.
1974   'The Significance of Discourse Analysis for New Testament
            Interpretation and Translation: Introductory Remarks with Special
            Reference to 1 Peter 1:3-13', *Neotestamentica* 8: 54-79.
1985   'The Pauline Letters—Orientational Remarks', in A.B. Du Toit (ed.),
            *Guide to the New Testament. V. The Pauline Letters: Introduction and
            Theology* (trans. D.R. Briggs; Pretoria: N.G. Kerkboekhandel): 1-21.
Du Toit, H.C.
1977   'What is a Colon?' *Addendum to Neotestamentica* 11: (1)-(10).
Ebeling, G.
1985   *The Truth of the Gospel: An Exposition of Galatians* (trans. D. Green;
            Philadelphia: Fortress Press).
Eckert, J.
1971   *Die urchristliche Verkündigung im Streit zwischen Paulus und seinen
            Gegnern nach dem Galaterbrief* (BU; Regensburg: Pustet).
Edwards, E.G.
1972   *Christ, a Curse, and the Cross: An Interpretative Study of Galatians
            3:13* (ThD dissertation, Princeton Theological Seminary; Ann Arbor:
            University Microfilms International).
Eichrodt, W.
1961   *Theology of the Old Testament*, I (trans. J. Baker; London: SCM
            Press).
Ellicott, C.J.
1867   *St Paul's Epistle to the Galatians: With a Critical and Grammatical
            Commentary and a Revised Translation* (London: Longmans, Green,
            Reader & Dyer).
Ernst, J.
1974   *Der Brief an die Philipper, an Philemon, an die Kolosser, an die
            Epheser* (RNT; Regensburg: Pustet).
Espy, J.M.
1985   'Paul's "Robust Conscience" Re-examined', *NTS* 31: 161-88.
Esser, H.H.
1976   'στοιχεῖα', *NIDNTT*, II, 451-53.
Fallon, F.T.
1979   Review of H. Hübner, *Das Gesetz bei Paulus*, *CBQ* 41: 650-52.
Farmer, W.R., C.F.D. Moule and R.R. Niebuhr (eds.)
1967   *Christian History and Interpretation: Studies Presented to John Knox*
            (Cambridge: Cambridge University Press).
Fensham, F.C.
1963   'Common Trends in Curses of the Near Eastern Treaties and *Kudurru*-
            inscriptions Compared with Maledictions of Amos and Isaiah', *ZAW*
            75: 155-75.

| 1966 | 'The Curse of the Cross and the Renewal of the Covenant', in *Biblical Essays* (Potchefstroom: Pro-Rege): 219-26. |

1966   'The Curse of the Cross and the Renewal of the Covenant', in *Biblical Essays* (Potchefstroom: Pro-Rege): 219-26.
1967   'Covenant, Promise and Expectation in the Bible', *TZ* 23: 305-22.
1971   'The Covenant as Giving Expression to the Relationship between Old and New Testament', *TynBul* 22: 82-94.

Fitzmyer, J.A.
1981   'Paul and the Law', in *To Advance the Gospel: New Testament Studies* (New York: Crossroad).

Friedrich, J., W. Pöhlmann and P. Stuhlmacher (eds.)
1976   *Rechtfertigung: Festschrift für Ernst Käsemann zum 70. Geburtstag* (Tübingen: Mohr [Paul Siebeck]).

Fuller, D.P.
1975–76   'Paul and "the Works of the Law" ', *WTJ* 38: 28-42.
1980   *Gospel and Law: Contrast or Continuum?* (Grand Rapids: Eerdmans).

Fung, R.Y.K.
1988   *The Epistle to the Galatians* (NICNT; Grand Rapids: Eerdmans).

Funk, R.W.
1966   *Language, Hermeneutic, and Word of God: The Problem of Language in the New Testament and Contemporary Theology* (New York: Harper & Row).
1967   'The Apostolic *Parousia*: Form and Significance', in Farmer, Moule and Niebuhr 1967: 249-68.

Furnish, V.P.
1968   *Theology and Ethics in Paul* (Nashville: Abingdon Press).
1972   *The Love Command in the New Testament* (Nashville: Abingdon Press).

Gaston, L.
1979   'Paul and the Torah', in A.T. Davies (ed.), *Antisemitism and the Foundations of Christianity* (New York: Paulist Press): 48-71.
1984   'Works of Law as a Subjective Genitive', *SR* 13: 39-46.
1987   *Paul and the Torah* (Vancouver: University of British Columbia Press).

Gese, H.
1981   *Essays on Biblical Theology* (trans. K. Crim; Minneapolis, MN: Augsburg).

Gordon, T.D.
1987   'The Problem at Galatia', *Int* 41: 32-43.
1989   'A Note on παιδαγωγός in Galatians 3.24-25', *NTS* 35: 150-54.

Grafe, E.
1884   *Die paulinische Lehre vom Gesetz nach den vier Hauptbriefen* (Freiburg: Mohr [Paul Siebeck]).

Greeven, H.
1968   'πλήσιον', *TDNT*, VI, 311-18.

Grundmann, W.
1964   'ἁμαρτάνω, ἁμάρτημα, ἁμαρτία', *TDNT*, I, 267-316.

Gundry, R.H.
1985   'Grace, Works, and Staying Saved in Paul', *Bib* 66: 1-38.

Gunther, J.J.
1973   *St Paul's Opponents and their Background: A Study of Apocalyptic and Jewish Sectarian Teachings* (NovTSup; Leiden: Brill).
Gutbrod, W.
1967   'νόμος κτλ', *TDNT*, IV, 1036-91.
Guthrie, D.
1973   *Galatians* (NCB; London: Marshall, Morgan & Scott).
Hall, R.G.
1987   'The Rhetorical Outline for Galatians: A Reconsideration', *CBQ* 106: 277-87.
Hamerton-Kelly, R.G.
1990a   'Sacred Violence and the Curse of the Law (Galatians 3.13): The Death of Christ as a Sacrificial Travesty', *NTS* 36: 98-118.
1990b   'Sacred Violence and "Works of Law": "Is Christ then an Agent of Sin?" (Galatians 2:17)', *CBQ* 52: 55-75.
Hansen, G.W.
1989   *Abraham in Galatians: Epistolary and Rhetorical Contexts* (JSNTSup, 29; Sheffield: JSOT Press).
Hanson, A.T.
1974   *Studies in Paul's Technique and Theology* (London: SPCK).
1988   'The Origin of Paul's Use of παιδαγωγός for the Law', *JSNT* 34: 71-76.
Harnish, W.
1987   'Einübung des neuen Seins: Paulinische Paränese am Beispiel des Galaterbriefs', *ZTK* 84: 279-96.
Haufe, C.
1966   'Die Stellung des Paulus zum Gesetz', *TLZ* 91: 171-78.
Hawkins, J.G.
1971   *The Opponents of Paul in Galatia* (PhD dissertation, Yale University; Ann Arbor: University Microfilms International).
Hays, R.B.
1983   *The Faith of Jesus Christ: An Investigation of the Narrative Substructure of Galatians 3:1–4:11* (SBLDS; Chico: Scholars Press).
1987   'Christology and Ethics in Galatians: The Law of Christ', *CBQ* 49: 268-90.
1991   'ΠΙΣΤΙΣ and Pauline Christology: What is at Stake?', in *Society for Biblical Literature Seminar Papers*: 714-29.
Heidland, H.W.
1967   'λογίζομαι, λογισμός', *TDNT*, IV, 284-92.
Heiligenthal, R.
1984   'Soziologische Implikationen der paulinischen Rechtfertigungslehre im Galaterbrief am Beispiel der "Werke des Gesetzes": Beobachtungen zur Identitätsfindung einer frühchristlichen Gemeinde', *Kairos* 26: 38-53.
Hester, J.D.
1967   'The "Heir" and Heilsgeschichte: A Study of Galatians 4:1ff', in F. Christ (ed.), *Oikonomia: Heilsgeschichte als Thema der Theologie:*

Festschrift für O. Cullmann (Hamburg: Herbert Reich Evangelischer Verlag): 118-25.

1984   'The Rhetorical Structure of Galatians 1:11-2:14', *JBL* 103: 223-33.

1986   'The Use and Influence of Rhetoric in Galatians 2:1-14', *TZ* 42: 386-408.

Hill, D.

1981–82   'Salvation Preached: IV. Galatians 3:10-14: Freedom and Acceptance', *ExpTim* 93: 196-200.

Hirsch, E.

1930   'Zwei Fragen zu Galater 6', *ZNW* 29: 192-97.

Hooker, M.D.

1971   'Interchange in Christ', *JTS* 22: 349-61.

1982   'Paul and "Covenantal Nomism"', in Hooker and Wilson 1982: 47-56.

1989   'πίστις Χριστοῦ', *NTS* 35: 321-42.

Hooker, M.D., and S.G. Wilson (eds.)

1982   *Paul and Paulinism: Essays in Honour of C.K. Barrett* (London: SPCK).

Houlden, J.L.

1983   'A Response to James D.G. Dunn', *JSNT* 18: 58-67.

Howard, G.

1967   'Notes and Observations on the "Faith of Christ"', *HTR* 60: 459-65.

1969   'Christ the End of the Law: The Meaning of Romans 10:4ff', *JBL* 88: 331-37.

1974   'The "Faith of Christ"', *ExpTim* 85: 212-15.

1979   *Paul: Crisis in Galatia: A Study in Early Christian Theology* (SNTSMS; Cambridge: Cambridge University Press).

Hübner, H.

1975   'Das ganze und das eine Gesetz', *KD* 21: 239-56.

1984   'Der Galaterbrief und das Verhältnis von antiker Rhetorik und Epistolographie', *TLZ* 109: 241-50.

1986   *Law in Paul's Thought: A Contribution to the Development of Pauline Theology* (trans. J.C.G. Greig; reprinted with corrections; SNTW; Edinburgh: T. & T. Clark).

Hultgren, A.J.

1976   'Paul's pre-Christian Persecutions of the Church: Their Purpose, Locale, and Nature', *JBL* 95: 97-111.

1980   'The *Pistis Christou* Formulation in Paul', *NovT* 22: 248-63.

Jeremias, J.

1963   *Der Opfertod Jesu Christi* (CwH; Stuttgart: Calwer Verlag).

1964   'Ἀβραάμ', *TDNT*, I, 8-9.

1967   'παῖς θεοῦ', *TDNT*, V, 677-717.

1971   *New Testament Theology*, I (London: SCM Press).

Jewett, R.

1971a   'The Agitators and the Galatian Congregation', *NTS* 17: 198-212.

1971b   *Paul's Anthropological Terms: A Study of their Use in Conflict Settings* (Leiden: Brill).

Johnson, H.W.
1987   'The Paradigm of Abraham in Galatians 3:6-9', *TrinJ* 8: 179-99.
Johnson, L.T.
1982   'Rom. 3:21-26 and the Faith of Jesus', *CBQ* 44: 77-90.
Käsemann, E.
1971   *Perspectives on Paul* (trans. M. Kohl; Philadelphia: Fortress Press).
Kaiser, W.C.
1971   'Leviticus 18:5 and Paul: Do This and You Shall Live (Eternally?)',
            JETS 14: 19-28.
1983   *Toward Old Testament Ethics* (Grand Rapids: Zondervan).
Kalusche, M.
1986   ' "Das Gesetz als Thema biblischer Theologie"? Anmerkungen zu
            einem Entwurf Peter Stuhlmachers', *ZNW* 77: 194-205.
Karlberg, M.W.
1986   'Israel's History Personified: Romans 7:7-13 in Relation to Paul's
            Teaching on the "Old Man" ', *TrinJ* 7: 65-74.
Keck, L.
1979   *Paul and his Letters* (Philadelphia: Fortress Press).
Kennedy, G.
1963   *The Art of Persuasion in Greece* (London: Routledge & Kegan Paul).
1984   *New Testament Interpretation through Rhetorical Criticism* (Chapel
            Hill: University of North Carolina Press).
Kertelge, K.
1967   *'Rechtfertigung' bei Paulus: Studien zur Struktur und zum
            Bedeutungsgehalt des paulinischen Rechtfertigungsbegriffs* (NTA;
            Münster: Aschendorff).
1984   'Gesetz und Freiheit im Galaterbrief', *NTS* 30: 382-94.
1989   'Freiheitsbotschaft und Liebesgebot im Galaterbrief', in H. Merklein
            (ed.), *Neues Testament und Ethik: Für R. Schnackenburg* (Freiburg:
            Herder): 326-37.
Kim, S.
1984   *The Origin of Paul's Gospel* (WUNT; Tübingen: Mohr [Paul Siebeck],
            2nd edn).
Klausner, J.
1956   *The Messianic Idea in Israel* (trans. W.F. Stinespring: London: George
            Allen & Unwin).
Klein, G.
1969   *Rekonstruktion und Interpretation: Gesammelte Aufsätze zum Neuen
            Testament* (BEvT; Munich: Chr. Kaiser Verlag).
Kline, M.G.
1968   *By Oath Consigned: A Reinterpretation of the Covenant Signs of
            Circumcision and Baptism* (Grand Rapids: Eerdmans).
Köster, H.
1959   'Häretiker im Urchristentum', *RGG*, 3rd edn.
Kramer, W.
1966   *Christ, Lord, Son of God* (London: SCM Press).

Kümmel, W.G.
1974   *Römer 7 und das Bild des Menschen im Neuen Testament*. (2 vols.;
            TBü; Munich: Chr. Kaiser Verlag).
1975   *Introduction to the New Testament* (trans. H.C. Kee; London: SCM
            Press; rev. edn).
Kuhn, K.G.
1968   'προσήλυτος', *TDNT*, VI, 727-44.
Ladd, G.E.
1968   'Paul and the Law', in J.M. Richards (ed.), *Soli Deo Gloria: New
            Testament Studies in Honor of William Childs Robinson* (Richmond,
            VA: John Knox): 50-67.
1970   'Revelation and Tradition in Paul', in W.W. Gasque and R.P. Martin
            (eds.), *Apostolic History and the Gospel: Biblical and Historical
            Essays Presented to F.F. Bruce on his 60th Birthday* (Exeter:
            Paternoster Press): 223-30.
1974   *A Theology of the New Testament* (Grand Rapids: Eerdmans).
Lambrecht, J.
1977–78   'The Line of Thought in Gal. 2.14b-21', *NTS* 24: 484-95.
1986   'Gesetzesverständis bei Paulus', in K. Kertelge (ed.), *Das Gesetz im
            Neuen Testament* (Freiburg: Herder): 88-127.
Lang, F.
1976   'Gesetz und Bund bei Paulus', in Friedrich, Pöhlmann and
            Stuhlmacher 1976: 305-20.
Lapide, P.
1981   'Der Rabbi von Tarsus', in P. Lapide and P. Stuhlmacher, *Paulus—
            Rabbi und Apostel: Ein jüdisch-christlicher Dialog* (Stuttgart: Calwer
            Verlag):
            35-61.
Lategan, B.C.
1978   'Structural Analysis as Basis for Further Exegetical Procedure',
            SBLSP 1: 341-60.
1985a   'Galatians', in A.B. Du Toit (ed.), *Guide to the New Testament. V. The
            Pauline Letters: Introduction and Theology* (trans. D.R. Briggs;
            Pretoria: N.G. Kerkboekhandel): 89-106.
1985b   'Paul and Jesus', in A.B. Du Toit (ed.), *Guide to the New Testament.
            V. The Pauline Letters: Introduction and Theology* (trans.
            D.R. Briggs; Pretoria: N.G. Kerkboekhandel): 187-200.
1988   'Is Paul Defending his Apostleship in Galatians? The Function of
            Galatians 1:11-12 and 2:19-20 in the Development of Paul's
            Argument', *NTS* 34: 431-41.
1991   'Formulas in the Language of Paul: A Study of Prepositional Phrases
            in Galatians', *Neotestamentica* 25: 75-87.
Lenski, R.C.H.
[1937] 1961 *The Interpretation of St. Paul's Epistles to the Galatians, to the
            Ephesians and to the Philippians* (Minneapolis, MN: Augsburg).

The Law in Galatians

Liechtenhan, R.
1946   *Die urchristliche Mission: Voraussetzungen Motive und Methoden* (ATANT; Zürich: Zwingli-Verlag).
Lightfoot, J.B.
1880   *St Paul's Epistle to the Galatians* (London: Macmillan; 6th edn).
[1891] 1980 *The Apostolic Fathers* (Grand Rapids: Baker).
Limbeck, M.
1971   *Die Ordnung des Heils: Untersuchungen zum Gesetzesverständnis des Frühjudentums* (KBANT; Düsseldorf: Patmos).
Lindars, B.
1961   *New Testament Apologetic: The Doctrinal Significance of the Old Testament Quotations* (London: SCM Press).
Linss, W.C.
1988   'Exegesis of Telos in Romans 10:4', *BR* 33: 5-12.
Lohmeyer, E.
1929   'Probleme paulinischer Theologie: II. "Gesetzeswerk"', *ZNW* 28: 177-207.
Longenecker, R.
1975   *Biblical Exegesis in the Apostolic Period* (Grand Rapids: Eerdmans).
[1964] 1976 *Paul, Apostle of Liberty: The Origin and Nature of Paul's Christianity* (Grand Rapids: Baker).
1982   'The Pedagogical Nature of the Law in Galatians 3:19-4:7', *JETS* 25: 53-61.
1990   *Galatians* (WBC; Dallas: Word Books).
Louw, J.P.
1973   'Discourse Analysis and the Greek New Testament', *BT* 24: 101-18.
1977   'The Structure of Mt 8:1-9:35', *Neotestamentica* 11: 91-97.
1982   *Semantics of New Testament Greek* (Philadelphia: Fortress Press).
Louw, J.P., and E.A. Nida, *et al.* (eds.)
1988   *Greek–English Lexicon of the New Testament Based on Semantic Domain*, I (New York: United Bible Societies).
Lührmann, D.
1965   *Das Offenbarungsverständis bei Paulus und in paulinischen Gemeinden* (WMANT; Neukirchen–Vluyn: Neukirchener Verlag).
1976   'Christologie und Rechtfertigung,' in Friedrich, Pöhlmann and Stuhlmacher 1976: 351-63.
1988   'Die 430 Jahre zwischen den Verheissungen und dem Gesetz (Gal 3,17)', *ZAW* 100: 420-23.
Lütgert, W.
1919   *Gesetz und Geist: Eine Untersuchung zur Vorgeschichte des Galaterbriefes* (Gütersloh: Bertelsmann).
Lull, D.J.
1980   *The Spirit in Galatia: Paul's Interpretation of 'Pneuma' as Divine Power* (SBLDS; Chico: Scholars Press).
1986   ' "The Law was our Pedagogue": A Study in Galatians 3:19-25', *JBL* 105: 481-98.

Luther, M.

[1891] 1979   *A Commentary on Saint Paul's Epistle to the Galatians* (Grand Rapids: Baker).

McComiskey, T.E.

1985   *The Covenants of Promise: A Theology of the Old Testament Covenants* (Grand Rapids: Baker).

McEleney, N.J.

1974   'Conversion, Circumcision and the Law', *NTS* 20: 319-41.

Malherbe, A.J.

1980   'μὴ γένοιτο in the Diatribe and Paul', *HTR* 73: 231-40.

Martin, B.L.

1983   'Paul on Christ and the Law', *JETS* 26: 271-82.

1989   *Christ and the Law in Paul* (NovTSup; Leiden: Brill).

Martyn, J.L.

1983   'A Law-Observant Mission to Gentiles: The Background of Galatians', *MQR* 22: 221-36.

Marxsen, W.

1968   *Introduction to the New Testament: An Approach to its Problems* (trans. G. Buswell; Oxford: Basil Blackwell).

Meeks, W.A.

1983   *The First Urban Christians: The Social World of the Apostle Paul* (New Haven: Yale University Press).

Menoud, P.H.

1953   'Revelation and Tradition', *Int* 7: 131-41.

Metzger, B.M.

1971   *A Textual Commentary on the Greek New Testament* (London: United Bible Societies).

Meyer, P.W.

1980   'Romans 10:4 and the "End" of the Law', in J.L. Crenshaw and S. Sandmel (eds.), *The Divine Helmsman: Studies on God's Control of Human Events, Presented to Lou H. Silberman* (New York: Ktav): 59-78.

Michaelis, W.

1931   'Judaistische Heidenchristen', *ZNW* 30: 83-89.

1968   'πίπτω κτλ', *TDNT*, VI, 161-73.

Michel, O.

1966   *Der Brief an die Römer* (KEK; Göttingen: Vandenhoeck & Ruprecht, 4th edn).

1967   'οἶκος κτλ', *TDNT*, V, 119-59.

1971   'συγκλείω', *TDNT*, VII, 744-47.

Migliore, D.L. (ed.)

1990   *The 1989 Frederick Neumann Symposium on the Theological Interpretation of Scripture* (PSB Supplementary Issue).

Minear, P.S.

1979   'The Crucified World: The Enigma of Galatians 6:14', in C. Andresen and G. Klein (eds.), *Theologia Crucis—Signum Crucis: Festschrift für*

                    E. Dinkler *zum 70. Geburtstag* (Tübingen: Mohr [Paul Siebeck]):
                    395-407.
Mohrlang, R.
    1984   *Matthew and Paul: A Comparison of Ethical Perspectives* (SNTSMS;
                    Cambridge: Cambridge University Press).
Mol, H.
    1976   *Identity and the Sacred* (Oxford: Basil Blackwell).
Montefiore, C.G.
    1914   *Judaism and St Paul: Two Essays* (London: Max Goschen).
Montefiore, H.
    1962   'Thou Shalt Love the Neighbour as Thyself', *NovT* 5: 157-70.
Moo, D.J.
    1983   ' "Law", "Works of the Law", and Legalism in Paul', *WTJ* 45: 73-
                    100.
    1986   'Israel and Paul in Romans 7.7-12', *NTS* 32: 122-35.
    1987   'Paul and the Law in the Last Ten Years', *SJT* 40: 287-307.
Moore, G.F.
    1921   'Christian Writers on Judaism', *HTR* 14: 197-254.
    1927–30   *Judaism in the First Centuries of the Christian Era: The Age of the
                    Tannaim* (3 vols.; Cambridge, MA: Harvard University Press).
Morris, T.F.
    1987   'Law and the Cause of Sin in the Epistle to the Romans', *HeyJ* 28:
                    285-91.
Moule, C.F.D.
    1944–45   'A Note on Galatians ii.17,18', *ExpTim* 56: 223.
    1963   *An Idiom Book of New Testament Greek* (Cambridge: Cambridge
                    University Press, 2nd edn).
    1967   'Obligation in the Ethic of Paul', in Farmer, Moule and Niebuhr
                    1967: 389-406.
    1967–68   'Fulfilment-words in the New Testament: Use and Abuse', *NTS* 14:
                    293-320.
Munck, J.
    1959   *Paul and the Salvation of Mankind* (trans. F. Clarke; London: SCM
                    Press).
Murray, J.
    1965   *The Epistle to the Romans* (NICNT; Grand Rapids: Eerdmans).
Mussner, F.
    1974   *Der Galaterbrief* (HTKNT; Freiburg: Herder).
Neusner, J.
    1971   *The Rabbinic Traditions about the Pharisees before 70*, I (Leiden:
                    Brill).
    1978   'Comparing Judaisms', *HR* 18: 177-91.
Nida, E.A.
    1975   *Exploring Semantic Structure* (Munich: Wilhelm Fink).
Nida, E.A., *et al.*
    1983   *Style and Discourse: With Special Reference to the Text of the New
                    Testament* (Cape Town: Bible Society).

Nolland, J.
1981   'Uncircumcised Proselytes?', *JSJ* 12: 173-94.
Noth, M.
1966   *The Laws in the Pentateuch and Other Studies* (trans. D.R. Ap-
                Thomas; Edinburgh: Oliver & Boyd).
O'Brien, P.T.
1984   'Principalities and Powers: Opponents of the Church', in D.A. Carson
                (ed.), *Biblical Interpretation and the Church: Text and Context*
                (Exeter: Paternoster Press): 110-50.
Odendaal, D.H.
1970   *The Eschatological Expectation of Isaiah 40–66 with Special
                Reference to Israel and the Nations* (BTSt; Nutley, NJ: Presbyterian
                and Reformed Publishing).
Oepke, D.A.
1937   *Der Brief des Paulus an die Galater* (THKNT; Leipzig: Deichertsche
                Verlagsbuchhandlung).
1967   'μεσίτης, μεσιτεύω', *TDNT*, IV, 598-624.
Perelman, C.
1982   *The Realm of Rhetoric* (trans. W. Kluback; Notre Dame, IN: University
                of Notre Dame Press).
Perelman, C., and L. Olbrechts-Tyteca
1969   *The New Rhetoric: A Treatise on Argumentation* (trans. J. Wilkinson
                and P. Weaver; Notre Dame, IN: University of Notre Dame Press).
Perrin, N.
1970   'The Use of (παρα)διδόναι in Connection with the Passion of Jesus in
                the New Testament', in E. Lohse, C. Burchard and B. Schaller (eds.),
                *Der Ruf Jesu und die Antwort der Gemeinde: Exegetische
                Untersuchungen J. Jeremias zum 70 Geburtstag gewidmet von seinen
                Schülern* (Göttingen: Vandenhoeck & Ruprecht): 204-12.
Petersen, N.R.
1987   'Prolegomena to a Reader-Oriented Study of Paul's Letter to Rome'
                (paper presented at the SNTS reader response seminar, Göttingen).
Rad, G. von
1966   *Deuteronomy* (trans. D. Barton; London: SCM Press).
1975a   *Old Testament Theology. I. The Theology of Israel's Historical
                Traditions.* (trans. D.M.G. Stalker; London: SCM Press).
1975b   *Old Testament Theology. II. The Theology of Israel's Prophetic
                Traditions* (trans. D.M.G. Stalker; London: SCM Press).
Räisänen, H.
1980a   'Legalism and Salvation by the Law: Paul's Portrayal of the Jewish
                Religion as a Historical and Theological Problem', in S. Pedersen
                (ed.), *Die Paulinische Literatur und Theologie* (SB; Aarhus: Forlaget
                Aros): 63-83.
1980b   'Paul's Theological Difficulties with the Law', in E.A. Livingstone
                (ed.), *Studia Biblica*, III (JSNTSup, 3; Sheffield: JSOT Press): 301-20.
1983   *Paul and the Law* (WUNT; Tübingen: Mohr [Paul Siebeck]).
1985   'Galatians 2.16 and Paul's Break with Judaism', *NTS* 31: 543-53.

1987   'Paul's Conversion and the Development of his View of the Law', *NTS*
             33: 404-19.
Ramsay, W.M.
1900   *A Historical Commentary on St Paul's Epistle to the Galatians*
             (London: Hodder & Stoughton, 2nd edn).
1951   'The Law and This World according to Paul: Some Thoughts
             Concerning Gal. 4:1-11', *JBL* 70: 259-76.
Rengstorf, K.H.
1964   'ἀποστέλλω κτλ', *TDNT*, I, 398-447.
Rhyne, C.T.
1981   *Faith Establishes the Law* (SBLDS; Chico: Scholars Press).
1985   '*Nomos Dikaiosynes* and the Meaning of Romans 10:4', *CBQ* 47:
             486-99.
Ridderbos, H.N.
1953   *The Epistle of Paul to the Churches of Galatia* (NICNT; Grand Rapids:
             Eerdmans).
1975   *Paul: An Outline of his Theology* (trans. J.R. De Witt; Grand Rapids:
             Eerdmans).
Roberts, J.H.
1981   'Righteousness in Romans with Special Reference to Romans 3:19-
             31', *Neotestamentica* 15: 12-33.
Robertson, A.T.
1919   *A Grammar of the Greek New Testament in the Light of Historical
             Research* (London: Hodder & Stoughton, 3rd edn).
Robertson, O.P.
1980   *The Christ of the Covenants* (Phillipsburg: Presbyterian and Reformed
             Publishing).
Roetzel, C.J.
[1975] 1983   *The Letters of Paul: Conversations in Context* (London: SCM Press).
Ropes, J.H.
1929   *The Singular Problem of the Epistle to the Galatians* (HThS;
             Cambridge, MA: Harvard University Press).
Sampley, J.P.
1976–77   ' "Before God, I Do Not Lie" (Gal. 1.20): Paul's Self-defence in the
             Light of Roman Legal Praxis', *NTS* 23: 477-82.
Sanday, W., and A. Headlam
1907   *A Critical and Exegetical Commentary on the Epistle to the Romans*
             (ICC; Edinburgh: T. & T. Clark, 5th edn).
Sanders, E.P.
1977   *Paul and Palestinian Judaism: A Comparison of Patterns of Religion*
             (London: SCM Press).
1978   'On the Question of Fulfilling the Law in Paul and Rabbinic Judaism',
             in E. Bammel, C.K. Barrett, and W.D. Davies (eds.), *Donum
             Gentilicium: New Testament Studies in Honour of David Daube*
             (Oxford: Clarendon Press): 103-26.
1983   *Paul, the Law, and the Jewish People* (Philadelphia: Fortress Press).
1990   *Jewish Law from Jesus to the Mishnah* (London: SCM Press).

Sandmel, S.
1955   *Philo's Place in Judaism: A Study of Conceptions of Abraham in
            Jewish Literature* (Cincinnati: Hebrew Union College Press).
1979   *The Genius of Paul: A Study in History* (Philadelphia: Fortress Press,
            3rd edn).
Schechter, S.
[1909] 1961 *Aspects of Rabbinic Theology* (New York: Schocken Books).
Schlier, H.
1971   *Der Brief an die Galater* (KEK; Göttingen: Vandenhoeck & Ruprecht,
            5th edn).
Schmithals, W.
1972   *Paul and Gnostics* (trans. J.E. Steely; Nashville: Abingdon Press).
1983   'Judaisten in Galatien?', *ZNW* 74: 27-58.
Schneider, E.E.
1964   'Finis Legis Christus', *TZ* 20: 410-22.
Schneider, J.
1967   'παραβαίνω κτλ', *TDNT*, V, 736-44.
Schoeps, H.J.
1961   *Paul: The Theology of the Apostle in the Light of Jewish Religious
            History* (trans. H. Knight; Philadelphia: Westminster Press).
Schrage, W.
1988   *The Ethics of the New Testament* (trans. D.E. Green; Philadelphia:
            Fortress Press).
Schreiner, T.R.
1984   'Is Perfect Obedience to the Law Possible? A Re-examination of
            Galatians 3:10', *JETS* 2: 151-60.
1985   'Paul and Perfect Obedience to the Law: An Evaluation of the View of
            E.P. Sanders', *WTJ* 47: 245-78.
1989   'The Abolition and Fulfillment of the Law in Paul', *JSNT* 35: 47-74.
Schrenk, G.
1964   'γράφω κτλ', *TDNT*, I, 742-73.
Schwartz, D.R.
1983   'Two Pauline Allusions to the Redemptive Mechanism of the
            Crucifixion', *JBL* 102: 259-68.
Schweitzer, A.
1931   *The Mysticism of Paul the Apostle* (trans. W. Montgomery; London:
            A. & C. Black).
Schweizer, E.
1968   'πνεῦμα κτλ', *TDNT*, VI, 389-455.
1970   'Die "Elemente der Welt", Gal 4,3.9: Kol 2,8.20', in O. Bocher and
            K. Haacker (eds.), *Verborum Veritas: Festschrift für G. Stählin zum 70.
            Geburtstag* (Wuppertal: Theologischer Verlag): 245-59.
1972   'υἱός, υἱοθεσία', *TDNT*, VIII, 363-92.
1988   'Slaves of the Elements and Worshipers of Angels: Gal 4:3, 9 and Col
            2:8, 18, 20', *JBL* 107: 455-68.
Seebass, H.
1976   'ἅγιος', *NIDNTT*, II, 224-29.

Selby, D.J.
1962   *Toward the Understanding of St Paul* (Englewood Cliffs, NJ: Prentice-Hall).
Smend, R.
1986   *Die Mitte des Alten Testaments*, I (BevT; Munich: Chr. Kaiser Verlag).
Smit, J.
1989   'The Letter of Paul to the Galatians: A Deliberative Speech', *NTS* 35: 1-26.
Snaith, N.H.
1944   *The Distinctive Ideas of the Old Testament* (London: Epworth Press).
Snodgrass, K.
1988   'Spheres of Influence: A Possible Solution to the Problem of Paul and the Law', *JSNT* 32: 93-113.
Snyman, A.H. (ed.)
1986   *Oor styl en retoriek by Paulus* (Acta Academica; Bloemfontein: Universiteit van die Oranje-Vrystaat).
Stambaugh, J., and D. Balch
1986   *The Social World of the First Christians* (London: SPCK).
Stamm, R.T.
1953   'The Epistle to the Galatians', in G.A. Buttrick *et al.* (eds.), *The Interpreter's Bible*, X (New York: Abingdon Press): 429-593.
Stendahl, K.
1976   *Paul Among Jews and Gentiles* (Philadelphia: Fortress Press).
Stoike, D.A.
1971   'The Law of Christ': A Study of Paul's Use of the Expression in Galatians 6:2 (ThD dissertation, School of Theology at Claremont; Ann Arbor: University Microfilms International).
Stott, J.R.W.
1968   *The Message of Galatians* (BST; Leicester: Inter-Varsity Press).
Stowers, S.K.
1986   *Letter Writing in Greco-Roman Antiquity* (Philadelphia: Westminster Press).
Strecker, G.
1976   'Befreiung und Rechtfertigung: Zur Stellung der Rechtfertigungslehre in der Theologie des Paulus', in Friedrich, Pöhlmann and Stuhlmacher 1976: 479-508.
Stuhlmacher, P.
1986   *Reconciliation, Law, and Righteousness: Essays in Biblical Theology* (trans. E.R. Kalin; Philadelphia: Fortress Press).
Styler, G.M.
1973   'The Basis of Obligation in Paul's Christology and Ethics', in B. Lindars and S.S. Smalley (eds.), *Christ and Spirit in the New Testament: In Honour of C.F.D. Moule* (Cambridge: Cambridge University Press): 175-87.
Tannehill, R.C.
1967   *Dying and Rising with Christ: A Study in Pauline Theology* (BZNW: Berlin: Töpelmann).

Theissen, G.
1983   *Psychologische Aspekte paulinischer Theologie* (FRLANT: Göttingen: Vandenhoeck & Ruprecht).
Thielman, F.
1989   *From Plight to Solution: A Jewish Framework for Understanding Paul's View of the Law in Galatians and Romans* (NovTSup; Leiden: Brill).
Thrall, M.E.
1962   *Greek Particles in the New Testament: Linguistic and Exegetical Studies* (Leiden: Brill).
Tolmie, D.F.
1986a   'Die aanwending van die formele briefelemente in die brief aan die Galasiërs', in Snyman 1986: 19-37.
1986b   ''n Stylanalise van Galasiërs 3:1-14', in Snyman 1986: 38-51.
Tyson, J.B.
1968   'Paul's Opponents in Galatia', *NovT* 10: 241-54.
1973   ' "Works of Law" in Galatians', *JBL* 92: 423-31.
Unnik, W.C. van
1973   'Tarsus or Jerusalem: The City of Paul's Youth', in *Sparsa Collecta: The Collected Essays of W.C. van Unnik* (NovTSup; Leiden: Brill): 259-320.
Van de Sandt, H.W.M.
1976   'An Explanation of Rom. 8.4a', *Bijdr* 37: 361-78.
Van Deventer, H.J.
1986   'The Semantic Field "Salvation" in Paul's Major Epistles: A Componential Analysis of his Soteriological Metaphors' (ThD thesis, University of Stellenbosch).
Van Seters, J.
1975   *Abraham in History and Tradition* (New Haven: Yale University Press).
Vos, G.
[1930] 1982   *The Pauline Eschatology* (Grand Rapids: Baker).
Wang, J.S.
1971   *Pauline Doctrine of Law* (PhD dissertation, Emory University; Ann Arbor: University Microfilms International).
Watson, F.
1986   *Paul, Judaism and the Gentiles: A Sociological Approach* (SNTSMS; Cambridge: Cambridge University Press).
Wedderburn, A.J.M.
1985   'Paul and the Law', *SJT* 38: 613-22.
Weima, J.A.D.
1990   'The Function of the Law in Relation to Sin: An Evaluation of the View of H. Räisänen', *NovT* 32: 219-35.
Westerholm, S.
1984   'Letter and Spirit: The Foundation of Pauline Ethics', *NTS* 30: 229-48.
1986   'Torah, Nomos, and Law: A Question of "Meaning"', *SR* 15: 327-36.
1986-87   'On Fulfilling the Whole Law (Gal. 5:14)', *SEÅ* 51-52: 229-37.

1988   *Israel's Law and the Church's Faith: Paul and his Recent Interpreters*
             (Grand Rapids: Eerdmans).

White, J.L.
1971   'Introductory Formulae in the Body of the Pauline Letter', *JBL* 90:
             91-97.
1972   *The Form and Function of the Body of the Greek Letter: A Study of
             the Letter-body in the Non-literary Papyri and in Paul the Apostle*
             (SBLDS; Missoula, MT: Scholars Press).

Whiteley, D.E.H.
1957   'St. Paul's Thought on the Atonement', *JTS* 8: 240-55.

Wilckens, U.
1974   'Was heisst bei Paulus: "Aus Werken des Gesetzes wird kein Mensch
             gerecht?"', in *Rechtfertigung als Freiheit: Paulusstudien*
             (Neukirchen–Vluyn: Neukirchener Verlag).
1978   *Der Brief an die Römer (Röm 1–5)* (EKKNT; Zürich: Benzinger
             Verlag).
1980   *Der Brief an die Römer (Röm 6–11)* (EKKNT; Zürich: Benziger
             Verlag).
1982a   'Zur Entwicklung des paulinischen Gesetzesverständnisses', *NTS* 28:
             154-90.
1982b   'Statements on the Development of Paul's View of the Law', in
             Hooker and Wilson 1982: 17-26.

Wilcox, M.
1977   ' "Upon the Tree"—Deut. 21:22-23 in the New Testament', *JBL* 96:
             85-99.

Williams, S.K.
1987a   'Justification and the Spirit in Galatians', *JSNT* 29: 91-100.
1987b   'Again *pistis Christou*', *CBQ* 49: 431-47.
1988   '*Promise* in Galatians: A Reading of Paul's Reading of Scripture', *JBL*
             107: 709-20.
1989   'The Hearing of Faith: ἀκοὴ πίστεως in Galatians 3', *NTS* 35: 82-93.

Wink, W.
1978   'The "Elements of the Universe" in Biblical and Scientific
             Perspective', *Zygon* 13: 225-48.

Wright, N.T.
1978   'The Paul of History and the Apostle of Faith', *TynBul* 29: 61-88.

Wuellner, W.
1977   'Paul's Rhetoric of Argumentation in Romans: An Alternative to the
             Donfried–Karris Debate over Romans', in K. Donfried (ed.), *The
             Romans Debate* (Minneapolis, MN: Augsburg): 152-74.

Yates, R.
1985   'Saint Paul and the Law in Galatians', *ITQ* 51: 105-24.

Young, N.H.
1987   '*Paidagōgos*: The Social Setting of a Pauline Metaphor', *NovT* 29:
             150-76.

Zahn, T.
1907   *Der Brief des Paulus an die Galater* (KNT; Leipzig: Deichert, 2nd edn).

Ziesler, J.A.
1972   *The Meaning of Righteousness in Paul: A Linguistic and Theological Enquiry* (SNTSMS; Cambridge: Cambridge University Press).

Zimmerli, W.
1978   *Old Testament Theology in Outline* (trans. D.E. Green; Edinburgh: T. & T. Clark).

INDEXES

INDEX OF REFERENCES

OLD TESTAMENT

INDEX OF AUTHORS

JOURNAL FOR THE STUDY OF THE NEW TESTAMENT

Supplement Series